# Common Nonsense

# ANDY ROONEY

# *Common Nonsense*

PublicAffairs

*New York*

Book Design by Jenny Dossin.

Library of Congress Cataloging-in-Publication data
Rooney, Andrew A.
Common nonsense / Andy Rooney.— 1st ed.
p. cm.
ISBN-10 1-58648-200-9 (PBK.)
ISBN-13 978-1-58648-200-8 (PBK.)
1. American wit and humor. I. Title.
PN6165 .R66 2002
814'.54-dc21
20020.1828

DHSB        08 09   10 9 8 7 6 5 4

# CONTENTS

PART 4.
SPORTS

PART 5.
ENTERTAINMENT AND THE ARTS

PART 6.
LEARNING

# PART 9.
# HOME LIFE

# PART 10.
# ANIMALS

# PART 13.
# PROGRESS

# PART 14.
# PEOPLE AND PLACES

# PREFACE

Almost everyone has in mind writing a book someday. The assumption by so many people that a book is easy to write—if they could only find the time—is irritating to writers who actually write books. Although there is no evidence one is any harder to do than the other, people who wouldn't think of operating on a friend for a brain tumor have no hesitation about trying to write a book. Most of them don't actually want to write anything, they just want to be authors.

I like being a writer but I also like writing. The only time I feel in control of my life is when I am sitting at my typewriter—computer now—typing.

This book was three quarters written when the publisher, Peter Osnos, started pressing me for a title. Coming up with the name for a book has never been one of my strengths. It doesn't seem important because the name of a book doesn't have anything to do with whether a book sells well or not. The title only seems like a good one after it becomes a best-seller. When John Steinbeck submitted his book during the great depression of the thirties, it seems unlikely that the publisher thought *The Grapes of Wrath* was a title that would become one of the best known of all time.

I tried to think of a name for this book. There is no orderly process to go through thinking of a name for a book. If you're naming a child, there are long lists of names you can look through. It's more difficult naming a book than naming a baby because of the multitude of options. Just to give you some idea, every child's name there ever was is the potential name for a book.

As my brain flipped through possibilities, it seemed as if all the good book names had been taken. I started making notes of titles I'd like to have for this book and in every case, someone had thought of it first: *War and Peace, Pale Horse, Pale Rider, Catch 22, Cry the Beloved Country, Heart of Darkness, The Joy of Cooking, Gone With the Wind, Never So Young Again, The Heart Is a Lonely Hunter, Brave New World, The Naked and the Dead, Darkness at Noon, Tender Is the Night, The Postman Always Rings Twice, From Here to Eternity.* Now those are great names for books. What could we come up with to match one of those in the unlikely event this becomes a classic?

We ended up with *Common Nonsense.* I cannot remember whose idea it was. Five of us were sitting around a table and it may have been mine. At first glance it's pretty good. It's short and mildly clever being a play on a cliché. As the others around the table agreed that *Common Nonsense* would be the name of the book, the problem with me giving the name *Common Nonsense* to a book I wrote, came to me. Why am I saying the material in it is both common and nonsense? I guess the answer is that the book comprises 154 essays about a wide variety of subjects and is a reflection of a flawed brain with a capacity for being interested in more things than it can comprehend. We need fewer mysteries in our lives though and holding up any subject, no matter how trivial or how profound, to the strong light of day, takes the mystery out of it. But we could have called it *154 Essays by Andy Rooney.* That would have been a good, straightforward name for the book. Making my name part of the title would have been a trick way of getting it mentioned more prominently than if the book was called *154 Essays* and then, down below in smaller type, "By Andy Rooney." Because of the exposure my name gets on the television broadcast *60 Minutes*, its prominence in the title is considered to be a sales tool.

We'll see.

# PART 1

*Daily Life in America*

*Further proof of the fact that hope springs eternal is everyone's anticipation that the mail will bring something wonderful even though it almost never does.*

# DO NOT PUT BOOK IN WATER!

The directions that come with any new appliance or tool must all be written in one place in some remote foreign country because they all sound the same. They also sound as if they've been written by a Japanese who went to college in the United States.

As part of my vacation pleasure, I have just treated myself to a new, heavy duty cordless drill. The book of instructions that came with it clearly states, in big, bold letters:

WARNING! READ ALL INSTRUCTIONS BEFORE OPERATING THIS TOOL!

I don't do that. From many years experience buying new tools, gadgets and appliances, I have learned that the best thing to do is ignore the instructions, put the manual aside and start trying to use the new toy right away. If you don't try to use it, you can't understand the instructions. If you fool with it for a while and run into some problems using it, then you are better equipped to understand what the instructions are talking about. I realize, of course, that I am never going to get a book of instructions that says:

FOOL WITH YOUR NEW TOOL FIRST, THEN READ THE INSTRUCTIONS!

Neither am I going to read a book of directions that says:

THIS IS NOT A DANGEROUS TOOL!

Or:

KIDS WILL ENJOY PLAYING WITH THIS TOOL!

As careful as they want me to be, the instructions I have in front of me now don't give me a lot of confidence in whoever wrote them. I already owned an electric drill but I decided it would be handy if I had one that didn't have to be plugged in so I got this cordless model with a big battery. The fourth paragraph in the manual advises me: DO NOT ABUSE CORD. NEVER USE CORD TO CARRY TOOL. KEEP CORD AWAY FROM HEAT, OIL, SHARP EDGES OR MOVING PARTS.

What's that all about? I bought this piece of equipment because I wanted a drill that doesn't have a cord. It has a battery. Why do they tell me not to abuse the cord when it doesn't have one? They must be saving money by writing a single, all-purpose manual for every tool they make. All they have to say is generalities like KEEP YOUR WORK AREA CLEAN AND WELL LIT.

Whether my work area is clean or not is my business and I'll thank this big corporation to mind its own business. Do I write telling them to keep their factory clean? First thing you know, the manual will be telling me to make my bed in the morning and wash the dishes before watching television.

DO NOT OPERATE TOOL WHEN YOU ARE TIRED.

Oh, fine. If I didn't operate the tool when I'm tired, I'd never operate it because woodworking is my hobby and I only do it when I'm tired of working.

DO NOT IMMERSE IN WATER!

Gosh, it's a lucky thing you told me that. I was just going to fill the bathtub and put my new drill in there to soak.

They ought to have an instruction manual you had to read before they'd allow you to buy a tool.

ATTENTION! DO NOT BUY THIS TOOL UNLESS YOU ARE CERTAIN YOU REALLY WANT IT. MAKE SURE THIS TOOL DOES WHAT YOU WANT IT TO DO BEFORE YOU WASTE A LOT OF MONEY ON SOMETHING YOU DON'T REALLY NEED!

I don't keep warranties, factory guarantees or promises of any kind that come with stuff I buy because I know from experience that if something goes wrong, there's nothing good to do but throw the thing away and buy a new one. I don't keep the box stuff comes in, either, even though they tell me to.

"For service," the booklet says, "contact your nearest factory service center. A list of the factory service centers nearest you appears on page 14."

My nearest factory service center is always someplace like Dayton,

Ohio. I suppose I could just drive by someday and drop the tool off in Dayton when it breaks except that Dayton just doesn't happen to be on my way to anyplace I go these days.

## THE UNREMOVABLE TOP

The problem and the joke about it is old now. We're used to it. They've beaten us down and we're no longer complaining.

The fact remains, tops of jars and bottles are too hard to take off. Stuff that comes packaged in plastic is too hard to open and get at. Even cardboard boxes have become more impenetrable than a cave in Afghanistan. You shouldn't have to go to the garage to get a hatchet. Big envelopes that say "tear along dotted line" don't tear there at all. How come companies are selling us stuff we can't get at?

Something as simple as the twist-off cap on a bottle of soda is often impossible to remove with the normal strength of your bare hands. I have normal strength in my hands. I work with them in my shop all the time. I'm not embarrassed about my strength. I just can't get the tops off about half the things I try without wrestling with them.

If the average person was on a desert island with boxes full of bottles and jars of food, he or she could starve to death simply because it was impossible to get the tops off anything. Anyone in dire need of medicine in the middle of the night could die trying to get at a pill in a bottle. They aren't just "child-proof," they are "adult-proof."

About half of the cardboard milk or orange juice containers that have arrows saying "push here" or "open here," do not push or open there at all. You have to pry them open with a knife which creates a spout that drips.

Do the manufacturers who sell us these products understand how angry we are? They may not know and I have one possible explanation. It may be that the people who can't get the tops off things feel inadequate. They don't want to admit they can't do it so they don't complain. They assume everyone else can get the tops off and, if they can't, they figure they must be too dumb or too weak. No one wants to admit either of those things so they remain silent.

Men, in particular, don't want to admit they aren't strong enough. My friend Garry Moore had a great sense of humor. He was married to a woman quite a bit bigger than he was and he liked to joke about her size and strength. When he couldn't get the top off something, he enjoyed needling her by handing her the jar and saying "Here, Dear. Would you take this top off for me?"

The other conspiracy I suspect is that the inventors of tops are in cahoots with the people who make a wide variety of gadgets designed to help people remove tops. Inventing new kinds of openers is a cottage industry and many of them don't work. Even if they do, no one should buy something like a jar of jam and then have to buy something else to get the top off.

Some of these gadgets are designed to remove small tops, others large tops and people have to buy a different kind of top remover, depending on their problem and the size of tops they want to remove. Sales of these faulty gadgets are brisk and top designers may be in on the profits.

When it comes to taking the tops off things, I'm a rapper. I give anything that resists a sharp rap with the handle end of a table knife and this sometimes loosens it. I have even taken a jar to the basement and inserted it in my vise while I try to twist the top with a pair of pliers.

Last week I bought a can of something that's supposed to cut through the buildup of baked-on grease in the oven. The top of the can says "TO REMOVE TOP, SQUEEZE, TWIST AND PULL." I squeezed, twisted and pulled with all my might and couldn't get the top off.

In a moment of fury, I had a wild idea. I was going to find out who designed the top, locate his home or office and then take off in my car with a camera crew. Once in the presence of this inventor of tops, I'd whip out the jar or can from my bag, push it at him with the camera rolling and say "Here. You invented this damn thing. Let me see YOU squeeze, twist and pull it off."

All this would be caught on camera. After the inventor failed miserably removing his own top, which I am convinced he would, I would come back with my pictures and sell them as an expose to one of the television shows that exposes things. I would have exclusive pictures of an inventor of tops who couldn't get one of his own tops off.

## HOW TO SAVE TIME

It's important to be on the lookout for ways to save time. Here are some tips:

- There is no sense in wasting time being open-minded about everything. Don't waste time listening to arguments in favor of something you thought through years ago and decided against.
- Dressing in the morning, make sure you have both shoes and two socks together in front of the chair so you only have to bend over once to put on all four of them.
- If the printer on your computer is slow and you're thirsty, press PRINT and then go get a drink. By the time you get back, the printing will be finished and you'll no longer be thirsty.
- When opening mail, slit open all the envelopes before reading anything. It takes longer to slit, read, slit, read, slit, read so it's quickest to slit, slit, slit, slit, slit, read, read, read, read. Save time by not reading anything in an envelope that says IMPORTANT!
- Read the newspaper during the commercials on television news.
- Never start a crossword puzzle. If you have that much time to waste, take a nap.
- When boiling water, put the water in two pans or one kettle and one pan. Use the first to boil to start the coffee.

- When driving on a road with no traffic, stay on the inside of every curve, thus straightening out the road thus saving both distance and time.
- While brushing your teeth in the morning, turn on the shower so you don't have to wait for hot water when you're ready to get in.
- If you work on an upper floor in an office building, wait until you have pressed the elevator button before starting to put on your coat. If it takes 15 seconds to button your coat and two minutes for the elevator to come, you're only losing a minute and 45 seconds.
- In the supermarket, don't pick the shortest line. Choose the line in which people have least in their shopping carts.
- This is personal but when I'm writing I save time by not putting apostrophes in words like "isnt," "dont," "arent" and "wouldnt." I estimate that in a 400-word letter, I save as much as five seconds by not putting in about 30 apostrophes.
- Don't put everything back where it belongs every time you use it. Wait until you have a lot of stuff out of place and put it all back where it belongs at one time.

## THANKS A LOT FOR NOTHING

Common courtesy has all but disappeared in many public places. We are no longer polite to strangers as a matter of course and that has contributed to the decline of what is called the quality of life in America. It varies in different parts of the Country but nowhere is common courtesy the same as it once was.

It may be simply because, on one hand, we are closer together physically than people used to be but farther apart in mind and spirit. In our cars we don't hesitate to blow our horn at someone in another car because we are remote from that person.

At one time it was quite usual in a crowd for both the jostled party and the jostler to say, "Excuse me." Or perhaps one would say "Excuse me" and, simultaneously, the other would say "Pardon me." It still happens but a much more common response than "Excuse me" to an unintended jostle now is "Why don't you watch where you're going." It's a comment, not a question.

Part of the new rudeness can also be attributed to the fact that we have diminished the importance of good words like "please" and "thank you" by using them indiscriminately and too often when we don't mean them.

We've weakened their meaning by using them always in some superlative form. We seldom say just "Thank you" anymore. We routinely say "Thank you very much." We say it for the most inconsequential things people do for us. When someone holds open a door for the person following, "Thank you" would seem an adequate acknowledgment of so routine a courtesy but we never let it go at that. It's always "Thanks a lot." If someone provides us with change for a dollar, we're apt to say "Thanks a million." Thanks ten, or at the most a hundred, would seem to be thankfulness enough.

Excessive thanks for a simple gesture leaves us nothing in reserve for the important occasions when we want to thank someone for some extraordinary courtesy they have extended us.

I stopped for gas last month in New Jersey where self-service is still illegal. A sign near the pump said "If our attendant fails to say 'Thank you,' the gas is on us."

Is that kind of "thank you" from the heart? I don't think so.

If the attendant didn't say "thank you" and I reported him for it and the owner had to make good on the sign's promise to give me the tank of gas free, the attendant would be fired. When the attendant thanks me, it doesn't come from his gratitude, it comes from his fear of the boss. It's a meaningless "thank you." Too many "thank you's" are these days.

When you get into a taxicab in New York City now, a recorded voice thanks you for using the taxi. Thanks for what? Thanks because we had to go someplace and needed transportation?

My trusty old Underwood typewriter and my Toshiba computer sit here on my desk side by side. The typewriter has the good taste not to say anything to me. It just does its job, silently and well.

My computer, on the other hand, won't shut up. I touch a few keys and the screen reads: PLEASE WAIT

Why "please"? Do I have a choice? Does my computer mean that it's grateful to me for being patient, which I am not? It's meaningless for a machine to ask you anything as if it were being polite. Traditionally, the word "please" has been used as the polite introduction a person uses before making a request that may or may not be fulfilled. The word has even acquired a whole new meaning in the last few years.

When someone starts giving a friend advice he doesn't want, the friend is apt to say "Please!" He doesn't mean "Please give me more." In this sense, the word retains some of its pleading quality but what the person using it means is "Please stop" or "Who needs your advice" or "Please knock it off with the advice."

The word "thanks" is used in the same ironic sense. You might say to me after reading this column, for instance "Thanks for not lecturing me again about courtesy."

## THE TRUTH ABOUT LYING

Lies are a part of life. In spite of the admonitions we get beginning in childhood to tell the truth, the whole truth and nothing but the truth, the most honest people among us don't live by that standard. It's too hard.

"How does this look?" a woman asks her husband as they're going out the door to a party. If he's lucky, he genuinely likes what it looks like. If he doesn't he's in trouble because either he has to lie or tell the truth and start the whole evening off on the wrong foot. He not only has to lie but has to add to the deceit by lying enthusiastically. "It's okay" is not enough.

It's at least partly the woman's fault for asking the question in the first place. Samuel Johnson put his finger on the problem when he said "Nobody has the right to put another under such a difficulty that he must either hurt the person by telling the truth or hurt himself by telling what is not true."

Truth has a much better reputation than lying. We propagandize ourselves in favor of it every chance we get. All the wise men have endorsed it:

Plato—"Truth will prevail."

H. W. Shaw—"Truth is the edict of God."

Emerson—"Every violation of truth is a stab at the health of human society."

Woodrow Wilson—"The truth always matches, piece by piece, with other parts of the truth."

Mark Twain—"When in doubt, tell the truth."

In spite of the lip service we pay truth, we spend a lot of time deciding when to lie. It's good that it doesn't come easily or naturally to most of us. We spend even more time trying to determine when we're being lied to and when we're being told the truth.

Advertising puts us to the test and gives us a lot of experience in detecting untruths. We know they lie so how good is this product they're telling us about? And what about politicians? Not many people pick up the newspaper and read a story coming out of Washington without wondering whether they're getting the truth or some altered version of it. The elected official who lies or tells less than the whole truth may, like the husband, believe that it's best for everyone if he doesn't go overboard being honest. He can get himself believing it's best for the American people if they do not know the whole truth. He is not lying for personal gain. This is called "Lying Made Easy."

It is even sadder to consider the possibility that many Americans know it and accept it. They don't want the burden of knowing the truth because they are then confronted with solving some of the problems.

Trying to discern whether we've been lied to or not is complicated when we start considering that maybe we were told part of the truth but not all the truth. Part of the truth is like a lie but worse because it's more devious and more difficult to detect.

As a guest on the Larry King show one night I said some things, in answer to his questions, that I would have been better off lying about or avoiding. My superiors at CBS were angry. It was not that the people who objected to what I said necessarily thought I was wrong. They simply thought I shouldn't have said it. It was, they thought, disloyal to be critical of CBS while I still took a salary from the company.

In my own defense, I told a boss of mine that I thought if all the truth were known by everyone about everything, it would be a better world. He scoffed. I think "scoff" is what he did. I know he rejected the idea.

I've thought about it and in retrospect decided he was right. It was a pompous statement that sounds true but probably isn't. Our lives could not survive all the truth about everything. If my boss asks me about it again though, I'm going to lie and repeat it. I like the sound of it. Maybe I can get my name in Bartlett's *Familiar Quotations* by saying "It would be a better world if everyone in it knew all the truth about everything."

## SMILING

Words are what we use most often to communicate information or a thought but we transfer a lot of ideas from one of us to another using means other than the written or spoken word. For example, we smile.

A smile is a complex way of indicating what we think to someone else because there are so many ways to smile, each with its own meaning. We smile when we are amused. We smile to indicate we are pleased. If we wish to let the person looking at us know that we agree with what he or she said, we smile and nod. We frown to convey the opposite of those ideas but we don't frown as often as we smile.

There are compulsive smilers. Even when they tell a sad story, they smile. I frown more than most people and smile less often although I don't think my reaction to the world is any less positive than people who smile a lot. Smiling just doesn't come naturally to me.

A smile loses its effectiveness if a person smiles too often. You can usually tell when a person is smiling for effect and when he or she is smiling naturally. At its best, smiling is one of the nicest things to do.

Laughing is an extreme smile. It doesn't have as many nuances as smiling has although you can laugh, you can chuckle or guffaw. Laughing can be nasty too. When you "laugh at" someone, you are not being friendly. You're putting the person down.

There are an infinite number of ways to smile. A smirk is a nasty smile. A grin is getting close to a laugh. A smile can even be evil. Mona Lisa's smile is enigmatic. You wouldn't ever say that someone had an enigmatic laugh. When you see someone laughing, it seems as though the eyes are laughing too although eyes don't change. Not even Irish eyes laugh. When the rest of the face, including even the nose, sometimes changes during a laugh, it gives the illusion that the eyes have joined in the fun.

The best smiles come unbidden. That's when you don't *decide* to smile. Your mouth just widens and, involuntarily, the corners turn up slightly. That's why smiles are so good. The best ones are unplanned.

You see a lot of fake smiles. People use their smile for a purpose. For example, I enjoy watching Goldie Hawn in a movie but I wish she'd stop smiling. The world isn't that funny all the time, Goldie. Although, come to think of it, the smile Goldie uses doesn't suggest she is amused. It suggests someone is taking her picture and she decided many years ago that she looked better in a picture if she was smiling. I don't know whether she does or not because I've never seen her when she wasn't.

Professional photographers almost always insist that you smile.

"Okay, look at the camera and smile."

Why in the world should I smile because a photographer thinks I look better doing it? I don't think I look better. If the smile didn't come naturally as the camera clicked, I look foolish, not friendly.

In newspaper pictures of businessmen, they are often seen smiling when in actual fact, they seldom smile on the job. When a corporation spends a fortune having its annual report printed in an elaborate brochure, it's full of hot air and the pictures fit the text. All the executives are smiling as if they were nice guys and they are not. I don't want a business executive smiling at me in his pictures. I know it's just a pose. It's known in song as laughing on the outside, crying on the inside.

## NO CLOTHES MAKE THE WOMAN

Unless you know a lot of people I don't know, you don't know anyone who looks like the women wearing the clothes in fashion magazines and newspaper ads. I stare in amazement at what I see, hoping no one will catch me looking.

Who are the women in your crowd who don't put on any underwear from the waist up and then get into loose-fitting, V-necked dresses cut down to their waistline?

It would be interesting to watch these women, wearing these so-called clothes, perform any normal, everyday chore. They certainly couldn't bend over to pick up a quarter if they dropped one on the sidewalk without falling out of what little they have on.

There are newspaper ads showing pictures of women in clothes so revealing that editors at the same newspaper would refuse to use them on grounds they were indecent if they were submitted by a staff photographer to illustrate a news story.

What I fail to understand is the theory behind fashion advertising. Do stores show their clothes on these glamorous, barely-covered models because they think the average American woman will be fooled into thinking she'll look like that if she buys the dress?

If that isn't the theory, what is? What does the average woman think? She's 53 years old, 5 feet 2 inches tall, weighing 141 pounds. She's neither homely nor beautiful. Does she look at the ad with the voluptuous model, 19 years old, 5 feet 7 inches tall, who weighs 103 pounds, and envision herself, in the mirror, looking like that if she buys the dress?

One Sunday fashion section carried a story saying that women are once again wearing high-heeled, high-fashion shoes to work. Several pictures accompanied the story, showing women wearing platforms attached to their shoes with elaborately cut leather straps. These shoes would inhibit the most athletic woman alive from getting out of her own way.

The thought I had seeing women in these ridiculously high heels is that someone in the shoe industry got to a fashion writer or an editor at the newspaper. That occurred to me because from my experience, women are clearly NOT wearing high heeled shoes to work. It is not a trend. It may be a wish that shoe manufacturers have but it is not a trend.

My office is on the same floor of a building with a lot of other offices that are occupied by at least 25 women. I see them come to work every day and none of them ever wears high-heels. High heels are as rare at work as slinky, low cut dresses. Some working women may keep a pair of shoes with high heels in their desk drawer in the event they have an evening date but they do not wear them at work.

Nothing has done more for the women's movement than when they moved out of high-heeled shoes and into flat-soled shoes. It changed their image and for the better. I looked at those pictures of what the newspaper called the latest thing and it reminded me of stories I'd read of the days when Chinese women bound their feet to misshape them into little arched stubs that they couldn't walk on.

The makers of women's shoes must be distraught over the move women have made toward wearing sensible shoes and sneakers. Shoe manufacturers would love a newspaper story suggesting that the new fashion among women is high-heeled shoes even if it is not. I'll bet they'd even be willing to pay someone to suggest women are returning to high heels as a trick to encourage it. I don't want to suggest a newspaper editor was less than honest but it comes to my mind as a possibility.

It's hard to say how much influence advertising has on what people wear. Obviously the people who design and sell clothes think it has a great deal. I can't help thinking though, that fashion has a mind of its own independent of designers or fashion section editors. There is no telling where the latest fashion comes from or where it goes when we're done with it.

## NAPPING

It isn't right for anyone to talk about the things he or she does well. It is for other people to point out your strengths.

Having said that, I want to tell you about something I do exceedingly well. If there were some way of ranking the people who do it in order of their proficiency at it, I believe I'd be near the top of the list. I'm that good.

What I do so well is nap. There are few people I know who nap as well as I do. I have a couch in my office and I often close the door, take off my shoes and lie on it. The duration of my nap time is seldom more than five minutes. An eight-minute nap would be like a night's sleep. I awake from a four-minute nap completely refreshed and ready to face a new day—even though the day is half over.

People who don't nap well miss one of life's great pleasures. I think they realize this because they try to make up for their disappointment over not being able to nap by making derogatory remarks about people who do nap. They assume a superior attitude.

"You didn't hear it because you were asleep" a family member will say to me in a holier-than-thou tone of voice if I miss a little of Jim Lehrer's *NewsHour*. A drink before dinner is nap-inducing and I enjoy dropping off briefly before going upstairs to bed. You might think that would take the edge off a night's sleep but it does not.

Last Sunday I made a three-hour drive from upstate New York down to The City and I had to pull over twice and doze briefly. I can be asleep in the car before the residual vibrations of a running engine subside.

There are several things that put me to sleep and driving with the sun in my eyes is principal among them. Other somnifacients are a bad movie, a dull concert or a company treasurer's report.

A book, *The Art of Napping* by William Anthony, a Boston University professor, has encouraged me to come out of the bedroom closet. Professor Anthony argues in favor of the recreational nap. Taking a nap not because you're tired or sleepy but simply because taking one is a pleasant pastime. (It seems possible that the phrase "taking a nap" might be responsible for napping's negative reputation. "Having a nap" might be better.)

For years I was a secret napper but *The Art of Napping* has changed all that. I am now an outgoing, up-front napper. I no longer feel I have to steal a nap or hide the fact that I am taking one. I nap with confidence and pride in how good I am at doing it.

## AVOID THESE WHEN POSSIBLE

There is solace in the fellowship of adversity. I am, therefore, undertaking the job of cataloging some of life's unpleasant little tasks in an effort to bring us all together:

The following are hard little jobs:

- Filling out a form that has boxes too small for what they want you to write in them.
- Washing the frying pan in which you've cooked scrambled eggs. It is difficult to remove the egg that sticks to non-stick pans.
- Mowing the lawn when the grass is wet.
- Pulling out the stem of a watch to reset the time.
- Cleaning the garlic press.

- Untwisting the wire that cleaners use to hold two hangers together when you don't know which way to twist.
- Plugging a cord into an outlet that's behind the couch or a dresser—which seems to be where they usually are.
- Programming a VCR to record a show you want to see that's being broadcast next Tuesday while you're out.
- Erasing anything you've written with a pencil.
- Looking up a word you don't know how to spell to find out how to spell it.
- Choosing the fastest lane at the checkout counter in the supermarket.
- Getting to talk to a real live person who can help when you call a store, an airline, a doctor's office, a bank or a big company.
- Picking a ripe melon.
- Remembering which side the gas tank is on if you have two cars that have them on opposite sides.
- Getting back to sleep if you have to get up in the middle of the night when there's a full moon.
- Finding anything you want to watch on television from the descriptions of them in the newspaper listings.
- Opening a carton of milk that doesn't open when you press where it says "Open here."
- Attaching a hose to the faucet and the nozzle to the hose so that neither of them sprays water all over you when you turn it on.
- Changing a light bulb in the ceiling from a short ladder.
- Separating the bottles, the newspapers, the cans and the garbage when you suspect the people who pick up your trash dump them all together wherever they take them.
- Keeping a canoe going in a straight line when you're the only one paddling it.
- Maintaining a handy balance of money in your pocket without ending up with too many dimes, nickels and pennies and not enough five and ten dollar bills.

- Finding anything in the Yellow Pages. If you look under "Doctors," it'll be under "Physicians." If you look under "Cars," it'll be under "Automobiles" but if you look under "Automobile Rental," it'll be under "Car Rental."
- Getting the wire on the back of a picture to catch the hook you hammered in to hang it from when you can't see the hook because of the picture.
- Cooking the right amount of rice or pasta without making either too much or too little.
- Not letting someone dumber than you are know that you think so.
- Throwing away something you've had for a long time that is of absolutely no use to you.
- Leaving the theater in the middle of a movie you hate but that you paid $9 to get in to see.
- Reading in bed when the table the lamp is on is too low.
- Doing anything just because it's good for you.

## UNEASY CHAIRS

There's a problem with chairs.

People almost never sit on chairs the way chair-designers intended they should and perhaps it's time to rethink the chair in relation to the shape of the human body and the positions it assumes while in or on them.

There is a difference between sitting *in* a chair and sitting *on* one. It depends some on the chair. There are chairs you sit *on* and chairs you sit *in*. The *in* chairs are more comfortable for lounging. They have arms and soft cushions. You wouldn't want to watch a long night of television seated *on* a chair. They are straight-backed and hard. On the other hand, you wouldn't be comfortable at the dining room table trying to eat while seated in the chair you like for television watching.

At a college graduation ceremony I attended, 500 students and 1,000 parents sat on card-table chairs temporarily lined up on the lawn of the campus quadrangle. During parts of the commencement ceremony that I didn't find compelled to give my total attention to, I stared at the sea of people and could tell they weren't happy with their seating arrangements. They fidgeted. They crossed their legs, twisted them like pretzels, put their arms over the back of the chair next to them, squirmed continuously. Some of the college girls curled one leg up under themselves and sat on that.

It concerned me because I was the graduation speaker and it's hard enough to keep the attention of an audience when they're comfortably seated. In a survey I made while waiting to speak, I determined that, at one time or another 84 percent of the seated audience crossed their legs. This is evidence of a chair's basic inadequacy. If chairs were comfortable and supportive of us where we most want support, we would not feel that great urge to lift one foot off the floor and hook the back of the knee over the other knee. Men often don't actually cross their legs, they place one ankle on top of the knee of the other leg and simultaneously rest the palm of one hand on the ankle that is on the knee. This is a ridiculous bit of contortion that points toward bad chair-design.

The average chair is a straight right-angle with four legs supporting the flat seat. The human body, seated, is not a perfect right angle. No straight chair can be expected to be much comfort to a round bottom.

The answer may be that each of us should choose our chairs to fit our body much as we choose our clothes. One-size chairs do not fit all. If we ever come to the time when we can order a chair to fit our size and shape, it should be a consideration when large groups are being seated at parties or meetings. Just below the RSVP address would be a discreet notation "Please indicate chair size." Theaters and ball parks should have seats small, medium, large and X-large. One airline has announced it's going to charge extra for over-sized people who need two seats. Anyone who has ever had to sit in the middle of a three-across airline row between two out-sized men or women will approve of this.

There are restaurants with excellent food and bad chairs. The most frequent problem with a restaurant chair is its height in relation to the table. No one wants the table up under his or her chin. The average table is 29 inches high. The seat of many chairs is only 17 inches off the floor and the disparity is too much for anyone short of six feet. Banquettes are softer and may be more comfortable but they are usually lower than the chairs. No one wants to eat lying down.

I propose a Congressional investigation into chairs.

## BARNS

There's nothing Americans of another age have built on the land that makes more difference to what our country looks like than barns. When you drive a long distance and get out of town, you look out your car window and what do you see? In many parts of the Country you see barns. You see lots and lots of barns.

Barns look good because they're built for what they do. Nothing fake about a barn. Skyscrapers have been tortured into shape by architects who had only some vague idea what would happen inside them. Barns, on the other hand, are purposeful. They provide a roof overhead for everything a farmer can't take into his farmhouse. A barn covers cows in winter, horses if a farmer has them, hay, machinery and, on a rainy day, the kids who play in it.

Barns are bigger than farmhouses and very often, better looking. A well-built barn is a thing of beauty. An 8 by 8 inch oak beam 14 feet long dovetailed into another is practically immortal and exceeds in beauty any picture ever hung on a wall.

The bad news is, wooden barns, like farmers, are disappearing.

There were once three million farms in the United States and every farm had at least one barn. Most farms had two, some had three and a few farms had a whole family of barns . . . big barns, middle-sized barns

. . . small barns. Barns can't move to the city so when the farmer does, barns stay where they are and fall first into disrepair and then down.

Barns don't give up easily but our countryside is littered with abandoned barns that are deteriorating. It's sad to see something so noble as a barn die a slow and painful death. They deserve better than what most of them get. There is no society devoted to saving them. Their roofs no longer keep out the weather but some barns were so honestly built that they last 50 years after they're left for dead. Old barn boards cling where they were nailed to old beams. Our houses should be so well built.

Barns age more gracefully than most buildings and certainly more gracefully than people. They actually improve in appearance with age. Their weathered wood turns silvery gray. Or if they were painted barn red, they never give up being red. Some farmers, in need of cash, sold the side of their barns to companies advertising chewing tobacco or some other commercial product. A sign painter spent a day applying a grossly commercial advertisement to the side of the barn most visible from the road. In many cases, the fading picture on the side of the barn outlasted the farmer and the product.

Barns last for another reason, too. They don't have to take indoor heating or leaky plumbing fixtures. A barn is pretty much the same temperature inside as it is outside so barns remain standing long after the farmers who built them have been laid to rest.

Everyone says they love the Country but everyone moves to the city. There are about 800,000 fewer farms in the United States than there were just 20 years ago. Most of the deteriorating barns are right where the farmers left them, evidence of their sad and desperate departure.


## PENMANSHIP WITH AN ACCENT

Do they really make glass by melting down sand?

I sat down at my typewriter—computer actually—and considered what I might write about. There is no shortage of things to write about but a writer has to settle on one. I looked up from the keyboard for a minute and idly stared out my window.

"What wonderful, absolutely amazing material," I thought to myself as I stopped looking through the window and started thinking about glass. There may be nothing we so routinely take for granted that is more important.

That this material we can see through, which stands between us in our homes and the threatening outside world, makes a loud noise when it breaks is, as Walt Whitman said of a mouse, "miracle enough to stagger sextillions of infidels."

We double-lock and bolt our doors when we leave the house or at night but all there is between the thieves and our treasures is that thin, fragile pane. We would be constantly vulnerable if it didn't register the kind of high decibels that discourages thieves when it crashes. I suppose eventually someone will invent glass that doesn't make a noise when it breaks but it'll never catch on.

It is absolutely incredible that we can see through something so fragile in one way and yet so strong and durable in another. We have windows in our house that were put in when it was built in the 1860s. It's a good thing windows don't get harder to see through as they get older.

If it were not for glass, we'd still be driving open cars because we couldn't sit inside a dark metal box on wheels without seeing where we were going and cruise down a highway at 60 mph. Imagine a house, an office, a factory or a school room without glass. Imagine a bar without a glass. Or people without glasses.

Here's this transparent material they can do optical tricks with so that when we put it in front of our eyes in little oval shapes, contained in a metal frame held in place with a hook that goes over our ears, we can see better.

If it were not for glass, Thomas Edison never would have invented the light bulb and nothing is more amazing about the property of glass than the fact that if we coat one side of it with a mercury solution, the material we could previously see through becomes opaque and something in which we can see our own likeness reflected, a mirror. Without mirrors, we could never have been able to see ourselves as others see us.

No historian has been able to put a finger on when glass was invented. In London, the British Museum has example of it 5,000 years old. The earliest glass was probably made in the Middle East in places like Syria and Palestine because the pure sand there was its principal ingredient although there's no mention of glass in the Bible. It's best if we don't worry our heads over how they make glass out of sand.

The Indians didn't have glass in their tepees when the Pilgrims got here but early settlers built a glass factory in Virginia in the early 1600s and started putting windows in their houses.

When I was in the third and fourth grades, the boys often got into fights out on the playground but even back then we had a code of honor: it was considered cowardly to hit a boy who wore glasses. It was okay to be mean to them though. We often called little Eddie Williams "Four Eyes."

In my teenage years, it was considered unfortunate if a girl needed glasses. Dorothy Parker made that memorable with her famous couplet:

"Men seldom make passes
At girls who wear glasses."

More recently glasses have been turned into a fashion item that people wear, not because they need them to see with, but for effect. There are Hollywood stars who wear dark glasses in the dark.

So much for glass.


## THE SOUND OF NOISE

There's a difference between sound and noise. Noise is objectionable. Sound can be objectionable sometimes and not other times. Good music is sound. Music you don't like is noise.

Saturday morning at 5:30 I awoke to the sweet sound of chirping birds. I lay there wondering why the birds were chirping. Were they communicating with other birds? If they were, what were they saying? Was it a form of singing or was it just an ode to joy, a sound they were making for the fun of it? Sound is impossible to describe with words. We fail when we try to name a bird after the sound it makes. Whippoorwills, don't say "whip poor will" anymore than chickadees say "chickadee" or cuckoos say "cuckoo." Ducks don't go "quack quack" but that's as close as the human voice can get.

After breakfast that morning, as we sat reading the paper, the woman across the street put her two dogs out in her yard and they started yapping. Yapping is a noise. These two dogs are not trying to say anything. They're barking their little heads off and driving everyone else crazy for the fun of it. Their owner ought to point out to these dogs that they are being a nuisance and should stop barking.

My plan is to hide a tape recorder in the bushes near her porch and record the barking dogs. That night, at 2 a.m., I'll sneak over, put the recorder on her porch and turn it on full volume.

I considered the possibility that the birds had awakened the dogs and wondered whether barking dogs annoy birds as much as they annoy me.

Dogs can vary the sounds they make almost as much as humans can. You know a lot about what your dog has in mind from the manner in which it barks, yelps or whines. It doesn't seem to me that birds can alter the noise they make but I don't know that. When a flock of them in a tree senses the presence of a cat, the bird noises are louder and more frequent but otherwise sound the same as their chirps.

The difference between sounds is often definite but not easy to define. We can tell a yell from a scream but couldn't say precisely why. A scream is more apt to be involuntary. One of its characteristics is the element of terror in it. If we hear a yell in our backyard, we figure there are some kids out there. If we hear a scream, we rush to the window, alarmed.

Not everyone agrees on which sounds are good and which are bad. I like the sound of great, rolling thunder with its promise of lightning and rain.

A squeak or a rattle is a bad sound because either means trouble. Something is loose, broken or needs oil.

The abrupt closing of an expensive car door is a good sound. You can tell how much a car cost by hearing one of its doors slammed shut.

The sounds of screeching brakes, skidding rubber wheels and the noise of metal hitting metal are some of the worst sounds.

The sound of a typewriter clacking away is a sound I miss now that everyone is writing on computers that just go ticky tack.

In summer I like the sound of a screen door slapping shut.

The eerie sound of a distant train whistle is distinctive.

Noises in war were important. A good infantryman could identify a dozen weapons by the noise they made. It was important for the soldier to know whether the sound he heard was from the rifle of a friend or a foe.

Ornithologists have certainly studied the sound birds make but no one, to my knowledge, has ever done a report on the sound a house makes in the middle of the night. Sometimes you could swear there's someone downstairs but there never is.

What mysterious force is it in a house that makes the sound of someone creeping up the stairs when there is no one creeping up the stairs?


## IS IT SOUND OR NOISE?

I have written the essays in this book over a period of about five years. No one has so many thoughts that the same ones don't keep recurring in your mind. I can't get noise out of my head.

Everything is too loud, that's what I notice most when I come back to the City after vacation.

There is some inevitable noise in our lives but we shun silence. We don't seem to want it even though silence is the natural condition of earth. We equate silence with nothingness and nothingness is like death. That scares us most of all. Young people, in particular, are uneasy if there's no sound. If it's quiet, they turn on the radio.

Radio was a great invention but it is more intrusive than television because it doesn't demand the attention that comes with watching so people have it on when they aren't listening. You can have noise without any obligation to listen.

There are gadgets sold that produce a barely audible sound called "white noise." They are supposed to help people who have trouble getting to sleep. Technically, white noise is sound whose emphasis is the same at all frequencies. It might be called "dull noise" because it's the opposite of the elaborately contrived difference in the emphasis on frequencies that make music.

It is almost as if we are afraid of silence. If I call a company with which I do business the person I wish to talk to is usually busy but will be with me in a minute. I am put on hold and immediately my ear is filled with music I don't want to hear. The company is afraid that a little silence will indicate to me that they aren't there or don't care that I'm waiting. I don't want to think about what their music makes me think of. I want to think my own thoughts in silence while I wait and I'll thank them to shut up and turn off their damn music.

There are good sounds but good sounds are not noise. Good sounds are those of a distant cricket, the chirping of early morning birds, a well-played instrument, a trained voice singing, a well-tuned engine running. Noise is the neighbor's power mower, a chain saw, jackhammer or an outboard motorboat on the lake early in the morning.

The greatest quiet of all is falling snow late at night in winter. You don't actually hear the sound of it, you sense it and it's pervasive. The sound of rain on the roof is pleasant although louder than snow. There is a pervasive quietness to rain. It drowns out noise.

Horn-blowing is worse in many foreign cities than it is in American cities. Would it be possible to ration horn-blowing? Maybe every car should come equipped with a counter that registers every toot. When the number hits some arbitrary figure, the horn would deactivate and the driver would have to submit an explanation for his horn-blowing to the motor vehicle bureau before getting it back. Notice of the horn reactivation would be entered on a driver's license, like a speeding conviction. I might use my horn twice a year.

The drivers of cars with their tops down and their radios blaring rock music ought to be given tickets. I look at the drivers of those cars and I'd be condemned as prejudiced if they knew what I was thinking. "They're stupid," I'm thinking. "They don't want to have to think because they're incapable of thinking so they're drowning out thought with noise."

It's difficult to think when noise is entering your brain through your ears. If someone made an audio cassette of beautiful quiet, it might sell to people who dislike noise. There's a marginal difference between quiet and silence. Quiet is beautiful and comforting. Silence can be scary.

There are people who seem oblivious to sound. They can edit it out. They leave their radios and television sets on while reading the newspaper. They find the sound of voices comforting. Well, I don't. I find soundlessness comforting. In the country this summer, I'd awaken every morning to the sound of absolutely nothing and the silence was golden.

## DON'T YOU HATE IT WHEN . . . ?

Don't you hate it when:

- You finally find time to go to the movies and the only thing playing is something you don't want to see?
- Your suitcase is the last one off the airplane?
- They put you on hold and play canned music you can't stand?
- You pay too much for a melon and find out at breakfast that it's hard and green?
- You let someone use your car and when you get it back the gas is below a quarter, the seat has been moved and the radio is on FM.

- The guy in front of you is moving at 10 miles an hour when the light turns yellow and he makes it but you don't?
- Or he starts to make a right turn and then flips on his right-turn signal?
- The bread in the toaster burns on the edges but doesn't turn brown in the middle where you want to put the jam?
- Your shoelace breaks when you're in a hurry?
- You try to look up a word in the dictionary to see how it's spelled and can't find it because you don't know how to spell it?
- You take your shoes off and find a hole in the toe of a sock, the rest of which would last another ten years?
- Someone is giving you a number and the ballpoint pen by the telephone won't write?
- The lines on the map you're reading don't seem to have any relation to the roads you're trying to find?
- Someone ahead of you in the 10-items, express checkout line at the supermarket has 20 items and wants to pay by check?
- You're walking down the street with a woman you don't know well and someone walking behind you starts using foul language?
- You need five scoops of coffee for breakfast but there are only three left in the old can so you have to open a new one and mix the tired old with the aromatic new?
- The flashlight doesn't work so you buy new batteries and find out it's the bulb that's bad?
- The only place to plug in an extension cord is down behind the couch?
- The mailman leaves a letter at your house that looks important but it's for the people next door?
- The bank buries your statement in an envelope with a fistful of advertising for some new service you don't want?
- You fail to stop the gas pump on an even number so you owe $17.03 and don't have any pennies?
- Cute "we-can't-answer-the-phone-right-now" messages on answering machines?

- You get a chance to watch a little of a game but it's halftime so all you get are commercials and a panel of sportscasters trying to be clever saying nothing?
- Your grass is brown and there's thunder and lightning but you don't get any rain?
- You put on a shirt you haven't worn in months and find it is no longer your size?
- The fire engine goes by your house and you don't know where the fire is?


## GARDENERS ARE GOOD PEOPLE

Farmers are good people. Gardeners are amateur farmers and they're good people, too.

There are millions of people who take pleasure from growing flowers or vegetables in their small gardens in the summer or keeping pots of them going inside their homes in the winter. They nurture life and offer hope for the world. There are some decent people.

Planting and encouraging a garden takes virtues most of us don't have. Let me count the ways:

- A gardener has to be sensible. I am not a gardener. On the few occasions I've tried to grow something, I've killed the plant with what I thought was kindness. If it was to be fertilized, I gave it too much fertilizer. If it needed water occasionally, I flooded it every day. The best gardeners know when the ideal treatment for a plant is benign neglect. They leave it alone.
- Gardeners have to love life. Love of life is what drives a gardener to grow things. A farmer may do it for money but there's nothing in it for a gardener. There are people with no respect for life and certainly no love for it. A gardener accepts death as part of life more gracefully than most people. They know when it's over.

- Gardeners are patient. If you're going to have flowers by summer, you have to plan ahead, do some work and then be prepared to wait for results. Most of us don't wait well. To win an election, the politician has to promise us he's going to make our world better by tomorrow. We lack the gardener's patience.

  Flowers won't be out any time soon when you plant the seeds today. It takes a special quality gardeners have to anticipate the reward of beauty that will come some day—not tomorrow. The gardener takes pleasure meanwhile from looking forward to the day the flowers bloom.

- A gardener has to have faith in his soil, in his seed and in nature. He or she has to believe that there is a miracle contained in that small, oval seed that will produce first a thin green stem, then leaves and finally, flowers. The seed is the egg of the flower.

  The mystery of genes is nowhere more mysterious than in the seed of a flowering plant. How does the seed of a zinnia, which looks so much like the seed of a rose, know enough to come up in all those dazzling colors? How does the seed of the rose know enough to be red? Doesn't a rebellious rose ever decide it wants to be a dandelion?

- A gardener has to be a nurturer. There's something of the good mother in a gardener, man or woman. Gardeners provide food and water for their young plants until they are able to gather it for themselves—water and nutrients from their root system and life-blood from the chlorophyll in their green leaves which so cleverly enables them to convert sunlight into the chemicals they need to flourish.

- A good gardener has to be practical and not a romantic. When the time comes, the gardener has to chop away and prune out stems that would produce flowers in the interest of better flowers on the stems that remain. It's a cruel process but the gardener knows is has to be done and does it.

  The flowers might survive without their gardeners but they're not apt to flourish. Flowers and gardeners need each other. Flowers need gardeners. Gardeners need flowers. You look up into the windows of decaying old apartment buildings in big cities and the residents may be holding on to life by the price of a welfare check but in half those windows, there sits a clay pot with a few flowers trying desperately to bring some color into the lives of those without any.

## HOT AIR AND WIND CHILL

Saturday it was 60 degrees and beautiful. The grass seed companies were advertising on the radio. I walked out to pick up the newspaper and had that great sensation that comes just once a year when we get that sensation that spring has arrived.

Monday morning I drove to work in a torrential rain. By afternoon the temperature had dropped and there was snow on the ground. I thought back wistfully to Saturday and wondered where Spring had gone.

It's a strange love/hate affair we have with hot and cold. When we're cold we wish we were warm and when we're hot we look for a cool breeze.

It seems as if we get accustomed to cold better than to hot but maybe that's because I hate hot. I still remember the shock, as a kid, of immersing my body in cold water by jumping off the dock into the lake to cool off on a warm summer day. I would thrash around, half swimming, half punching at the water for 30 seconds until the sensation of cold gradually faded. From then on, the water and my body seemed to be the same temperature. I felt nothing. The water temperature seemed neutral. I could stay in the lake, playing tag or racing with my friends for hours with no sensation of cold.

Years later, it was much the same on days that seemed too cold to ski when we arrived at the mountain. We'd park the warm car in the lot next to the lodge and dread getting out to free the skis lashed to the rack on top of it. Our fingers became numb as we buckled on our boots and we wondered why we came. It was hard to force yourself to get to the lift that took you to the top of the mountain. In the lift chair, you sat huddled and cold, wondering why you came.

By the end of the first downhill run, you felt exhilarated. Your body was cozy warm inside your goose-down parka and you never wanted to stop skiing.

Those experiences with hot and cold continue all your life. It is a mystery why a bed can feel so uninviting and freezing cold when you first climb between the sheets and yet so warm and toasty seven hours later when you have to force yourself to get out of it.

There is no question in my mind that cold is better than hot but not everyone agrees. We've all had the Florida argument. The people who hate the heat cannot understand the people who love it.

It's hard to understand how people got any work done before air-conditioning. There are office buildings in every big city that were built before it was possible to cool them and it must have been terrible to have to go to work every day in a hot box of an office, sometimes without even a window. Factories, with the added heat given off by machinery, must have been excruciating places to work with temperatures above 100 degrees. "Sweatshop" didn't acquire its own meaning for no reason.

Weather information is a salable commodity because everyone is interested in how hot or how cold it's going to be and whether they're going to get wet if they go outside. The more extreme the weather, the more salable information about it is. For this reason the people who sell weather information have worked up fake ways to make it sound interesting on dull days. You shouldn't say, "Have a nice day" to a weatherman because for him a nice day is no news.

There are plenty of examples of inflating weather numbers. When the radio report says, "humidity is 100 per cent" that sounds as if the air was water. In fact the phrase does not refer to the actual amount of water in the air but to the percentage of water in the air in relation to the amount it can hold. It can hold more when it's warm than when it's cold. If humidity is called "100 percent" and the temperature is 60 degrees, it means the air can't hold any more but it's less than 5 percent water. Calling the humidity "100 percent" sounds more interesting than saying it's 5 percent.

The same is true of "the wind-chill factor." That refers to the effect weather experts estimate that the combination of temperature and wind speed has on people. It's a ridiculous guess but it makes a weather reporter on television sound more interesting when it's 41 degrees outside, if he can say "the wind chill factor makes it feel nine degrees below zero this morning."

"Wind chill" is hot air.

## THE THIRD BEST MONTH

Some good things about the month of June:

- It's warm enough so you don't need a coat but it's not so hot that you need air-conditioning.
- The leaves on the trees are young, fresh and green-looking. They don't look anything like what falls in the fall.
- The name is good to write because we don't use any ugly, truncated abbreviation the way we do for Feb. or Sept. The dictionary claims the abbreviation for "June" is "Jun." but there wouldn't be any point in using it because, by the time you put the period in, denoting an abbreviation, you've used the same number of spaces.
- May and June are months used by women as a first name—unless you count April. April is a name a press agent gives a young woman who wants to be an actress.
- You can put away your winter clothes that seem so old and tired and get out your old summer clothes—which seem so fresh and new after their winter vacation.

- No one who doesn't live there has to go to Florida this month.
- It rhymes with moon.
- You don't have to rake leaves or shovel snow.
- We can all sit home at night after dinner and enjoy deciding what to do with our upcoming vacation—without actually having to go to all the trouble and expense of going on one yet. Vacations are often better anticipated than taken.
- A lot of the good things about June are negative. Taxes aren't due, we don't have to buy Christmas presents, there are no parades blocking the main street and no major holidays like Thanksgiving, Christmas or the Fourth of July.
- The almanac says June 10th is Children's Day but it is no longer celebrated as it was in the 1800s. They still have it in some Protestant churches. It's surprising that the makers of greeting cards never promoted its continuation. My guess is that Hallmark will be pushing it any year now.
- Through the years, June has been a month of remarkable events: on June 6th, 1816, ten feet of snow fell in Vermont and New Hampshire; in 1786, a New York company started making ice cream commercially; Station WGY, Schenectady, started televising regular programs three times a week on June 28th, 1928; *Gone with the Wind* was published June 30th, 1936.
- June is the only month that has a bug named after it. There's no July bug or August bug. Up in the country at this time of year, the big, harmless, hard-shelled June bugs batter away at the screens in the bedroom when the light is on there. They must be afraid of the dark.
- The summer solstice occurs June 21. Almost every year I look up the word "solstice" and I'm still not clear about it. The summer solstice is the longest day of the year and the shortest night— "when the sun is at its zenith over at the tropic of Cancer." To me, all solstice means is, it's easier to get up in the morning because it's light out.

## FALL HAS SPRUNG

There is only one time of year that has two names. September, October and November are known as both fall and autumn. I like the word "autumn" but never use it because it's a little florid for my prose style. Autumn is for poets not for essayists or journalists. "Autumn" is actually the correct word because "fall" is nothing more than a nickname taken from one of the major events of the season—the fall to the ground of leaves from the trees.

Fall has acquired a bad name because it's associated with the end of things. Flowers die, trees lose their leaves. My dictionary calls it "The time of year between summer and winter. A period of maturity verging on decline." That's not a very positive definition. It's about where I am in life and I don't want to be reminded of it. The dictionary doesn't disparage summer by calling it "The time of year between spring and fall."

Walter Huston didn't do fall any good with his sad rendition of *September Song*. In a haunting and mournful tone, he sang "Oh, it's a long while from May to December . . . but the days grow short when you reach September. . . . Oh, the days dwindle down to a precious few . . . September, November." The song is enough to make a person in the fall of life consider suicide.

A lot of poets of the past have used autumn to ring their death knells. Robert Browning wrote "Autumn wins you best by this, its mute Appeal to sympathy for its decay."

William Cullen Bryant was a lot of fun writing about it, too.

*The melancholy days are come, the saddest of the year*
*Of wailing winds and naked woods*
*and meadows brown and sere.*

(Like "autumn," "meadow" is a poet's word. No one I know calls a field a meadow.)

Percy Bysshe Shelley was toughest on fall.

*The warm sun is failing, the bleak wind is wailing*
*The bare boughs are sighing, the pale flowers are dying*
*And the year*
*On the earth her deathbed, in a shroud of leaves dead,*
*Is lying.*

Oh, come on, Percy Bysshe, things aren't that bad. I wish poets would lighten up on fall.

There's a lot to be said in favor of fall—autumn, if you wish. If anyone kept statistics, I suspect we'd find that more work gets done between Labor Day and Thanksgiving than during any other 80-odd day period of the year.

Fall is good for working because it's cool enough so you have to keep moving but not so cold you have to spend half your energy staying warm. An ideal fall day has the best temperature for getting anything done.

I've read about why leaves change color but I keep forgetting. The encyclopedia says that the red and yellow colors are always there in a leaf but during the growing season, they are covered by the green chlorophyll. When the chlorophyll dies, the reds and yellows come through. There's something wrong with that explanation but I don't want to know about why leaves change color badly enough to look into it further.

## "HAPPY HOLIDAY" DOESN'T DO IT

The following things are true about Christmas:

- Sometimes it's joyous and merry but it's never easy.
- Old weather records do not substantiate the suggestion, given by today's Christmas cards, showing scenes from old-fashioned Christmases, that it used to snow more than it does now. Horses

did not dash through the snow pulling sleighs on the way to grandmother's house any more a hundred years ago than cars do now. It almost never snows on Christmas even in northern parts of the Country and if it does, the snow is wet and slushy and not conducive to horses pulling sleighs through it.

- It's a sign of the new sensitivity to political correctness that, more and more, the greeting "Happy Holidays" is replacing "Merry Christmas." Most Jews I know accept "Merry Christmas" in the spirit in which it was intended without adding any heavy religious baggage to it. Most atheists or agnostics I know use "Merry Christmas."

- I never get over feeling bad about tearing open a beautifully wrapped present. It takes ten seconds to destroy a work of art that took someone ten minutes to accomplish.

- Someone in the family is always better at wrapping than anyone else. My sister stays up in the back bedroom in our house and we all deliver presents to her to be wrapped as if she was the package room behind the scenes in a department store.

- Of course it's true that some presents are better to get than others but some are better to give, too.

- Some people are easy to give to, others are hard and there's always one who's impossible. Usually it isn't that the person has everything, it's that he or she is not enthusiastic about gifts.

- The knowledge that the sales will start the day after Christmas doesn't deter many people from buying presents before Christmas.

- When you buy a piece of clothing for someone, it's more apt to be too small than too big. Clothes look bigger on the rack than they do on someone.

- The store clerk who asks "May I help you with something?" can hardly ever help.

- You read and hear a lot of advice about how to keep your Christmas tree to keep from getting dry so the needles don't fall off but most Christmas trees are cut in November and nothing anyone does can keep them from drying out and dropping their needles all over your living room floor.

- It's interesting how good orange and black seem for Halloween and how wrong they'd be as Christmas colors.
- In spite of the old sayings to the contrary, the best presents come in large packages.
- A quarter of the Christmas cards we get are from some commercial establishment. There ought to be a law against a company or anyone with whom you have a business arrangement, sending you a Christmas card. "Happy Holidays from all of us at the First National Bank" doesn't make me feel warm all over toward the bank. I don't want cards from any real estate brokers, dentists, insurance salesmen or car dealers, either. I don't want a Christmas card from anyone I don't know personally.

I'd include in this group the President of the United States. When Bill Clinton was President, we used to get two cards from Bill and Hillary, one at home and one at the office.

The Clintons wished us "a beautiful holiday season." I was flattered and touched until I came to the note in small print on the back of the card that read "PAID FOR BY THE DEMOCRATIC NATIONAL COMMITTEE." That's not in the Christmas spirit.

Apparently the Clintons didn't leave their Christmas card list with the Bushes. We haven't received one from them.


## ASHES TO ASHES

My friend Judy told me she had asked her husband, Sam, to drive out with her to the cemetery last weekend where her father was buried.

On the way back, they got arguing about whether they wanted to be buried or cremated.

"Don't throw my ashes to the wind," Judy said she told Sam. "I want some tangible evidence left that I was here. A stone marker and a grave in a cemetery."

About 20 percent of Americans who die are cremated. The other 80 percent are buried in ridiculously expensive oblong wooden or metal boxes. I have never faced the question of my preference in this matter because I still entertain the possibility I may not die—although I understand the odds are against that.

It seems likely that the time may come when there isn't room left to bury everyone in a plot that takes up a piece of the earth eight feet long and four or five feet wide. There are now about six billion people alive in the world. One billion is a thousand million. This is more people than have lived and died in all the earth's long history. If each of them occupies a plot of land when they go, there might not be any land left for the living. The earth would be one solid cemetery.

I have never returned to the cemetery where my parents are buried. It is not out of disrespect. I loved them and think of them frequently but placing a wreath or a bouquet of flowers on their grave strikes me as a waste of flowers. It doesn't make them feel good and it doesn't do anything for my psyche so who beside the florist benefits?

The ultimate living memorial to a dead person is Lenin's Tomb in Moscow's Red Square. Vladimir Lenin died at the age of 54 in 1924 and through some secret process, the Russians have preserved his body so that he lies there in state looking exactly as he did when he was alive— and probably better dressed. Is this something we'd all like to have done to what's left of us when we die? It would appeal to our ego.

The fact is, there is just so much remembering any of us can or should do. Being constantly aware of friends and relatives who are gone would be too depressing to live with. We have to move on.

The best thing we could all do for relatives and friends we loved who die is make certain there is some written record of who they were and what they did. It is dismaying to me how little I know of my ancestors. Once I pass my grandparents back there, I'm lost. I would much prefer to have something on paper about them and about their parents and grandparents than a headstone in a cemetery.

What we need is a government agency that records the life and death of every American just as certainly as we all have birth certificates but with details of the person's life. The government bureau in charge would have a staff of reporters whose only job would be searching out and writing down for the record, everyone's life story.

## YOUR GRANDFATHER'S GRANDMOTHER

It is an American character flaw that genealogy doesn't interest most people. We aren't much concerned with searching out the records of family members who preceded us to find out what they were like. It may be because the British always made too much of heredity so, after we revolted, Americans decided not to make anything of it.

Some of us have a casual interest in relatively recent family members but we have lost track of anyone who lived long ago enough to be called "ancestors." (I don't know what the cutoff age is.) We lose interest two or three generations back.

Most of us know something of our grandparents but ask us about their fathers or grandfathers and we're ignorant of them. We don't know who they were, what they were like, what they did with their lives or even where they came from and went to. Great-grandparents are ancient history to Americans.

In the year 2001, 1,300,000 babies were born without live-in fathers. We use the euphemism "single mother" for the child's only visible parent. That's nicer than several things we used to call women who had babies without husbands but it makes genealogy a lost art. If you don't know who your father was, how are you going to track down your great-grandfather?

It may seem inconsequential for anyone to search out a family tree but knowing where we came from provides clues to where we're going. It gives us insight into our character and personality that might not otherwise have occurred to us. Keeping track is evidence of a civilized society, too.

One of the problems with tracking down long-gone family members is that it always seems too late to start. The trail is cold. There are things about our parents that few of us can answer and it's a mere two generations back. We should all start by writing down anything we know even if it seems inadequate.

It isn't long ago that the parents of my grandparents lived in England, Ireland and Scotland but I know little or nothing about them and haven't tried to find out. The selfish thought has occurred to me that I'd like to be remembered a few generations after my demise but—fat chance, I suppose.

There is no stronger influence on the character and personality of each one of us than the transmission of genes from one generation to the next and then to the next and to the next. Each human comprises a grab bag of genes from relatives that contribute to who we are and what we're like. We should know them so we know ourselves.

The inevitability of inherited characteristics is alternately exhilarating and depressing to consider. The same things keep happening to the same people because of their genes. We're trapped in who we are, good and bad. There was a biology teacher in the Albany Academy who told me about a family, with a fairly common name, and more than 25 percent of all of them were in prison. Dishonesty, he told me, was an inherited characteristic. A teacher would be fired for saying that today but I've never forgotten it.

My most talented grandparent lived with us for several years when I was young so I try to remember details about him. I'm looking for evidence that I inherited some of his ability. I can't find anything. What talent I have bears no resemblance to his.

The mystery of inheritance is that while I can't find it in myself, I see a little of my grandfather in our son. I see a touch of my mother in a daughter. It is a good feeling for a parent to watch a granddaughter doing some simple thing and suddenly recognize in her a flash of something, a look, a gesture that reminds you of a father, a mother or even an uncle or an aunt. Dad died forty years before this little girl who reminded me of him was born. She knows nothing of him but here is that fleck of him in her. Genes have incredible tenacity. It's as close as we come to immortality and that makes genealogy worth something.

## NOT DYING TO DIE

If you were given an envelope containing the day and date you were going to die, would you open it? Most people would rather be surprised even though there would be advantages to knowing.

If you knew you could organize your treasures in the basement, the garage and in closets and drawers around the house. Knowing would—you'll pardon the expression—be a deadline.

There are several other things you'd do and not do. You'd probably cancel the appointment to have your teeth cleaned. You certainly wouldn't buy four new tires for the car if your demise was imminent.

Since the World Trade Center terrorist attack, airline ticket sales, which were already down, have dropped again. People, thinking of life expectancy, are not only afraid to fly, they are not willing to endure a two-hour wait to board a crowded plane.

All the other ways people die in the United States make flying look like a walk in the park. Or, wait a minute! It might be true that more people die walking in the park than in airplane accidents.

Anytime you look at statistics involving 280 million people, all the numbers are high. Last year 2,337,256 Americans died of one cause or another. If we could choose, most of us would opt for dying quietly in bed, at some ripe old age, of a heart attack. A great many of us go that way, too. Heart attacks account for about half a million deaths a year.

Most of us don't choose our manner of death so between 1980 and 1999, 14,500 people died in airplane accidents. That's an average of 725 a year. During that same period 750,000 people—three quarters of a million—were killed in car crashes . . . almost 40,000 a year. Even so, you don't hear people saying they're not going to travel by car any longer. If you figure deaths-per-mile-traveled, the statistic is astronomically high in favor of airlines. The figure varies more for airplane accidents than for cars because the number is relatively low and one big crash sends it way up. Nonetheless, airplane crash fatalities are far below almost any other way Americans die. In spite of the scare headlines every July 4th and Labor Day weekend, the percentage of people killed in car accidents is lower than on an average weekend. The actual number is higher because of the millions of extra cars on the road.

One of the things that makes the thought of an airline crash terrifying to us is knowing that we'd have several minutes, while the plane was plunging to earth, to think about our all-but-certain death.

There are a lot of ways to die accidentally, and 54,331 people died in different kinds of accidents that didn't involve driving or flying in 2001. This includes things like falling off a ladder or getting hit by a brick dropping off a building on a windy day.

In an average year, more than 30,000 people are shot dead by someone else with a gun. The "else" is because in addition to that figure, 17,000 people kill themselves, most of them with guns. That figure doesn't change much year after year. More people commit suicide with guns than get killed by someone else with guns. The murder number hangs around 13,000. It's comforting to know there are fewer murders than suicides.

Mankind has made considerable progress against death. Our life expectancy from birth has increased by 35 years over what it was before 1900. This has been brought about through improved medical knowledge, better nutrition, safety measures imposed on a reluctant population by various government agencies in charge of things like vaccinations, gun laws, speed limits and health care.

The single most amazing statistic about death is difficult to verify but a few years ago a panel of historians issued a paper concluding that there are more people alive in the world today than have ever died in all its history.

# PART 2

## *Food and Drink Health and Doctors*

*The idea of having a cup of coffee is usually better than the coffee.*

# NE BOUVEZ PAS DE L'EAU

It seems possible from what I see of their drinking habits that not one of our five grandchildren has ever had a drink of water.

If you forced the average American kid to take a glass of water, the child might not be able to identify what it was. Give a taste test asking them to say which was Coke and which was Pepsi and they'd have no trouble. If parents had all the money they've spent on soft drinks by the time their children get out of high school, there would be enough to send all of them through four years of college . . . and in the case of our granddaughter Alexis, medical school, too. A gas station that sells regular for $1.25 a gallon probably has a cooler with soft drinks inside where they sell a pint of water for $1.25.

Americans drink 51 gallons of soft drinks per year per person. There's no way to keep track of how much water they drink free from the tap at home but it's less.

Like most Americans, I seldom draw a glass of water from the faucet either. It does happen occasionally in the middle of the night when I want to take an aspirin but otherwise I go to the refrigerator for Perrier. I don't know what there is about bubbles. There are "designer" brands of water that are used as hip accessories, like handbags, by young working women. They won't go anywhere without one.

Part of the reason people avoid tap water is that in many areas it isn't very good. Water all over Earth has had so much dumped into it that, in order to make it safe, authorities have had to make it antiseptic with massive infusions of chlorine. Chlorine kills the bugs but makes water unpleasant to taste. And, anyway, who wants to drink dead bugs.

Good water doesn't taste like anything and there isn't much of that left anywhere. The sparkling clear mountain stream or the pristine lake is becoming a thing of the past. Wherever there's water, we've polluted it. We're slowly changing our habits but since the Nation's beginning, a body of water, a lake, a river or an ocean has been considered a place to put anything noxious that we don't want.

In the summer we have a house with a well 350 feet deep and it keeps fresh my memory of what good water tastes like. I grew up spending summers on Lake George, one of the world's great bodies of water. For 75 years my family ran a pipe down into the water, pumped it out and drank it. My sister and our children use the cottage now and they still pump water directly from the lake and use it, untreated, but we don't drink the water anymore except in coffee.

Lake George water is what's known as "soft," meaning without a lot of minerals in it. The well water is "hard." The lake water makes better coffee. I often fill several bottles with it and bring it home for making coffee during which process it is boiled.

Details of drinking habits in the United States are strange. The story of Coca-Cola and its successful imitator, Pepsi-Cola, is amazing. Here's this mysterious concoction of water, sugar, artificial coloring and some hard-to-identify flavoring that is infused with carbon dioxide bubbles and it becomes one of the great business enterprises the world has ever known. We drink oceans of it.

We don't drink as much beer here as they do in European countries and the reason is simple; most of our beer isn't any good. You'd think the major breweries would fix that but they have not. It is a mystery why some countries make some things better than other countries make them. I would not buy a watch made in Russia.

I like beer but I'm not much of a beer drinker. I've never understood how anyone could stand at a bar and drink enough beer to get drunk. More than one beer makes me bilious and sleepy. On a hot summer day I like one but a person who drinks just one beer isn't considered much of a beer-drinker.

The sale of hard liquor is down. Restaurants that used to add substantially to their profits with a big and active bar are having to push wines harder. The waiter in an expensive restaurant invariably asks whether you want bottled water. He asks it in a manner that suggests you are an inferior customer if you want plain tap water.

Some hard liquors that were popular just 20 years ago, have all but disappeared. Drinks like Four Roses, Seagram's blended whiskey or Canadian Club, which were blends of bourbon whiskey and alcohol are all but gone. There are several good brands of bourbon, an excellent and uniquely American drink at its best, but sales have dwindled. The martini has staged a surprising comeback among young drinkers in recent years, offering hope that theirs is not a lost generation.

Alcoholics and drunk drivers have given drinkers a bad name and those of us who enjoy a drink in the comfort and safety of our homes before dinner, will never forgive them. I look for the newspaper stories from medical authorities that extol the virtue of alcoholic drinks. There are two or three stories a year that detail the life-lengthening or brain-enhancing properties of a daily portion of liquor.

I cut them out and save them.

I take the position that not drinking is bad for your health.


## HAVE A GOOD BREAKFAST

The good people of the world, like mothers, have traditionally insisted that we should "eat a good breakfast." It sounds like sensible advice although there may not be any solid medical evidence that we should start our day's work on a full stomach.

Whether it's true or not, mothers have failed to impress us with its importance. All of us have the same thing for breakfast today that we had yesterday whether it's sensible or not. You can't get a cereal-eater to switch to toast and jam or a bagel-eater to try scrambled eggs and bacon.

The monotony of breakfast diets comes from the fact that we don't want to waste time considering what to eat when we get up. We have other things on our minds. We know what we're having, where it is in the kitchen and what plate it goes on. We have no intention of experimenting.

In the days when more people were working with their hands and fewer people were selling things or working in sit-down jobs in what's called "the service industry," people ate substantial breakfasts of bacon and eggs, pancakes, waffles or corned beef hash with a poached egg. That was for farmers, builders, cowboys or lumberjacks. If a family sits down to a breakfast like that now it's usually only on a Saturday or Sunday morning.

Most people going to work in an office now eat one of several dozen of the boxed cereals made by just four huge corporations that keep buying each other out and putting more sugar in their cereals. Nabisco is owned by Kraft Foods but Kraft is owned by Philip Morris. Nabisco sold its Shredded Wheat to Post. Kellogg still has Corn Flakes but Quaker Oats is owned by Pepsi-Cola.

The biggest seller among the breakfast cereals is Cheerios followed by Frosted Flakes and Raisin Bran. Corn Flakes and Rice Krispies still make the top 10 although Shredded Wheat isn't on the list and Wheaties are no where to be seen. Kellogg's Special K and Fruit Loops are still fairly popular.

People have read that grain is good for them as a cholesterol reducer so a lot of people eat what is called "cereal." The trouble with that is commercial brands calling themselves cereal are probably not what doctors had in mind. Anyone who eats one of the popular brands thinking it's "a healthy breakfast" ought to read the list of ingredients. The word "fiber" sounds good and it's on the box but many brand name cereals have more sugar in them than fiber. Kellogg's Number 2 Frosted Flakes for example, has just one gram of fiber in it but 14 grams of sugar. You look at the label and wonder where the cereal is. The box they come in might be healthier to consume than what's inside.

The traditional breakfast in a cookbook or in a hotel dining room menu does not represent what people eat at home either. The buffet steam table is laid out with scrambled eggs, bacon, sausage, fried potatoes, pancakes, French toast, muffins and bagels. If you order breakfast from a waiter, it usually comes with a portion of fried potatoes. Where did hotel kitchens get the idea that most Americans eat fried potatoes for breakfast? In the South, they used to eat grits but even grits have had their day.

A commercial loaf of American bread made by one of the baking conglomerates is so poor that toast has diminished on the breakfast menu. There are small bakeries in many cities that make good bread but it is not usually in the shape of a loaf that can be sliced for toast. Many who once had toast and jam have turned to bagels.

For years I worked with a man who sat down morning after morning with nothing but the newspaper, a cup of coffee and a cigarette. You couldn't talk to him about it. You can't talk to anyone about what they eat for breakfast. The young people's equivalent today of "a cuppa coffee and a cigarette" is simply a Coke or some other sugar-loaded soft drink and nothing else. What ever it is someone has for breakfast, don't try to change it.

## ABOUT FOOD

The following thoughts have occurred to me from time to time about eating in a restaurant and about food in general.

- I don't dine in a restaurant, I eat. Eating is less expensive.
- The more outside leaves of lettuce the cook throws away, the better the salad is.
- In 1987, you couldn't have told me I'd come to prefer broiled salmon rare. It's just better.
- You can tell a lot about a restaurant from the bread it serves. Commercial bread in the United States is the worst in the world.
- A lot of restaurants charge $8.50 for a drink of scotch or bourbon. They get 16 one and a half ounce drinks out of a fifth, which is 24 ounces. That comes to $120. for a bottle that cost them maybe $16. It's no wonder the first thing the owner wants a waiter to ask is "Can I get you anything from the bar?"

- When you sit down in a strange restaurant, you can tell in the first three minutes whether it's going to be any good or not.
- Restaurants that have "Caesar salad" on their menu often don't have the vaguest idea how to make a Caesar salad. If a people don't like anchovies, they shouldn't order it.
- I don't eat hotdogs anymore. I want to know more about what's in them.
- I fail to understand why gelatin desserts got popular.
- The two things a microwave oven does best are bacon and popcorn.
- The appetizers on the menus of fancy restaurants often cost more than I want to pay for the whole meal. They don't whet my appetite, they kill it.
- Paper tablecloths cut to exactly fit the top of a table in a restaurant are a nuisance because you keep catching your sleeve on them.
- A lot of restaurants that have candles in the middle of their tables, give you a huge menu that you have to hold up in front of the light from the candle so you can't read it.
- Bus boys in expensive restaurants are too anxious to refill your water glass.
- The tables in the average restaurant are too high for the height of the chair they give you to sit on. If you sit on the banquette against the wall, they're much too high.
- I've eaten in a thousand restaurants but I still have trouble figuring the tip. I should tip good waiters more than bad ones but I tip them all the same.
- Chinese restaurants have gone out of style.
- In New York there are French, German, Italian, Chinese, Japanese, Indian, Thai, Scandinavian, Mexican, Greek, Hungarian, Vietnamese and Spanish restaurants. I have never heard of an English restaurant.
- When I travel, I never eat in the dining room of the hotel I'm sleeping in.

- If the waitress says, "My name is Linda" I want to leave. I am not interested in Linda's name.
- In a good restaurant, the owner is usually there, watching. In the best restaurants, the owner is out in the kitchen cooking.
- The size of the portion is of relatively little importance to a restaurant because food is only about 30 percent of a restaurant's costs.
- Bad murals painted on the walls are not necessarily a sign that the restaurant is bad.
- I don't eat in a restaurant that has a sign outside saying "HOME COOKING." If I wanted home cooking, I'd eat at home. I don't eat in a place that has a sign in the window saying "WAITRESS WANTED," either.


# THANK YOU
# BUT I'M NOT HUNGRY

There are things I don't eat:

- Sandwiches or hamburgers on buns too thick to get your mouth around.
- Hot dogs, even when they are called frankfurters. I'm suspicious of what they grind up to put in them. I'm sure they're sanitary but sanitary isn't good enough.
- Sweetbreads. A terrible name for an animal part.
- Marshmallows. We used to toast them over a wood fire on the end of a stick. We called them "marshmallows." I'd probably still like them.
- Canned peas, turnips, snails, frog legs—each for a different reason.
- Peanut butter and jelly sandwiches. I like peanut butter and I like jelly but I don't like peanut butter and jelly.
- Deviled eggs. My mother always used to make these when she was

having a party. There are only a few things that are bad for me that I don't like and deviled eggs are one of them.

- I used to love chocolate eclairs. They were made by the good neighborhood bakery and good little neighborhood bakeries are scarce.
- Banana cream pie, chocolate-covered doughnuts, tapioca pudding, Nesselrode pie.
- Pomegranates.
- Pasta before the main course in an Italian restaurant. Do Italians really eat a plate of spaghetti first and then have a main course?
- I don't eat sugar-coated cereal.
- I don't put anything called "non-dairy creamer" in my coffee.
- Jell-O. I don't like the rubbery consistency or the artificial flavor. I know it's good for your fingernails but my fingernails are okay without eating Jell-O.
- I avoid any ice cream that's a cute flavor. You won't catch me eating rocky road or tutti fruitti. Chocolate, vanilla and coffee are so good there's no need to get clever with flavors.
- Honey. Everyone says they like honey but when we buy a jar it sits in the cupboard for a year. Sticky, too.
- Ketchup or catsup. I don't care which you call it, I don't eat it or anything that needs it.
- Chocolate chip cookies. It's like peanut butter and jelly, I like chocolate and I like cookies but not together.
- Strips of red or green peppers as decorations.
- Tofu.

## FRUIT

- How do they get a grape to grow without seeds?
- You can't lose weight by eating sensibly. You must do something

drastic that may not be good for you. I've been losing weight by eating nothing but a grapefruit until 12:30 p.m. It must be bad for my stomach but I have to weigh that against my loss of weight.

- I don't know what's happened to bananas. They go bad before they get ripe.
- My fruit stand is selling kiwis three for a dollar. That's a good buy. The only down side to that is, I don't like kiwis. It's a designer fruit with more good looks than taste.
- I forget the difference between a mango and a persimmon but I don't eat either. I've made mango ice cream in the summer but otherwise a mango is not worth the trouble.
- Melons look good but they are almost never ripe.
- Pineapple is hard to fix but good and you can tell when one is ripe because it's yellow, not green.
- Grapefruit have changed for the better in my lifetime. My mother used to cut them in two at night, sprinkle them with sugar and put them in the ice box overnight. They are sweet enough now so you don't have to do that.
- Driving to the country two weeks ago, I bought three pounds of Concord grapes with lots of seeds. They were the only grapes I ever ate as a kid. We used to squeeze them into our mouth, throw away the skin and spit out the seeds.

   I took the grapes off their stems, put them in a pot with two cups of sugar and a little water and brought them to a boil. It was a messy operation but I poured them through a sieve and separated the juice from the seeds and the skin and got a rich, deep, dark blue liquid. It's the start of grape jelly but I didn't make jelly. I pour a couple of inches of juice into a glass with ice cubes and fill it with club soda.

- Watermelon is available all year around but it's an insipid fruit.
- I like the idea of apples better than I actually like eating one. An apple doesn't satisfy me for breakfast.

## PACKAGES IN PACKAGES

Friendly types strike up a conversation with the person next to them on an airplane. Others fall asleep or read a newspaper, ignoring the person with whom they are rubbing elbows. I don't want to be best friends with a stranger but it seems polite to exchange a few words.

Last week I sat with an attractive woman in her late forties (I'm guessing) and we started to talk. She said she frequently flew from New York to California and back in her job as "marketing director" for a company that makes potato chips.

She had something to do with their advertising and I've always been curious about the relationship of the advertising budget to the cost of the product itself so I asked her about that.

"Which costs the most?" I asked. "The potato chips or the advertising?"

"Oh, the advertising," she said without hesitating. "Far and away."

"And what about the packages the potato chips come in?" I wanted to know.

"The package costs more than the potato chips, too," she said. "It's an expensive process."

When you think about it, you can see how it would cost the potato-chip makers a pretty penny to pump all that air in their bags and seal it tight enough to make it look as though it had more in it than it does.

This is the same idea that candy-bar makers have when they put the candy on a piece of cardboard twice the size of the candy bar, and wrap that to make it look roughly three times bigger than it is.

We all know advertising is out of control but so is packaging. Manufacturers put their products in plastic, wax paper or foil, put that in a box, wrap the box in paper with advertising or nutritional information or warnings on it, cover the whole thing with another layer of thin plastic film and at the checkout counter, the store puts the whole thing in a bag for us to bring home.

I don't want to buy crackers, cereal or toothpaste loose but we are consuming huge amounts of material wrapping things that are already in three or four other kinds of wrappings or containers.

It's what accounts for the mountains of junk we all put out by the street in front of the house on the day the garbage truck comes. We couldn't wait to buy all the stuff and now we can't wait to throw away all the debris attendant to its packaging. Wrapping paper and the boxes stuff comes in expands when it's removed from whatever it was covering so our trash takes up more room than the products it held.

There are laws now that make manufacturers inform consumers of things like the nutritional content of their product and potential dangers for people with special medical problems. I'd like to have them add to those laws by making manufacturers tell us what percentage of the price we pay is for the product itself and what percentage of the total is for advertising and packaging.

Too many of the packages stuff comes in are more convenient for the manufacturer than they are for the consumer. While I was talking to the potato-chip lady, the flight attendant came around with a basket containing foil bags of peanuts. These bags are also blown up like a balloon to give the impression of more peanuts than they contain. There is a mark on the top of the bag designating the spot where you are supposed to tear open the bag. If I had to depend on getting into the bag in the manner suggested by the words "TEAR OPEN HERE," I could starve to death trying to get at my peanuts.

Last week I bought a toothbrush, a comb and a pair of scissors. I made the mistake of trying to open the plastic packages the comb and the toothbrush came in first. It took me about 10 minutes. When I went at the heat-sealed plastic container that enclosed the scissors, I realized I should have tried to open that first so I could have used the scissors to open the other two.

We're being packaged to death.

## THROUGH THICK AND THIN
## WITH DIETS

In the past six months I've lost 20 pounds. I don't have any dread disease that I know of. I lost weight on purpose.

If 20 pounds seems like a lot, keep in mind that it isn't as if I weighed 135 pounds to start with. I weighed 226 a year ago and this morning the scale tottered between 205 and 206. It's been down there for almost six months so I may have licked that 20 pounds. If I lost another 20, I'd be only slightly overweight.

I mention all this not because you care how much I weigh but because everyone thinks about his or her weight.

Doctors advise us to lose weight sensibly by eating the same things you've always eaten but less of them. Like so much advice doctors give us, it's good but impossible to follow. That's its only shortcoming as a plan for dieting. No one can do it.

If you're going to lose weight, you can't be sensible about it. You have to do something extreme—and usually unhealthy. You have to believe that losing weight is going to be better for you than your way of doing it is bad for you. When you cross the street or drive a car, you take a chance with your life. You measure the desirability of getting somewhere against the minuscule chance you'll get killed traveling and you invariably decide to go. That's what you do when you decide on a diet. You balance the good things about losing weight against the chance of some bad things happening as a result of almost any diet you go on.

It seems likely that, when it comes to weight we are once again victims of our genes. It is as impossible to be thin by resolve as it is possible to be six feet tall by trying.

Even if it's true that fat parents are apt to have fat kids—and it is true—it is also true that one of the ways you get fat is by eating too much. Even if it turns out that some people get fat on less food, it's still true that if they get fat, they're eating too much of it. I've never read anything that says whether the fat gene controls your desire to eat too much or controls your system's ability to convert what you do eat to fat. It doesn't matter.

It does seem strange and unfriendly of God to have made most of us with an appetite that exceeds our need for food. If we get thirsty, we drink water and our thirst disappears. If, on the other hand, we eat a big meal containing everything we need to sustain us, we often have a desire to eat more.

For breakfast I've been eating nothing but a whole grapefruit and drinking a lot of coffee. I peel the grapefruit with a little gadget I got years ago and it's a satisfying thing to do quite aside from the pleasure of eating the grapefruit. If I eat cereal, I want cream or half and half. If I start eating toast and butter with jam, I eat too much of it. So I don't eat cereal or toast.

Most doctors are enthusiastic about one or two health measures and my urologist—I call him mine although he isn't mine, of course—is high on water. Every time I've seen him, he's told me to drink more water and that's what I'm going to do. If, next time you see me, I'm back up to 226 pounds, you'll know what's fattening. It's water.

## DEATH BY CELERY STALK

Last Monday I went to my doctor for my annual physical. I say "annual" but I usually push it to 14 or 15 months and things are looking up for me. My weight is up, my cholesterol is up and my blood pressure is up. I'm flirting with a heart attack and my doctor was insistent that I lose weight. My doctor of many years was ten years younger than I am. He used to insist on my losing weight, too. He is in poor health and retired. No one should go to a doctor fewer than 20 years younger than himself.

Here my new doctor said as I was leaving his office after my first visit: "Take these with you. Bedtime reading." He handed me two brochures. One was from the American Heart Association and called *SODIUM RESTRICTED DIET*. The other one was put out by Morton's Salt telling you how to measure the salt, potassium and calories you're eating.

With due respect to my new doctor and to the good intentions of both the American Heart Association and Morton's Salt, let me say in the nicest way I know how—they're ridiculous and if they've published ten million of them, I'd be willing to bet there aren't three people whose demise will be delayed because of them.

If you really want to help someone with a diet, you don't tell them how much salt or how many calories there are in half a bouillon cube, one ounce of animal crackers or five-sixth of an ounce of shredded wheat. To do that, you couldn't eat with a knife, a fork and a spoon. You'd be eating with tweezers off a scale on the table in front of you.

I'm suspicious of the Morton Salt pamphlet anyway. If their business is selling salt, are they really trying to help me restrict my intake? Is this a company that's really thinking of my welfare ahead of its profits? My suspicious nature asks "What's in this for you, Morton's?"

Morton's also gives advice on the sodium, potassium and calorie content of strawberries. Half a cup of strawberries, they say, has only one mg of salt and 23 calories. I'd like to watch the Morton Salt people measure out half a cup of strawberries. Do you mash them down, Morton's?

Between Morton's Salt and the American Heart Association, it appears there isn't much I can eat. If I take their advice, don't expect to be seeing much of me in the future. Or, expect to be seeing a lot less of me anyway because I'll be a shadow of my former self.

The American Heart Association's bulletin is, I'd say, at least as helpful and realistic as the Morton's Salt's bulletin. The American Heart Association has a good reputation as far as I know—although, of course, I don't know very far.

I hate myself for being so skeptical and suspicious but I am and I can't help it. For instance, I don't know why this booklet keeps telling me to see my doctor before I as much as chew a stick of gum.

"Do not use any salt substitute that your doctor has not recommended."

"The important thing is to keep in touch with your physician while you are on a diet and to see him as often as he suggests."

Well, my doctor, good as he is, doesn't suggest I come in and chat all the time. He's a busy man with a lot of patients and some of them are sick. He doesn't want me calling all the time to ask if it's okay for me to eat 200 milligrams of pitted olives or "two tablespoons of low-sodium dietetic peanut butter," one of the items in the Heart Association's brochure.

Caviar is on their list of things that are bad for you so I have sworn off caviar. I will give them that.

My doctor thought I might be consuming salt I didn't know about. That's why he gave me these brochures and I must admit, there are a couple of surprises in here. It turns out celery is lethal. I have to swear off celery.

Listen to this "You may use carrots and celery sparingly to season a dish—one stalk of celery to a pot of stew."

The other day at a party, before I saw this bulletin, I ate two stalks of celery. If I drop dead of a heart attack anytime soon, don't blame me, blame the celery.

## THE BETTER
## TO SEE YOU WITH

They seemed to have printed the small type in the telephone book smaller this year. At night, sitting in the living room, it seemed to me that they aren't making light bulbs as bright as they used to. They changed the type in my newspaper and made it harder to read, too. I was reading less and watching television more. I finally faced the fact that I needed new glasses. I needed new glass in my glasses, but they won't usually sell you that.

I looked under OPTOMETRIST in the Albany Yellow Pages because Albany is the nearest big city to the little village where we spend our summers. The Albany phone book gives the impression that Albany is a bigger city than it is. There were 22 listings under OPTOMETRIST.

Margie had urged me to go see an ophthalmologist but, proud as I am of being able to spell it, I had been to an ophthalmologist in Albany with an elderly aunt six years ago. We waited two hours and ten minutes before she was finally seen, not by the doctor with his name on the door, but one of his assistants. I was on vacation and only take a month. I didn't want to spend three hours of that in an ophthalmologist's waiting room.

I jotted down the names and addresses of six places listed under "optometrist." The first was in an upscale shopping mall. There was another store I wanted to go to there anyway and I thought I'd kill two birds with one parking place. The optometrist's "office" looked neat and efficient. There were slick pictures everywhere of beautiful women too young to need glasses wearing glasses. I walked in and was approached by a pleasant young woman.

"May we help you?" she asked. Just the way she said "we" I knew she couldn't help but figured it meant she knew someone else in the place who could.

"I'd like to have my eyes examined," I said. "I think I need new glasses."

"Won't you please sit down," she said. "Mr. Frointz will be right with you."

I am never inclined to sit down when I'm not tired. I didn't need rest, I needed new glasses. I don't know why people always insist that you sit down while you wait.

Within a few minutes the man I thought was the optometrist appeared and greeted me.

"I'd like an eye exam," I said, trying to get at the point quickly. "Are you an optometrist?"

"What seems to be the trouble?" he asked, not answering my question.

"The trouble is," I said with obvious irritation, "I can't see as well as I'd like to. Are you an optometrist?"

"We can arrange an appointment for you with an optometrist," he said unctuously. "What day would be good for you?"

I had been reading all the ads for eyeglass stores that said "ONE HOUR SERVICE" and that's about when I wanted new glasses, in an hour. I didn't need anyone to arrange an appointment for me. It's like going into a store that doesn't have something you want and they say "We can order it for you." I can order it myself. I go to a store so I won't have to order it.

In the next two hours I visited four places that were listed in the Yellow Pages under OPTOMETRIST that did not have an optometrist on the premises. One must make the rounds.

Opticians have taken a two-year course in things like how to cut a lens to fit the frame you order and they know their business. The blank lens has usually been ground to some standard prescription at the factory. Opticians cannot test your eyes. They can determine what your prescription is from your old glasses and make new ones from that if all you want is a duplicate pair.

Optometrists are better educated than they used to be but all they're allowed to do is test your eyes. In recent years their license has allowed them to do diagnostic work. They can dilate your pupils and look in there with those little flashlights to see what's going on but if there's anything wrong, they can't fix it. They call themselves "doctor" but they are only sort-of doctors.

Ophthalmologists are doctors. If you have a problem with your eyes, you should go see one. I just wanted to be able to read the newspaper. On my fifth stop I found an optometrist who was actually in the shop that said OPTOMETRIST outside. "GLASSES IN ONE HOUR" the sign read. I'm to pick them up Thursday.

## DON'T TOUCH ME!

There are few greater problems any of us face in life than the question of whether or not to scratch an itch. To scratch is one of life's most urgent urges. At its best, it can be one of the most satisfying sensations available to us and yet we know that, more often than not, scratching what itches is the wrong thing to do.

How can anything that feels so good be bad? Something wrong there in the whole scheme of things. A scratched itch can be an agonizing delight. An itch isn't really a pain. You can't say it hurts but, on the other hand, an itch unscratched can drive you crazy.

Is God testing us? Is he daring us to itch to see what we're made of? What did he have in mind when he came up with poison ivy, anyway? Everything on earth must have a purpose. What's the purpose of itchy poison ivy? Where's Billy Graham or Robert Schuller when we need them?

This comes to mind today—I can't get it OFF my mind today—because I have a mild case of poison ivy. It itches and I don't dare scratch it because the rumor is that scratching it will cause it to spread to parts unknown.

I was cutting down wild grape vines that were strangling some trees I like along a small road I take and inadvertently got my hands into the ivy. I have since returned to look and, sure enough, down low to the ground there it is, that innocent-looking little three-leaved devil. I must have reached down close to the ground to pull up some of those damnable young wild grape vines by the roots when I got into the poison ivy.

There are several things people say to you when you have poison ivy. For instance, almost everyone says "I had it once."

You itch so bad, you don't care whether they ever had it or not.

They also say "This has been a bad year for poison ivy. There's a lot of it around."

The third day after contact, I woke up and wasn't sure whether it was morning or not because my face was so puffed up my eyes were swollen shut. That made me nervous because I didn't know what other body part might swell shut so I drove into town to see a doctor. I looked him up in the Yellow Pages under PHYSICIANS: ALLERGIST; SEE GUIDE. They never tell you where the "GUIDE" is.

The doctor was Jamaican and he seemed knowledgeable but I was not convinced that he had firsthand knowledge of it because I don't believe they have poison ivy in Jamaica. I decided he had never had it because he was one of the few people who didn't say to me "I had it once." Of course a doctor can deliver a baby even though he's never had one himself.

He took my pulse and my blood pressure, neither of which were bothering me, and gave me a prescription for some pills. They have been variously described to me by non-doctor friends as cortisone or steroids. They were most impressive to me not because of their content but because of the elaborate schedule laid out on the little bottle, for taking them.

"Four for four days, three for three days, two for three days, one for two days and a half for two days." That's 29 pills. I count the ones left every day to make sure I'm doing it right. The consequences of getting out of order, I suspect, are dire.

This is the sort of direction though that gives me confidence in a pill and I waited expectantly for the results.

In an effort to understand my problem better, I went to our book-shelves and took down the learned tome, *A FIELD GUIDE TO TREES AND SHRUBS.*

"Poison Ivy" it says. "Rhus radicans. All parts contain a dangerous skin irritant. Leaves . . . variable. They may be stiff or merely thin . . . shiny or dull, coarse-toothed and wavy-edged or neither." That's a big help.

The treatise ends with this unscientific legend: "leaflets three, let it be."

That's fine for the leaflets three but now what about my itch? Do I leave it be or scratch it?

## WHEN DO YOU GO TO BED?

There's no general agreement on how much sleep we need and the amount of it that people get varies greatly. The amount they say they get varies even more. People don't tell the truth about how long they sleep. It is not necessarily true that the person who goes to bed early gets up early.

What we need is some kind of gauge like a thermometer that we could put in our mouths to tell when we're done as far as sleep is concerned. A green light might come on indicating we'd had enough. When the battery on a computer needs charging, a red light comes on. If you plug it in a green light appears when it's charged. Is it asking too much of them to make us a comparable sleep gauge? Feeling sleepy is not an accurate indication that you're tired.

Years ago, a California professor who studied sleep all his life said that if you read a random list of names and try to remember them eight hours later, you won't be able to recall as many as you will 24 hours later following a night's sleep.

No one has done a poll that I've seen that showed what time Americans go to bed. One key to our national bedtime is what's called "prime-time" and "late-night" television. The hours between seven and ten are prime-time, meaning the hours most people watch. Surprisingly, morning television shows on the networks have lower ratings than the late-night shows beginning at 11:30 p.m.

The late shows have more than twice as many viewers, indicating that more people stay up after 11:30 than get up before 7 a.m. There probably aren't many who go to bed after 11:30 and get up before 7 a.m. But I don't know.

The body and the brain seem to know a lot about how much sleep they need even without a green light. If I get sleepy at work after lunch, I know that I've either eaten too much lunch or didn't get enough sleep the night before. The difference between getting six hours and six and a half can do it. Eight hours is too much. Anyone who regularly gets eight hours sleep is hiding under the covers from the real world that's waiting out there for him to get up.

People speak of catching up on their sleep. Once you've lost sleep, I don't think you can ever catch it. You can't get it back by sleeping longer the next night. It's gone forever. If you normally get six hours, you need no more than six on a night following one during which you got only four. Sleep isn't cumulative.

Some of the best sleep I've ever had has been in movie theaters or in front of the television set. Falling asleep in the movies or your living room is more civilized than falling asleep during a play with real actors on the stage or during a concert where the musicians can see you. This is rude and I try not to do that—often unsuccessfully.

Considering how much we all enjoy sleeping, it's strange that the person who falls asleep easily and at various times and places, is made to feel inferior to the person who does not.

# PART 3

---

# *Politics*

*Everyone doesn't have a right to his opinion. The person who doesn't know what he's talking about does not have a right to his own opinion. It's why I'm never too much in favor of getting everyone out to vote on election day. Some people are too dumb or know too little about the issues and I hate to have one of them negating or canceling out the vote of someone who has bothered to inform him- or herself.*

# BASEBALL AND POLITICS

In every election year there are inevitable television scheduling conflicts between baseball games and political debates. Often a debate we feel obliged to watch as responsible citizens is on opposite a baseball playoff game.

There is plenty of time when nothing is happening in both a baseball game and a political debate and a knowledgeable viewer can switch back and forth at strategic times without missing anything of either.

Here I am in my living room comfortably seated in my chair, ready for baseball and politics intertwined. The pitcher steps to the mound. Does he throw the ball immediately? He does not and I know he's not going to. He has all those nervous twitches pitchers have . . . he tugs at the peak of his cap . . . he kicks at the dirt on the mound with his toe . . . he looks behind him at second base. Sometimes it looks as if a pitcher is afraid to throw the ball. I know this so the second the last play is over, before the pitcher even gets the ball back, I switch to the debate.

I'm watching the debate. I listen to the beginning of a question from the moderator. I hear the first few words and I know what the question is going to be. It's a long question and I've not only heard the question before, I've heard the answer. I get back to the ball game just in time to see the pitcher wind up and throw the ball. I haven't missed anything. The hitter swings and knocks the ball out of the park. I have seen one of the highlights of the game.

Now, here comes the manager. You know when the manager leaves the dugout and walks out on the field to tell the pitcher he's finished that it's going to take a long while. He tries to break it to the pitcher gently that he's through. He talks to him like a father although we can't hear what he's saying.

We do know though that it's going to be a while before play resumes . . . quite a while. Changing pitchers, including getting the new man in from the bullpen where he's been warming up, can take up to four minutes. People in the stands get a hot dog. At home, I go back to the political debate.

I've heard the candidates say almost everything they are ever going to say but I am interested in seeing whether either of them is going to make a fool of himself so I listen briefly. My finger is poised over the remote control button that will take me back to baseball. When one of them starts an old, familiar line I'm gone.

After the third out in the inning for either team you have time to go to the refrigerator before the first batter for the other team comes to the plate. If you are more interested in the debate than something to eat, skip the refrigerator and go back to the debate. You may have time for both.

You know you can leave the debate permanently when the moderator asks the candidates for their final statement. He tells them they'll have to do it quickly. I have never heard anything new in "a final statement" so it's back to the ball game for good.

The arguments on the field are often more interesting than the arguments at the debate. The networks should find a way to let us in on those. No reason why all the players and the umpires couldn't wear little microphones. To those who object because of the language used on the field, it seems certain that ball players don't say anything worse than what we hear in the average R-rated movie.

Switching back and forth between two programs or games is something we all do. It's so common that you'd think the networks would have thought of doing it for us. They know as well as we do where the lulls are going to be in both a baseball game and a political debate. By going back and forth, they could save us time and improve both events.

## A VOTE AGAINST CANDIDATES

We're all agreed on two things about politicians and Presidential elections. First, we agree the campaign for reelection starts too soon after the last election is over. President Bush started running again about 20 minutes after he was elected in 2000. They all do.

The second thing we agree on is that candidates spend too much money trying to get elected. If you took all the money that all the candidates spend, it would be enough to get a good start paying off the National debt. The buying of the White House is a national disgrace and it is not limited to either party.

The candidates don't have much trouble raising money because big businessmen don't dare turn down a candidate who asks them for a contribution. It accounts for why thousands of contributors give money to both candidates. This is so transparently sleazy that it ought to be illegal. These big-time contributors to both candidates want whichever one wins to be indebted to them.

The candidates could save millions if they concentrated on speaking only to voters who disagree with them. They never do. The Republican candidate speaks exclusively in front of Republican audiences and the Democrats speak to Democrats. It is idiotic. Why spend money trying to convince the convinced? President Bush, seeking reelection, will address the Republican Convention. There won't be one person in the crowd whose mind he's going to change.

If candidates made their arguments to audiences who disagreed with them, they could save 90 percent of their campaign money and maybe even pick up a few votes. Even that is doubtful. In all the years I've voted, no political candidate has ever changed my mind about who to vote for by any statement made in a campaign speech.

One reason candidates like to speak in front of a friendly audience is because the people in it applaud at the slightest provocation. If the speech is televised, it creates a good impression. There isn't a boo for the

Democratic candidate at a Democratic rally or a hiss for the Republican at a Republican dinner. That makes it seem to everyone watching at home on television as though the whole world approves of what the politician is saying.

Politicians put great faith in the bandwagon but Americans don't vote for a candidate because someone else is voting for him or her. They make up their own minds. Most competitors like to be seen as the underdog. A politician, on the other hand, tries to convince us that he or she is the favorite.

What gets into people who run for office? Why do they so misjudge what makes people vote one way or the other?


## NO MORE MR. NASTY GUY

Years ago someone on Richard Nixon's campaign staff asked if I'd work on some of his speeches. This was before he was President and I didn't do it because I knew I wasn't going to vote for him.

That was a pretty weak reason. I needed the money and, if you write for a living, you ought to be able to write a speech for someone whether you agree with him or not. Somewhere I read a line I've never forgotten about comedians, "A comedian is someone who can be funny when he doesn't feel funny." Same idea writing political speeches for politicians. You don't have to agree with them.

Still, it didn't seem honest so I refused the job. How did I ever get the idea that honesty had anything to do with a political campaign? Even though I've never written one, in the quiet of my own mind I often think to myself that I could improve on the political speeches I hear being delivered by the candidates.

My mistake is thinking I'd actually be writing about the issues. That isn't what a candidate wants. The candidate's purpose when he talks is to keep from saying much at all. Anything he says of substance will lose him votes. He isn't so much trying to get new votes, he's trying to hang on to the ones he has.

A writer couldn't sit down and write a speech for a candidate explaining his position on abortion because most of them don't have one and don't want to talk about it if they do. They don't want to make their position clear. The fuzzier they are when they talk about abortion or anything else, the better it is for them. About half of all Americans accept abortion and half oppose it. A candidate needs more than 50 percent of the votes and by really saying what he thinks, he can only lose some of them.

We keep asking candidates to tell us what they really believe but half the time they don't really believe anything. All they want is to say something that will get them elected. They can go either way on anything. Their speeches are not designed to address the issues, they're designed to tiptoe around them.

Walter Cronkite has been trying to get the television networks to give the candidates air time when Election Day gets close. Several of the networks have agreed to do that. Each candidate, on successive nights, is going to be given time on camera to say what he wants. It won't work. They'll give us the same old stuff. They'll avoid saying anything of substance that we can pin on them. We need a good inquisitor like Mike Wallace, Jim Lehrer or Cronkite himself to push them up against the wall and make them reveal themselves.

One thing I feel sure of, about speeches and campaigning, is that politicians should be nicer to each other. If there is any single reason one of them falls behind in a campaign it's because he gives the impression he's nasty. They should all start saying nice things about each other even if they don't mean it because it sounds better to the rest of us.

If one candidate absolutely refused to say anything bad about the other and flat out wouldn't do it, I'll bet that candidate would walk away with the election. Saying nasty things about an opponent does more harm to the person who says it than to the opponent.

When I write the speeches for both candidates, they're going to sound sweet as pie. Never is heard, a discouraging word. "He's good but I'm even better" will be their theme. When Election Day comes around, voters would be saying "Gosh, George Bush and Al Gore are both such nice, honest, capable guys . . . I hate to vote against either one of them."

## BLACK MAN FOR
## THE WHITE HOUSE

Last Monday I came to work early and parked my car near where I work in the CBS News building. As I was going in the door, a mile-long limo pulled up, three men jumped out, followed by a fourth. That last man out was obviously the reason for the other three and for the limo.

My instant thought, with all this hubbub and security was that the President of the United States was going to be interviewed on the CBS *Early Show*. I was slightly ahead of them so I pulled the glass door open and stepped back to let them go through. Even if it wasn't the President I knew it was someone more important than I was.

"Hi, Andy!" a voice said and I recognized the beaming, bespectacled face of General Colin Powell. He, not the President, was coming in to answer questions on the *Early Show*. I was so flattered he knew me I could hardly remember what floor I was on when I got in the elevator.

We all look for reasons to vote for or against someone and that friendly moment did it for me. Ever since, I've been thinking he's who I'd most like to see be our next President.

The thought had already occurred to me when I'd seen him being interviewed about a book he wrote by Jay Leno and several talk show hosts. In each case he was attractive, thoughtful, funny and . . . I thought, Presidential.

It doesn't matter much to me that I don't know where he stands on the issues. If you trust someone and believe he's bright, then you trust him to take the right stand on the issues. (By "the right stand" I mean the stand you take, of course.)

It might be a great thing for the United States to have a black man in the White House. It could happen. There's no doubt we're polarized as a nation. We have racist thoughts even if we suppress them but in spite of all the hate and bigotry in America, Colin Powell would have a good chance of being elected. White Americans would vote for him without giving his color a second thought just as they have accepted Tiger Woods as a sports hero without thinking of his ethnicity.

There would be the inevitable bigots who wouldn't dream of voting for a black man but they would be at least offset, and maybe more than offset, by the unanimous black vote. That the black vote would be all but unanimous is one of the few down sides to the idea but it's inevitable.

If we could ever elect a black President as good as Colin Powell seems to be, it would erase all the hate and pent-up anger so many black people have for white Americans. It would be the end of their being able to claim discrimination or suppression and it would go a long way toward eliminating this internal black/white war we've been fighting for so long. We wouldn't have to listen to Jesse Jackson, Al Sharpton or Louis Farrakhan anymore if Powell was elected.

For years when I was growing up, people said, "A Catholic can never be elected President." John F. Kennedy ended that talk.

Then they said, "A divorced man will never be elected." Ronald Reagan disproved that. Powell could be elected. He would be the 10th general to hold the office. You can probably name three—George Washington, Ulysses Grant and Dwight Eisenhower.

The fact that Colin Powell doesn't want to be President, is further proof that he's the right man for the job.

# POLLED TO DEATH

Polls suggest they reveal what America is thinking and it's insulting that they think we're so predictable. They're often wrong announcing what we think because half the time we have no idea ourselves what we think. Those of us who don't agree with the results of a poll are expected to think we're out of step and ought to get with it.

Taking a poll has become a popular and relatively inexpensive way for the organization that takes it to call attention to itself. Little-known colleges have started to do polls to make themselves known. The television networks do them. They put 50 people in a room with telephones, call a few hundred numbers, ask a few dozen questions and announce in a few hours what America thinks. They never take into account the fact that the only people they get answers from are those who have so little to do or are so stupid, that they willingly respond. A poll would probably show that the people who hang up are 37 percent smarter than the people who answer the questions.

Polls are an amusing but superficial indication of what a lot of people think. If any member of Congress accepts a poll as a mandate for how he or she ought to vote, then we've got the wrong form of government. Our democracy was never meant to be ruled by popular opinion. Things are too often popular without being right and half the time the public doesn't know what it's talking about on issues of importance. We don't take a vote on everything in a democracy. We elect representatives who we hope know more about it than we do.

It seems unfortunately true that too often politicians do pay attention to the polls. Particularly around election time, they determine what their constituents want and then try to please them by saying what they want to hear. Our legislators ought to know more about what's good for us than we know ourselves. If they don't, God Bless America because we're in trouble.

Elected officials ought to have better information on all the issues than we have and should vote for what's right whether it's popular or not. It doesn't sound democratic but democracy is a flawed concept. It doesn't always work perfectly and this is an example of one of its imperfections.

The ideal of our democracy assumes that if everyone knew everything about everything, we'd all come to the same conclusion, which would be the right one. The trouble is, we don't all have all the information. It's wrong when a Congressman tries to be so specifically representative of our thinking that he accepts a poll as gospel and acts in accord with it. We don't want a representative who's about as smart and knowledgeable as we are. We want someone a lot smarter than that who knows the right thing to do and does it even if it's unpopular with us.

Fortunately we're all saved by the fact that quite often there's a happy coincidence of what public opinion says it wants and what's actually good for us.

There are things about which it would be interesting to have poll results. We'd all like to compare our lives with the lives of other people. Never mind the political polls.

Here's a sample poll that might give interesting results on things that really matter:

- What time do you go to bed weeknights?
  8–9 ___, 9–10___, 10-11___, 11–12 ___, after 12 ___?
- If you stay up to watch Letterman, Ted Koppel or Jay Leno, do you get up later?
- Which do you like best, DOGS___ CATS ___?
- Do you like going to work? YES___NO___
- Has too much or not enough attention been given to sexual harassment in the workplace?
  TOO MUCH___ NOT ENOUGH ___
- Which do you prefer? VANILLA___ CHOCOLATE___
- If you were alone on a desert island, without a drop to drink, would you like an ice-cold COKE ___ PEPSI ___ BUD ___ LEMONADE ___ TEA ___WATER ___?
- Do you think there's a possibility that nuclear weapons or a bio-

logical plague will destroy all of civilization within the next 100 years? YES___ NO___
- Saddam Hussein is the dictator of IRAN___ IRAQ___.
- Do you eat dinner between 5–6 ___ 6–7 ___ 7–8___?
- Do you lie? Never___ Hardly ever___ Often ___
- Do you use profanity? YES ___ NO ___
- Vulgarities? YES ___ NO___
- Are beer-drinkers SMARTER ___ DUMBER ___ than average?
- Do you normally exceed the speed limit on a major highway?
- Have you ever been polled? YES ___ NO ___
- Do you trust polls? YES___ NO ___

## TELLING IT LIKE IT ISN'T

Reporters went anywhere our soldiers went in World War II. The American public got good, firsthand accounts of what was happening. The Army helped reporters, fed them, put up tents, gave them jeeps. Reporters followed along as close to the fighting as they dared go. Ernie Pyle was one of the reporters who kept Americans back home informed about what the soldiers were doing.

There isn't going to be another Ernie Pyle if the Pentagon continues to keep reporters from knowing what American forces are doing.

Two Army censors traveled with the press corps and read all copy that was sent out. There were just a few rules and reporters all knew what they were. It was obvious that they were not to write information that would help the Germans if they had it. Reporters rarely argued with censors.

The Defense Department has no censors with our men in the field during any recent battle we've fought. They don't need them because there are no reporters. The Pentagon stonewalled the efforts by newspapers and television news organizations to get reporters into Afghanistan with our troops so that they could tell the American public what was going on. This policy of operating in secret, even from the American people, was set by the Pentagon during the Gulf War.

There has always been animosity between journalists and generals. Generals don't like being watched. If they bomb the wrong target or alienate several million people in a foreign country by killing innocent civilians by mistake, they don't want anyone back home to know. The way to cover their mistakes is by not allowing reporters to be where the action is. You won't read of any military disasters in the bulletins issued by any Army public relations office.

Our military commanders have bitter memories of Vietnam where reports from correspondents in the field with our troops made it clear to the American public that we ought to get out. The Pentagon wasn't going to have any negative stories about the progress of the war in the Middle East or in Afghanistan because they would not allow reporters to do any reporting. The only information the public got was from Secretary of Defense Donald Rumsfeld and he has brought the art of "No comment" to a new level.

Here are a few excerpts from typical Rumsfeld's briefings during the Spring of 2002.

RUMSFELD:

"I am really not the person to ask about that."

"I know what I know, I know what I don't know and how can I stand up here when I know I don't know?"

"If I wanted to discuss any single element, I would have brought it up."

"I liked what I said and the way I said it."

"I do not think it would be useful at all to answer individual questions."

"I don't know that I want to get in to exactly what we would do."

"There are clearly a lot of people who are willing to guess at those numbers. I am not one of them. I could but I won't."

"We don't talk about future plans we might have."

"I'm not going to get into a daily assessment."

"I don't know that I want to give a day-to-day report."

"I'm not giving daily reports."

"I've answered that to the best of my ability."

"I think I've said as much as is appropriate."

"I don't care to respond."

"I have no desire to discuss the issue."

"I have no information whatsoever."

"I have no information on this."

"I have no idea."

It is apparent that the Secretary of Defense loves giving these reports. He's charming, funny and bright . . . but he's no Ernie Pyle and the American public has been kept in the dark about what its soldiers are doing.

## BETTER TELEVISION

It is disappointing how often junk sells better than quality. It doesn't seem to matter what the product is. The bad ones drive out the good ones. Usually it's simply because junk's cheaper. Other times, it's because junk appeals to our baser instincts.

In the grocery store, soft, commercial, pre-sliced bread sells better than the crusty, quality loaves made by the small, independent bakery in town. In bookstores, the cheap, sexy thriller sells more copies than the classy novel.

There is too much junk on television because that's what a lot of people like to watch either because they are too young to know any better or because they have too little education and no taste. Culturally deprived kids are exposed to a barrage of inane violence, sex and stupidity. Some of it rubs off on them. Violence, crime and sex attract a crowd of all ages.

The populist governor of Minnesota, former professional wrestler and showman Jesse Ventura, wanted to eliminate Minnesota's subsidization of public radio and television. Presumably this bright, likable ignoramus would like to bring television down to the level of professional wrestling.

Americans like to complain about the intrusion of government in their lives but there are things government does for us that we can't do for ourselves. Instead of eliminating or reducing it, we ought to quadruple the money spent on public television and radio. Television isn't a classroom but kids are learning more of what they know from the tube than from their schools. There should be a second public television operation to compete with the present. It would keep the Corporation for Public Broadcasting on its cultural toes.

CBS bought King World Productions for $2.5 billion because King owns three of the biggest moneymaking programs—*Jeopardy, Wheel of Fortune* and the *Oprah Winfrey Show.* The yearly budget allowed by Congress to the Corporation for Public Broadcasting is $250 million. At that rate, what CBS paid for King would pay for all of public television for 10 years. The King shows are as culturally uplifting as a freight elevator.

Republican members of Congress are always trying to reduce the money for public television because they think public television is philosophically and politically liberal and they don't think government should be involved anyway.

Why not? Government is involved with all sorts of things that are for the public's benefit. We don't hesitate to pay for our school system. We'd be lost without our court system which is paid for with tax money. We pay for everything good with public money. There isn't a city in the Country that doesn't support a museum because even the most ignorant of its town council members understands that it's worth using public money to support cultural standards. We support the great cultural standard bearers like the Smithsonian Institution, the Library of Congress, the National Gallery of Art, the National Archives. None of these is more important than what the American public is exposed to on television every day.

There isn't a price Congress could put on the value to be gained by our Country if we could raise the general level of public taste by exposing ourselves to more of the best of everything on tax-paid-for television. It's peanuts compared with what we spend on other things.


## WORKING THE GOVERNMENT

There was a time not so long ago, when our Government printed the money, fought our wars, made sure we didn't die of small pox and delivered the mail. Half of all 600,000 Government employees were mailmen in 1930.

Today there are about three million Government employees trying to do everything for everyone but if you try to get one of them on the telephone to ask a question, they're out that day. Other times they are at lunch, in a meeting or they have "stepped away from my desk."

For whatever reason, when I want to talk to one of our 3,000,000 Government employees, they aren't there.

In talking to a good friend who works for the Federal Government, I mentioned this and to help me understand, she sent me several Government memos regarding work schedules. If the employees of private companies worked by these rules, the companies would be out of business in six months.

One single-spaced, five-page memo is entitled:

"ALTERNATIVE WORK SCHEDULES (AWS)"

It sets out to explain "flexitime" and "a compressed work week." I've read it and it's no wonder no one's ever there in Washington when you try to get hold of them. Anywhere else "flexitime" and "a compressed work week" would be called "goofing off."

"Credit hours," the memo says, "are unique to the flexible work schedules. Credit hours are hours which an employee requests to work in excess of the basic work requirement in order to be able to take time off . . ." Time off is the key to everything in these Government guidelines. "Credit hours," the memo says, "may be used to take time off from work at any time . . . ".

"A flexible work schedule, referred to as 'flexitime,' replaces a fixed time and departure work day."

The Government allows employees to work longer hours so they can pile up time off and not come in at all on other days. A system called "a flexitour schedule" allows workers to work nine hours instead of eight for nine days and then take the second Friday off. Over a year, that would be 25 days off in addition to vacation and "sick" days.

If the day off falls on a holiday, the employee can choose to take some other day off in place of that.

In addition to "flexitour" and "flexitime," the Government offers its workers a feature called "FLEXIPLACE." Any American worker would jump at he chance to take advantage of it. "FLEXIPLACE" means he or she can stay home and work. Nice? You can imagine all the work being done in Government by employees who choose to work at home—quite often in bed, I imagine.

Government workers get sick a lot, too. No one I work with gets sick more than once every twenty years and then they're usually out for one day with a bad cold. Government workers are sick 13 days a year, year after year.

In a Government job they refer to "earning" sick leave. An employee "earns" four hours of sick leave every two weeks. The employee can save up those "sick" hours and stay home 13 days whenever he or she feels like being sick. Sickness is more prevalent in Washington on warm, sunny days than on cold, wet days.

A brochure for Government workers by the President's Council on Management Improvement offers tips for workers: For example:

"How can I convince my boss that I should be allowed to work at home . . . ?

"A: Here are some tips: Explain to your boss how it will benefit his/her organization. Start off small by suggesting working home a day or two a week."

The idea of working for the Government is beginning to appeal to me. I think I'll suggest to the boss that I work at home. I'll be working about 16 hours a day for a week. With the credit hours I've built up in my flexiplace with my compressed flexitime, I'll be able to take off half a year. This credit time I've acquired, plus my regular vacation added to my sick leave should enable me to work a three-week year.

So, don't call me at the office. I'm off that day.

## EXPERIENCE GOING TO WASTE

We waste our ex-Presidents. Whether a President was your choice or not while he was in office, you have to concede that by the time he leaves office, a former President knows more about what's going on in the Country and knows more about problems and possible solutions than anyone alive. We should provide a way for ex-Presidents to remain active in Government so they can give back to the Country the expertise and experience it gave them.

The way it works now, an ex-President wanders around the Country, gets applause and quite a bit of money for good causes and himself by making speeches at corporate dinners, charity affairs and political fundraisers. A former President is often paid $100,000 for a 20-minute speech. The money's good but the work is demeaning. And what a waste!

Former Presidents are seen playing golf, yachting or attending state funerals. Their pictures are in the papers not doing much of anything because they don't do much of anything.

We have five ex-Presidents: Ronald Reagan, Gerald Ford, Jimmy Carter, George Bush and Bill Clinton. They all seem lost with nothing but make-work jobs to do. Ronald Reagan's medical condition would preclude him from being active in Government but the others seem healthy and as bright as they ever were—which I recognize as a double entendre.

Bill Clinton still has a few years to go before he'll be 60. Whatever else we all think of him, it's hard to deny he's bright and experienced. There ought to be a place for him to contribute. Being a Senator's husband is not a full-time job for him.

Jimmy Carter has kept himself busy helping good causes but he has more to offer than that. Gerald Ford was an effective and experienced Congressman before he became Vice President and fell into the Presidency when Nixon was forced to resign. He's out around mostly having himself a good time. George Bush is busy being George W. Bush's father.

Every former President has more to contribute than the conventions of being a former President now allows for. It should have an important name. What we need is an official Government position specifically set up for each of them to occupy. They should at least have the rank of senator with real authority and pay to supplement their retirement income so they can stay off the lecture circuit. A cabinet of ex-Presidents might work. They'd meet and discuss problems and then offer their advice to the current President—and to us.

This new Government office would be occupied by all living ex-Presidents. The Senate now comprises 100 members. We could expand that to include the former chief executives.

As an ex-President, with no further political ambitions and no lust for power, he could vote according to his informed opinion. He'd have nothing to win, nothing to lose. He could be absolutely honest and above being influenced by partisan interests.

The only ex-President who ever used what he knew later on was John Quincy Adams. Adams was defeated after one term in office, by Andrew Jackson in 1828. He went back home to Massachusetts, sulked, hung around and did some make-work jobs. He hated it. A few years later, someone who knew how smart and experienced he was suggested he run for Congress.

This was a new idea, a former President running for a lower office, but Adams didn't think it was demeaning. He ran for the lesser office and took his chances on being defeated. Adams was elected and did more good things for the Country during the 17 years he served as a Congressman than he had during the four he was President.

If making all former Presidents Senators is for some reason impractical, I have another idea. We are desperate for good Vice Presidents. A Vice President who once had the #1 job would be the perfect adviser and stand-in for the President. In case of emergency, he'd be best equipped to take over. If we voted for nothing but the Presidency, the outgoing President might automatically assume the job of being adviser, confidante and Vice President to the newly elected Chief Executive. We'd eliminate a terrible waste of experience.

Of course, if the outgoing President said "I wouldn't take that job for all the tea in China," my idea might not work.

# THERE ARE LIBERALS
# AND CONSERVATIVES

There has never been a time when the country was more evenly divided between people who are liberals and people who are conservatives, and this can be confusing. For example, not all liberals are liberal about everything and not all conservatives are conservative about everything.

I've made some notes, trying to separate the two camps in my own mind:

- Republicans are conservative. Democrats are liberal.
- Conservatives want less government so people can do it for themselves.
- Liberals think we need government because there are too many people who can't do it for themselves.

- Conservatives are certain they're right.
- Liberals are thinking it over.
- Liberals are optimists. They think the best is yet to come.
- Conservatives are pessimists. They think things are getting worse.
- Conservatives are careful to lock everything.
- Liberals are more apt to leave the door unlocked. They may even leave the keys in the car in their driveway.
- Conservatives keep track of every check they write.
- Liberals hope they have enough to cover it.
- Liberals keep going when the light is yellow.
- Conservatives stop when they think the light is about to turn yellow.
- Behind on fourth down and inches to go in the fourth quarter of a football game, a liberal coach goes for it.
- A conservative coach punts.
- It is unknown whether more conservatives or liberals are college graduates. It is almost certain that more liberals have been thrown out of college.
- There are not many liberal farmers, but there aren't many liberal insurance salesmen, either.
- There are more rich conservatives than there are rich liberals.
- More really rich people than you'd think are liberals and more low-income laborers than you could believe are conservatives.
- Conservatives are more apt to own a gun but they're quicker to call the cops.
- Conservatives believe the government takes away an individual's liberty.
- Liberals believe the government protects their freedom.
- Conservatives are more religious than liberals—although there is no evidence that they're nicer people because of it.
- Conservatives are liberal about using up our natural resources because they don't think we'll run out before they die.
- Liberals are conservative about saving our natural resources because they think it makes them nicer people.

- Conservatives oppose abortion and liberal Democrats do not. No one knows why this is a liberal/conservative issue.
- Conservatives do not favor conserving when it comes to cutting down trees, digging for coal or drilling for oil.
- Liberals are more liberal with government money than with their own.
- With the exception of a few, most Hollywood actors are liberal.
- Liberals are more musical.
- Conservatives are better with numbers.
- Conservatives can't cook without a recipe.
- Liberals don't cook; they go out to dinner.
- Conservatives are practical.
- Liberals are dreamers.
- Conservatives plan their day.
- Liberals wait and see what happens.
- Conservatives think we do too much business with foreign countries but they buy Mercedes-Benzes and BMWs.
- Liberals buy Fords, Chevrolets, Hondas and Toyotas.
- Conservatives write notes with a fountain pen.
- Liberals scribble with a pencil.
- Conservatives complain that most television newspeople are liberals.

# PART 4

---

# *Sports*

*If all you care about is winning, you aren't a real fan.*

# THE TRIUMPH
## OF A SPORTS FAN

People who aren't sports fans don't understand sports fans and, as a sports fan, I can understand that.

Being a sports fan is mindless. What non-fans don't understand is, the mindlessness of it is what's so attractive. It isn't hard to be a sports fan, you don't have to think much—or even think at all, really. It doesn't cost anything to watch a game on television or read about it in a newspaper. Who wins doesn't matter and when someone gets hired or fired, the sports fan may find it interesting but it doesn't make a damn bit of difference to the fan's life or income.

When watching a game, the fan may get emotionally involved by hoping, or even cheering, for one of the contestants but, in the end, who wins and who loses does not have any effect whatsoever on the fan's life. The drama is contrived.

After a New York Giants football game last year, I felt vaguely depressed because they lost. I got thinking about it and started laughing. Why did I care? It was fun to go to the game and I went, not to see the Giants win but to see the game played. I did have one big winner the day Green Bay beat the Giants in their last game and I'll tell you about it with the hope that I don't end up in prison because of it.

January 6th was a nasty cold day. The temperature was in the '30s and there was a threat of rain. I enjoy defeating the weather's attempt to make me uncomfortable and I knew I had to bring enough clothes to keep me both warm and dry.

The "security" measures include a prohibition against fans carrying in any kind of a bag or container. You could not carry a canvas bag with clothes, a thermos or sandwich bag. This does more for the sale of the bad and expensive concession stand food than it does for security.

I was determined to bring hot chicken broth to drink at halftime no matter what the restrictions were so I filled a thermos. In my arms I carried an extra jacket, a down-filled vest and a four-by-four-foot Mylar blanket with which to cover myself in the event of rain.

As I stood in the mob pushing through the security funnel, I watched the guard scanning fans with his magic wand. He invariably had a fan hold his hands over his head so he could run his scanner up and down under his arms, looking for lethal weapons. I knew my thermos might be confiscated and I was plenty nervous about losing my chicken soup.

I needed a plan. What would a terrorist trying to get a thermos of chicken soup past a guard do in a situation like this, I asked myself. As I watched the actions of the security guard, a devious plan formed in my head. I tied a loose knot in the sleeve of the extra jacket and dropped the thermos down the sleeve.

Just as I got to the guard, I deliberately dropped the slippery Mylar blanket at his feet. He instinctively bent over to pick it up and, although I hated myself for taking advantage of a polite guard, I thanked him, held my arms, jacket, chicken soup and all, high over my head so he could scan my rib cage.

"Go ahead!" he said.

In my seat, I was the envy of all my friends who have been sitting around me at Giants Stadium for 25 years now. They all wanted to know how I got my chicken soup to the game and I was so embarrassed by the deviousness of my tactics, I didn't tell them.

I just smiled—and sipped my soup.

## SPORTS RULES

There's no game I ever watch without thinking of rule changes that would improve it. Here's a list of some suggested changes, by sport.

FOOTBALL:
- Calling the plays is part of the game and should be left to the play-

ers. It should be illegal for a coach to signal, send in by substitute or otherwise convey information to the quarterback. The quarterback alone should be responsible for calling plays and for making other tactical decisions. For example, when given the option by officials, the quarterback or captain should decide whether or not to take or decline a penalty. In the event one of the guards or other players was smarter than the quarterback but was a guard because he couldn't throw a football very far, the guard could call the plays.

It can be a crucial decision bearing on who wins or loses and, as part of the game, that decision should be made by a player, not by a coach. Up until 1963, coaches were not allowed to send information in to the players and they should return to those rules.

- In 1900, the football rulebook said a maximum of five people would be allowed to stand along the sidelines of the playing field. All others, including water carriers, would have to be seated on the bench. Today the sidelines are a mob scene. Anyone with a seat low down in the stadium can't see the game because the field is obscured by the people standing on the sidelines.

- Because the helmet, once a protective device for the head, has been made a weapon, all helmets worn by players should be made of leather, not plastic the consistency of steel.

- When a pass is tipped or touched by a player and then caught by someone on the opposing team, it should not be entered on the quarterback's record as an interception. It wasn't his mistake.

BASEBALL:

- There should be no substitutions in a game. Baseball isn't that taxing physically. All players, including the starting pitcher, should finish the game he starts even if the opposing team gets 50 hits off him. In the case of serious injury to a baseball player, the team should have to continue with eight men. This is comparable to the European soccer rule.

- Any baseball player caught spitting tobacco juice should be removed from the game. Once removed, he should be given a mop with which to clean up the mess he made.

BASKETBALL:

More than 90 percent of the players in the NBA are over six feet tall. Thirty-two NBA players are seven feet tall. The basket is fixed to the backboard 10 feet above the floor. At seven feet, with a three-foot arm stretched over his head, a player can drop the ball into the basket. The idea of having the basket over the players' heads was to make it necessary for the ball to be thrown upward toward the basket, not dropped through it from above. The basket should be raised one foot six inches to reduce the advantage to players whose principal contribution to the team is their height.

A team should be limited to a maximum height of 370 inches for five players. This would be an average of 6 feet 2 inches per player. If the Lakers played Shaquille O'Neal at 7 feet 2 inches, they would have to have a player 5 feet 2 inches or four players 5 feet 11 inches to make up for his height.

TENNIS:
- All shirts, skirts, shorts and shoes should be white. Shirts should be worn tucked in.
- Women should wear pleated white skirts.

HOCKEY:
- Too many hockey games end up 1–0. To increase interest in the game by increasing the scoring, the opening of the net should be widened by six inches so that more good shots would get past the goalkeeper.
- The goalkeeper's pads, which now present a virtual wall to anyone trying to get the puck into the net, should be substantially reduced so that, while they would protect the goalie, they could not exceed by more than an inch the size of the goalie himself.

GOLF:

- Every able-bodied player should walk the entire course carrying all the clubs he or she plans to use.
- The size of the hole in the green should be increased to double its present diameter of 4 and one-fourth inches to encourage holes-in-one and generally reduce the time it takes players to get the ball in the hole 18 times.

There should be a few rule changes common to every professional sport.

No player should be allowed to wear any emblem, trademark or symbol identifying a piece of his clothing or footwear with a commercial corporation.

## QUOTH THE RAVEN, "BALTIMORE!"

The nicknames for professional sports teams make no sense and there are so many teams needing nicknames now that the problem is out of hand. Most of the names teams get are dull or uninspired.

You might think that all the teams in a league would have nicknames in the same category. They might, for instance, all be named after birds like the Eagles, the Falcons, the Cardinals, the Blue Jays or the Orioles. There are plenty of other birds that could be used as nicknames but they don't do that. There's no pattern. Six teams in a league may be named after a bird then the next one will be named after an animal—preferably a vicious one like a tiger, a lion, a wolf or a bear. There are no conditions in real life when a blue jay or even a falcon, would be caught dead playing with a tiger.

Other teams have names that are in no particular category like the Angels, the Royals or so dull and prosaic a name as the Red Sox. Why would you name a team after a pair of socks?

You'd think there was a shortage of good nicknames the way they are repeated. Hundreds of professional, college and high school teams are called "the Tigers" but some animals are never used as nicknames. I've never heard a team called "the Elephants," "the Hippopotamuses" or "the Jackasses."

After a period of time, the silliest names become familiar and seem right for the team to which they are applied. The Cowboys, Celtics, Red Sox, Steelers and Bears were all names that were probably hard for fans to get used to when they were first given to the teams.

The real question is why a sports team has to have a nickname at all. Because of space problems, a newspaper listing hundreds of scores after a busy weekend, usually refers to a team in the listings by the name of the city it represents. If it's a college team, the paper lists it alphabetically by name of the college. It does not, for example, list Syracuse under O for "Orangemen," Tennessee under V for "Volunteers" or Notre Dame under F for "Fighting Irish." It is "Chicago 107–Seattle 94"—not "Bulls 107"–"SuperSonics 94."

The leagues in every professional sport are expanding and it's apparent that management is hard pressed to come up with names. Several years ago when Art Modell moved the Cleveland Browns to Baltimore, he was not allowed to take the name "Browns" with him. Modell had to choose a new nickname and he decided on "the Baltimore Ravens."

The reason Modell gave for naming the team after a bird with a bad reputation was that Edgar Allan Poe, who wrote the poem *The Raven*, died and is buried in Baltimore. I doubt if Modell read the poem or knew anything about Poe before he named his team. Edgar Allan Poe was an orphan who had a terrible life.

Poe was living in New York when his wife died and he moved to Baltimore to flee sorrow and to look for the recognition his work was not getting in New York. Nothing worked. Sorrow followed Poe wherever he went. His drinking got out of control and he died at age 40 shortly after he finished writing *The Raven*. He never made any money from the poem—which was not part of Modell's plan for his football team.

So my question about that nickname is this: Is a funky poem about a talking bird, written by an egotistical alcoholic who died drunk and delirious on the floor of a saloon in Baltimore, what you should name a football team after?

## COACHES NEED COACHING

The first time I went to a concert played by a big symphony orchestra, there were things about it that impressed me more than the music. I was fascinated by the man with the long, dramatically shaggy grayish white hair, standing with his back to the audience, holding a thin stick in his right hand. His tailor, I thought to myself, must design his tailcoat to look best from the back. He raised both arms and, as he brought them down sharply, the musicians blew into their instruments, drew bows across the strings or fingered the keys and the hall burst alive with music.

After watching him just before that initial blast, the players then seemed to ignore him and concentrate instead on the page of music on the stand in front of them. It appeared to me as though the orchestra leader was doing more following than leading. He looked good but the musicians didn't seem to pay any attention to his gestures.

I was about 15 years old and spent most of that two-hour concert thinking about the man on the podium, waving his arms at the players. Was he really necessary? That was the question I asked myself and, because I didn't know, never got an answer and never have since.

In sports, coaches are their teams' orchestra leaders. I find myself thinking I could manage a baseball team in the World Series. It is not clear why the person who directs a baseball team is called the manager while the same position on a football or basketball team is called coach. Neither is it clear why the baseball manager wears a baseball uniform but a football coach wouldn't think of wearing a football uniform as he paced the sidelines.

The qualities that make a great orchestra leader are unknown to most concert-goers. They don't fire a leader like Leopold Stokowski or Leonard Bernstein when an orchestra has a bad year but coaches get fired all the time when the team is unsuccessful. It's not unusual for eight or ten big league baseball managers or NFL football coaches to be fired in one year. NBA coaches come and go but mostly go.

Firing the coach is a way for a team with bad management and mediocre players to save face and put the blame somewhere else. Firing a coach is a favorite thing for team owners to do to placate angry fans but it seldom helps. A team with good players makes the best coach.

Red Auerbach, the legendary Boston Celtics coach, lost in the play-offs for seven straight years between 1950 and 1956. How long do you think Red would have lasted with a team today? In his eighth year as coach Auerbach won the first of nine NBA championships for the Celtics. Today, he'd be teaching physical education in high school after his second losing year.

It all makes me wonder how many games a basketball team would lose if I was coaching and had Michael Jordan playing for me. It makes me wonder what the New York Philharmonic would sound like if I was standing in front of it waving my arms.

Football coaches have been given increasing power and influence over the game and it's wrong. When I played football, it was illegal for a coach to send in a play. If the coach sent in a substitute, the player could not join the huddle until after the first play was called. This was to prevent the coach from sending in a player with a message. A player on the field, usually the quarterback, decided which play the team would run and that's the way it should be today. Deciding on the play should be part of the game and the game should be played by players, not by coaches.

The rule prohibiting coaches from sending in plays was changed in their favor because most of the people on the rules committee are coaches.

If I had to choose between having great players and a great coach, I'd take the players and if it was my orchestra, I'd ask the director to step aside so I could see the musicians.

## MUSICAL CHAIRS
## IN SPORTS

Owners and players of professional teams have been so abusive to their fans that it's surprising that fans have remained loyal.

It's not even clear what fans are loyal to. I'm a loyal New York Giants football fan but don't know why. It amuses me and I'm proud of myself for it, a sensation common to millions of sports fans.

Loyalty is an admirable trait even when a person is loyal to something that doesn't deserve it. Loyalty is independent of its object. You are loyal to your team no matter what they do to you. That's why I am still loyal to the Giants even after being so miserably treated by them. Being a fan is not a condition arrived at through intellectual consideration.

Several years ago Giants season-ticket holders got a lecture in the form of a letter from the Giants' management advising us to behave at games.

The letter was prompted by an incident involving fans who threw snowballs onto the field to protest a poor team performance. They threw snowballs because the seats they paid to sit in were covered with five inches of snow when they got to the game.

Management didn't apologize to fans for failing to clear the snow off the seats for which we had paid $37.

There was a time when the Giants' ownership was special because of its loyalty to its players. It had a family quality. It took care of its own. Old players were often rewarded with staff jobs after their playing days were over.

While Giants ownership has not changed much, no professional team can afford to be sentimental now. Players are fired or traded on a coach's whim and players are as unsentimental as owners. Money is all.

There was a time when the players on any team were almost permanent. New York Yankee fans knew from one year to the next who the players were. They were Ruth, Gehrig, DiMaggio and Mantle. I knew our Giants players would be Frank Gifford, Kyle Rote, Andy Robustelli and Rosie Grier.

The great Wayne Gretzky became famous playing for Edmonton but ended up playing for the New York Rangers. He left Edmonton for the Los Angeles Kings who sold him to New York. How can a fan be loyal to so evanescent an entity as a professional sports team? There's nothing to be loyal to that lasts.

It isn't anyone's fault. The courts determined that professional teams could not "own" or buy and sell players on the teams' own terms. For many years professional teams had special dispensation that allowed them to ignore anti-trust laws. When the rules were changed and players were allowed to declare themselves free agents at the end of a contract, salaries went through the roof. Ticket prices followed. Teams with the most money paid to get the best players and the players with the most skill demanded the most money. It got so out of hand for owners of some sports that the rules were changed to establish a maximum that any team could pay for players. It's called the salary cap.

There's some justice for players with a system that allows them to move from one team to another or for a team to move from one city to another but it's not as much fun for fans.

Fans get the worst treatment from professional sports. Baseball's World Series regularly shuts out the average home team rooter because he can't get tickets for the games. They either cost too much or they go to businessmen who give them to other businessmen with whom they want to do more business. Most people who watch the World Series are not from either of the cities represented by one of the teams. It has a dampening effect on the response from the crowd.

The New York Yankees have been in more World Series games than any other baseball team over the years but New York isn't the favorite city of many people who don't live there so their victory is not always greeted with thunderous ovation.

When the Giants play a team from any other city, I'm for the Giants but I like beating some teams better than others. As a fan, it's more fun to watch a game if you can find a way to hate the opponent. I don't like to have the Giants play Green Bay because I like the Packers. Packer fans retain some of the best of what loyalty in sports used to mean.

The first big change in professional sports took place in 1958 when a team whose fans were legendary, the Brooklyn Dodgers, moved from Ebbets Field in Brooklyn to Los Angeles. The owners thought more fans there would pay to come and see the games. They were wrong.

The only thing that has saved professional sports from being abandoned by the fans they have abused so badly is the thing that makes being a fan such a good off-duty activity: whatever happens doesn't make one damn bit of difference to your real life.

## COLLEGE NAMES

I almost never cheer for a college football team that has a state for a name. Call me pig-headed but if the game is between Stanford and California, I cheer for Stanford just because of that prejudice. I make an exception sometimes for Michigan but I wouldn't cheer for Michigan State. I never cheer for Nebraska, Alabama or any of the teams with the word "Florida" and "State" or "Texas" and "State" in their names.

To enjoy football, you have to have a rooting interest and there are so many teams, your favoritism has to be based on pretty inconsequential things. You dislike the color of their jerseys, someone you knew got thrown out, the coach talks too much.

The football teams I like are hardly ever among the best in the Country. When I look at the Associated Press list of the top 25 teams, quite often Auburn, Miami and Notre Dame are the only ones that don't have a State association.

It seems as though more colleges should have unique names like Amherst, Pomona, Dartmouth, Duke, Rutgers, Antioch, Villanova, Rice or Cornell. In the Big Ten, I'm always for Purdue and Northwestern because they're the only teams with names that don't have a State in them. Not that the name "Northwestern" makes much sense. It's neither very far west or northerly.

One reason not to cheer for a Texas or Florida team is, there are too many of them. Both Texas and Florida must have a dozen Florida-something or Texas-something colleges and a person like me who is from somewhere else, can't keep them straight. There is, for example Texas A&I, Texas A&M, Texas Southern, Texas, Texas Tech and the University of Texas in five different cities with the name of that city tacked on.

In addition to those, there is also Texas Wesleyan, Texas Tech, Texas Southern, Texas Lutheran, Texas Wesleyan and Texas Christian. There is no Texas Jewish or Texas Muslim. There is a Texas Woman's University ("Woman's" not "Women's") which does not have a football team but no Texas Man's University. I am at a loss to understand why a Texas Man's University would be considered sexist while a Texas Woman's is not.

Texas football teams have been good for a long while but the football teams from Florida have begun to excel only recently and I haven't had time to sort them out so I'm unclear about the difference between Florida State University, the University of Florida and half a dozen more good college football teams with Florida in their name. We do get some relief from the proliferation of "Florida's" with the University of Miami. The only possible confusion here is with Miami University—which is a whole other ball game because Miami University is in Oxford, Ohio. I think Miami of Ohio lets students play on their team—a mistake they don't often make at the University of Miami.

A football team has always been a way to bring attention to a college and to provide a rallying point for alumni. I don't know where it all went so wrong. It's becoming more and more difficult to distinguish some college teams from the professional teams. The best college players often quit before they finish school to play in the NFL and I wouldn't be surprised if some of the NFL players who are dropped started going back to play a few more years of college football to get the experience to try the NFL again.

If college football is an amateur sport played by genuine students, every player in the Country should be given some standard examination. We ought to know when players are bona fide college students and when they are not. We should know they can spell and count to ten.

The same test should be administered to every college team in the country and it might be possible to work out a handicap system. A team whose players averaged lower than 500 on their SAT scores, would have to concede a touchdown or two to any team whose players average above 500. A team whose players averaged 600, might get a two- or three-touchdown advantage over a team with a lesser collective score. Yale might get as many as a nine-touchdown handicap if it played Nebraska whose players have not been distinguishing themselves recently in the academic area.

## KNOW YOUR FOOTBALL PHRASES

In the style of the humorist Frank Sullivan, I offer this dialogue, a compendium of cliches, between a fan and a football game announcer:

FAN: What does a team have to do to win the game?
ANNOUNCER: To win this football game, you mean. We like to say "football game" or "the football." We hardly ever say just "the ball" or "the game." These are two good football teams playing this football game. They never kick the ball. They kick the football.

To win they have to come out ready to play football. They have to get on the scoreboard first.

FAN: What if the other team scores first?

ANNOUNCER: Then they'll have to play catch-up football.

FAN: Is there anything special they can do to win?

ANNOUNCER: They'll have to play well on both sides of the ball. I make an exception there and just say "ball." They're going to have to contain the run. They're going to have to have better pass protection so the quarterback has time to throw the football.

FAN: Where will he throw it?

ANNOUNCER: He'll throw the football downfield—to move the football into scoring position.

FAN: What if someone drops the pass thrown to him?

ANNOUNCER: We'll say he should have had that one. You have to catch a ball like that. You don't see him drop many.

FAN: Why do you think he dropped it?

ANNOUNCER: He didn't concentrate. He heard footsteps. He started to run before he had the football.

FAN: Have you talked about that?

ANNOUNCER: We've talked about that before. We've talked about that all day. Also, we talked about that earlier. We'll be talking about that later, too.

FAN: What does a team that's ahead do?

ANNOUNCER: They keep the ball on the ground. They rely on their running game to eat up the clock.

FAN: Sometimes the quarterback throws to a player on the other team and it's intercepted. What do you say about that?

ANNOUNCER: He wishes he had that one back.

FAN: What do you say when a team is about to score?

ANNOUNCER: They're in scoring position. They're down in the red zone. They haven't had much success in the red zone this year.

FAN: Does the quarterback favor one of his receivers?

ANNOUNCER: Yes. He has his go-to guy. That guy's got good hands.

He runs good routes and has a way of getting open.

FAN: It must be hard to hold your audience when the score is 34 to 6 in the fourth quarter isn't it?

ANNOUNCER: Not at all. This game is far from over. There's still a lot of football left to play. Anything can happen.

FAN: What will you say about the team that loses?

ANNOUNCER: We'll say it's going to be a long ride home but this football team has nothing to be ashamed of.

FAN: Thank you.

ANNOUNCER: Thank you. We'll be back with our locker room report after these commercial messages.

## GOLF OR TENNIS?

Tennis is a better sport than golf. It's better to play and better to watch. Golf can be a pleasant social occasion for a small group of friends to get together in the open air before drinking but, strictly speaking, it is not a sport.

The word "sport" suggests the expenditure of energy. It should involve active movements of the body, sweat, aching muscles and competition with another player. Tennis provides all of these, golf none but benign competition. It is an indication of the kind of game golf is that players add up numbers and the one with the lowest number wins.

Has anyone ever gotten out of breath playing golf? Are their muscles stiff or sore the day after a match? The exercise golf provides consists of swinging a short, expensive stick with a metal head on it, once every eight or ten minutes for several hours, at an inert white ball on the ground, in order to hit it in such a manner as to send it flying in the general direction of a small hole several hundred yards away.

A great deal of the golf in the United States is played in country clubs that proliferate in the wealthy suburbs of big cities. Snobbery is part of the clubs' charm. I am an enthusiastic defender of the kind of snobbery associated with excellence or special knowledge. A wine snob, for example, may be objectionable but he knows wine so, while I may dislike his attitude, I admire his expertise and concede. I concede his right to be snobbish. Golf club members have no such license. Their snobbishness emanates, not from any special quality members have, but from artificial rules of exclusion at their club.

Tennis is a game that can be played in a reasonable time—something short of all morning or all afternoon. It does not frustrate or infuriate the players of it as golf does. A golfer never wins because until he plays 18 holes in 18 strokes, there is room for improvement. He or she could always have hit it longer and straighter and that knowledge leaves the player feeling dissatisfied.

Tennis is better when you win but satisfying whether you win or lose because you have exercised. For that brief period in your day, no matter how old you are, you were an athlete again. No caddie has to choose a different racket for your next shot or carry it until you serve again.

Golfers are no more athletes than Bobby Fischer, the chess master. The act of taking a walk, once the best thing about a game of golf, has been all but eliminated. Golf course managers push more and more players around their courses faster and faster to make more and more money. Walking slows a golfer's progress and golf clubs want no part of walking players. In many clubs, it is mandatory that they ride in a cart. The quicker the better. Wheels have no part in tennis.

Tennis is not only a better sport to play, it is better to watch. While the placement of multiple camera positions around a golf course enables a director to take pictures of Tiger Woods on all of the 60 or more times he strikes at the ball, golf as a spectator sport can only be matched by the tension a viewer feels watching a sailboat race two miles off shore.

The closest I ever came to playing golf was when I was about eight. Alfie Gordon and I found an old golf ball and, after bouncing it around the street for several hours, we became curious about what made it bounce. We got a sharp knife from Alfie's kitchen and cut off the hard, white casing. The core was wound with what must have been a mile-long rubber band. This was the most fun I ever had with a golf ball. When I told my father what we'd done, he told me never to do that again because if you cut into the center of a golf ball, it might explode.

I wonder if Tiger Woods knows this?

## WORST AWARD
## OF THE CENTURY

As the 20th Century ended *Sports Illustrated* chose Muhammad Ali as "Sportsman Of the Century" and the newspaper *USA Today* called Ali "The Athlete of the Century." No magazine has ever been so wrong and no newspaper so far from the truth.

The dictionary says "Sportsman: a person who can take loss or defeat without complaint, or victory without gloating and who treats his opponents with fairness, generosity and courtesy."

While Cassius Clay, renamed Muhammad Ali after he decided he was a Muslim, has been fey and interesting in his limited public appearances since the onset of Parkinson's rendered him close to speechless, at the peak of his career no one could call Muhammad Ali generous in either victory or defeat. He was a bumptious braggart whose words spoke louder than his fists.

His current reputation is based, not on his excellence as a boxer, but on his charm and the sympathy for him evoked by his deteriorating mental and physical condition. He was a pretty good boxer who won 56 and lost five fights. The greatest athlete of the Century does not lose almost 10 percent of his contests. Rocky Marciano was a heavyweight champion who never lost a fight. I was at ringside during two Joe Louis fights and two Muhammad Ali fights. Muhammad Ali couldn't have laced up Joe Louis's gloves.

For both *Sports Illustrated* and *USA Today*, naming Ali was more of a promotional stunt than an honest attempt to do the impossible, name the best or most sportsmanlike athlete of the past 100 years.

Both *USA Today* and *Sports Illustrated* ignored the possibility that there ever might have been a good athlete who wasn't an American, too. You'd have a hard time convincing any South American sports fan that Ali was a better athlete than the legendary soccer player, Pele, or a Finnish fan that he was superior to Paavo Nurmi, their great distance runner. Both publications also ignored the fact that boxing is a disgusting sport that doesn't deserve to have anyone in it honored.

There are only a handful of sports that are truly international and none of them is suited the purpose of the two publications. Baseball, football and basketball are American sports. Hockey is a Canadian sport that is met with limited enthusiasm south of the border. Track and field is international but except at the time of an Olympics, not many people follow it.

There are a dozen runners and jumpers more worthy of "the Greatest Athlete" title than Ali but many of them have died. What kind of a television show and awards dinner would it have made for a magazine to have named Jesse Owens the greatest athlete of the Century? He is not alive to show up at the award ceremony. Ali filled the publishers' needs because he is alive and appealing. He just isn't anywhere near being as good an athlete or sportsman as 1,000 others that could be named.

Boxing's heavyweight champion is one of the few athletes known beyond the borders of his own country and Muhammad Ali, talent aside, is a well-known international person. His personality is unique.

My biggest complaint about calling Ali "best athlete" is based on having seen him beaten by a light heavyweight nonentity named Doug Jones. There was simply no question that Ali, then known by his pre-Muslim name, Cassius Clay, lost to Jones. All the sportswriters there in Madison Square Garden that night thought so and all the fans thought so, reacting to the decision with thunderous boos. Ali was given the decision.

Ali seems like a good guy but any sports fan could think of many athletes more deserving of the title "Athlete of the Century."

# KENTUCKY NOT
# MY OLD HOME

Until last year, there were only seven things I'd never seen. Eight at the most. Now there is one less. I went to my first Kentucky Derby. Getting to Louisville and then to Churchill Downs with 140,000 other people is a lot of trouble simply to watch 13 horses you can't see well enough to distinguish one from another, run around an oval track for two minutes.

We got up at 4:30 Friday morning to catch a 6 a.m. flight from New York to Cincinnati. In Cincinnati we changed planes and flew to Louisville. From Louisville we took a helicopter to Loretto, about 25 miles away, where we were going to a party.

The helicopter pilot was a veteran of thousands of hours in the air but unfortunately, all his hours were in the air over Michigan and we got lost in Kentucky. Finally, he put the helicopter down in an open field and ran across the road to ask directions of a truck driver who was stopped there. I was relieved when I saw the truck driver nodding and pointing down the road.

Our host at the party greeted us dressed in an Elvis Presley costume and a Presley wig which was kind of a bad start even though I'd already heard that local residents were relentless in their determination to have fun on Derby weekend.

Bill and Nancy, our host and hostess, were great to us. They have a beautiful home on 14 acres of rolling, green land. We were put in a guest bedroom suite so comfortable that I would rather have spent the two days in it and watched the Derby on television. There was a well-stocked refrigerator with a bar and I've stayed in hotel rooms that weren't as big as its bathroom.

Saturday, we parked a mile from the track and began the long walk loaded down with clothing and equipment that one or the other of us felt necessary or had been advised to take. Most of the ladies had hat boxes. Big hats are mandatory for ladies at the Derby but it was raining and windy so they couldn't wear them. Instead, they kept them in their boxes, presumably to prove they were ready to be well-dressed if the wind and rain gave them the opportunity by stopping. One woman in our group, when congratulated on the attractive design on her hat box, said that it matched the wallpaper in her bedroom.

The crowd was good-natured and ruly. There was less pushing and shoving than there would have been if the Derby were held in New York. Along the streets leading to Churchill Downs, soapbox ministers proclaimed the greatness of Jesus and beseeched us to pray that we not lose our souls. One woman in the group said that when she goes to a horserace, it was her shirt, not her soul, that she was most afraid of losing.

We had good seats high up in the wooden clubhouse, not far from the finish line but Churchill Downs is a disaster waiting to happen. The aisles leading up into the stands are only 30 inches wide and jammed. I was claustrophobic. I kept looking for an emergency way out in case of fire. Fire officials in New York would not tolerate conditions at Churchill Downs and the only thing that makes it work at all is the temperate nature of the crowd and a management that tries with some success to please everyone.

*The Star-Spangled Banner* is gotten out of the way in a perfunctory manner early so that the musical focus will fall on *My Old Kentucky Home* which is played immediately preceding the race.

Beautiful horses were not the best-looking thing I saw at the Derby. When I entered an elevator to get to the press room, one man came in with me, followed by two extraordinarily beautiful women. One looked at me, broke into a smile that improved her good looks and said "Andy Rooney! I'm Bo Derek. I love you. This is my sister, Kelly." Even Kelly wasn't what I'd call real homely.

The elevator stopped. Bo and Kelly smiled demurely and left. I think it was "demurely" they smiled. As the two disappeared down the hall, the other man in the elevator shrugged and said "I didn't recognize her with her clothes on."

We bet on the race, lost our money and came home happy we'd gone but pleased to be able to cross off the Kentucky Derby from our list of things we'd never been to.

## HUNTING THE HUNTERS

Tony Blair, the British Prime Minister, caused an uproar when he said he was going to support a bill in Parliament that would make all hunting illegal in England.

If any proposal like it was made here Charlton Heston and the National Rifle Association would declare war on Congress.

Fox hunting in England has always been the "sport" of kings— meaning the upper class. Oscar Wilde referred to "The English country gentleman galloping after a fox—the unspeakable in full pursuit of the inedible." The movement to ban hunting was brought by animal rights activists who apparently outnumber the landed gentry who do it and the law was passed in Scotland but not in England.

The fox has been driven out of the English countryside by hunters and developers, something like deer in some parts of this country. Deer in the East have fled to the suburbs and there are occasional foxes in backyards in London.

With the shortage of wild foxes in the fields, the hunting clubs breed foxes and release them while the hunters sit by on horseback. The dogs are let loose to follow the foxes and the hunters follow the dogs, shouting "Tally Ho!" (The meaning of the phrase, if it ever had one, is long gone.) When the dogs catch the fox, if they catch it at all, they torture it for 10 minutes, tearing it to pieces, and then the horsemen arrive. They do not carry guns so the fox is never put out of its misery with a shot.

There are so many people who genuinely enjoy hunting that it's not easy to condemn but it is amusing to see grown men dressed in camouflage costumes headed into the woods to slay a frightened, mild-mannered deer. It's strange that deer even know enough to be frightened. What experience have they had that makes them aware the are about to be shot? Deer have not done their public relations image any good in recent years with their invasion of suburban gardens.

Every year in the fall in upstate New York, you see targets set up in backyards with the outline of a deer on them. The hunters practice shooting at this stationary image with bows and arrows. The idea of shooting an animal with an arrow is hard to accept as a sport. Even Robin Hood could not have directed one to the heart or the head where the deer would have been killed instantly. You can only think of all the deer wandering the woods after the hunting season, hit but not killed by arrows that are still protruding from their thighs, their chests, their eyes and other organs.

If you assume, as most of us do, that mankind is more civilized than it was 500 or 1,000 years ago, it is easy to understand why a lot of people in a civilized society like England's, would think that banning the cruel act of killing animals for fun was another step away from the times when man had to kill or be killed, eat or be eaten. It is not hard to imagine a society just a few hundred years from now in which people will look back with revulsion on our practice of raising millions of animals every year to be slaughtered under barbaric conditions, cut into parts and eaten.

Hunters think those who object to hunting live by a double standard if they eat meat. They are right, of course. If most of us thought about slaughterhouses and the cruel ways in which the animals we eat live and die, we could swear off eating the flesh of animals forever. We don't think of steak as an animal.

It seems inevitable that, as civilization continues to mature, hunting will be banned in more and more places in the world. The idea of killing an animal to eat will become socially unacceptable. Vegetarians will be mainstream. The appeal of saving the few wild animals left in our diminishing wild will be a factor.

Hunters endow what they do with an almost mystical reverence for what they think of as a natural way of life and death. They don't think the rest of us understand. Men who hunt have some sense of being part of nature while they're at it. They feel masculine and like traditional providers. It doesn't matter that they don't like venison, that the quail was just released from its cage at their hunt club or that the pheasant still has buckshot in it when it comes to the table. They are hunters.

# PART 5

*Entertainment and the Arts*

*I'm impressed by people who love the opera but I don't. It sounds silly to me and I have the feeling that if they sang it in English, it would sound silly to everyone.*

# HOW TO WATCH
# GOOD MUSIC

Carnegie Hall is one of the great civilized places in the world. Going there to a concert gives you the feeling that we are living in a civilized world.

To tell you the truth, Carnegie Hall is more civilized than I am. It makes me feel guilty but I have small tolerance for "good music." The only thing I can say in my defense is, I don't like bad music, either. There are people who are born without some faculty that is necessary to listen to music and take pleasure from it.

Sitting in front of an orchestra in a concert hall makes me uneasy. One night at a concert I watched the first violinist closely. He contorted his face at times and it was hard to tell whether his expression had something to do with the intellectual and physical effort he was putting into the music or from some deep-down meaning he was getting from it that I was not. It was a good sound but I didn't get any meaning out of it. It didn't make me want to screw my face out of shape or smile. I hold this backward opinion that nothing has real meaning if you can't say what it is or write it down.

It's hard to know where to look when you're at a concert. There's just so long you can stare at the lead violinist or the semi-beautiful blonde viola player. You can't close your eyes or people will think you're asleep so you have to look as though you were seeing while you do nothing but listen.

Inevitably you get watching the back of the conductor. My mind wandered from the music because I found myself thinking about whether he had his cutaway jacket specially tailored to accommodate the motions he made with his arms. You can't think and listen at the same time and while I considered all these things the sound didn't get through to me as it should have. I forgot to hear the good music.

I've always been suspicious of the great composers like Beethoven,

Brahms, Bach, Mozart, Chopin, and so forth, because the great phil-harmonic orchestras of the world keep playing the same music over and over again, year after year. It must be great music but while they have occasional revivals on Broadway, most of the plays are new every year. They don't keep doing the same ones over and over and over. It's the same with opera. They don't occasionally perform one of the old ones. They almost always perform one of the old ones and occasionally run in a new one.

Painters like Picasso, Matisse or Jackson Pollock come along to make people forget, for a little while at least, about Rembrandt, Rubens and Michelangelo. Where are the modern composers comparable to Beethoven? I know of Aaron Copland and Béla Bartók but I don't hear their work challenging or replacing the old masters of music. Is there a composer of opera in a league with Verdi, Faust, Wagner, Puccini or Bizet?

Most concert-goers prefer the familiar and the strains they know and can hum. The majority of Americans are as unsophisticated about sound as I am and it probably accounts for why orchestras are so slow to accept new music.

The featured piece at the Carnegie Hall concert one week was a composition called " a symphonic suite" written by the wonderfully talented Marvin Hamlisch. If you don't know his name, I can assure you that you know his work from the Academy Award–winning scores he's written for motion pictures.

Because I recognize his talent from the popular music he's written, I listened attentively in Carnegie Hall, to see if Marvin is the next Beethoven. I have to report to you that I don't know. Don't ask me to whistle a tune from his symphony. It sounded good but I have no idea whether it was good or not and I certainly don't know whether orchestras will be playing it 175 years from now as they play Beethoven.

## ART FOR MONEY'S SAKE

Good should not be so hard to understand. When I see a painting that's meaningless to me, I'm puzzled and worried. Is it the painting or me? Is it obscure or am I obtuse? Over the years I have become more aggressive about art. If I don't like it, I no longer assume it's my fault.

The photographs by Andres Serrano of a cross in urine, which attracted so much attention, bothered me but not for the same reason it offended Jesse Helms and the mayor of New York at the time, Rudolph Giuliani. The picture was offensive to me because it was supposed to be filled with great meaning and significance and I couldn't figure out what the meaning or significance of it was. I'm as suspicious of Serrano as I am of anyone who suggests there's more meaning to his or her art than I can perceive. I don't like to be conned.

W. S. Merwin is recognized as one of the best poets alive but not by me. I don't doubt he's great, I just don't understand his poetry. I accept his greatness because people who are smarter than I am say he's great.

It was troubling to me when I read a magazine article Merwin wrote about a poet named James Merrill who had recently died. Merwin quoted excerpts from a few of Merrill's poems. A reader had to assume Merwin picked some of Merrill's best lines. For example:

*O heart green acre sown with salt*
*by the departing occupier*
*lay down your gallant spears of wheat*
*Salt of the earth.*

Or, how about this:

*The blond child on*
*The bank, hands full of difficult marvels, stays*
*Now in bliss, now in doubt.*
*His lips move: I love the black swan.*

This was some of Merrill's best work?

Merwin's own poetry is often unfathomable to me:

*I am in the old room across from the night*
*the long scream is about to blossom*
*that is rooted in flames*
*if I call It is not me would it reach*
*through the bells*

Hello! Mr. Merwin? Are you there? Is anybody home?

Frankly, W. S., I don't know what the hell you're talking about.

The real trouble is that a few of these obscurant artists like Merwin and Merrill *are* truly great. This fact was impressed on me while I was reading Merwin's article in *The New York Times Book Review* section because it was so well-written.

"This I understand," I thought to myself. "He's a good writer. If he writes prose that well, why can't I understand his poetry?"

Incompetent artists, bad poets and inept playwrights think that painting or writing something that is unintelligible adds a weight to it that qualifies it as art. It is not art and it ruins the game for genuine artists. Their work may be beyond the comprehension of some of us but it should not be confused with the junk issued by the fakers.

People who read poetry, look at pictures or listen to music, often add a meaning of their own to the work. They see or hear something the artist didn't put into it. That seems right. A good poem should make you think of something the poet never thought. I'm tired of searching for meaning in art that is meaningless.

# IT DOESN'T HAVE
# TO MAKE SENSE

My most frequent reaction when I'm exposed to the noise that passes as popular music is to say "I can't understand a word they're singing."

While I assume my problem with popular music is the age differential between me and the people singing, it doesn't pay to think much about the meaning of the words in the music and poetry of any age. Many of our most familiar old songs or much-loved poems don't make sense if you analyze them.

When I was in high school and listening to popular music three of the big hits were *Mairzy Doats* (and dozy doats and liddle lamzy divey), *Flat Foot Floogee* (with the floy floy), and *Bibbidi-Bobbidi-Boo*. That music would be as foreign to Hootie and the Blowfish or the Smashing Pumpkins as their music is to me. I would have to concede it didn't make any more sense.

The familiar lines in our patriotic or religious music often get to have a meaning for us that exceeds any literal translation of it. For example, *The Star-Spangled Banner*'s first two lines evoke a love-of-country in us when we sing them but don't sit down and analyze them and expect them to makes sense unless you were with Francis Scott Key when he wrote them while he was a prisoner on a British battleship looking at Fort McHenry off the coast of Maryland.

"OH, SAY CAN YOU SEE BY THE DAWN'S EARLY LIGHT
WHAT SO PROUDLY WE HAILED AT THE TWILIGHT'S
LAST GLEAMING?"

It's strange that a song with such arcane language should mean so much to us as a Nation. And why, for goodness sakes, did he begin the song with the word "Oh" and end the first sentence with a question mark?

What the lines in the first stanza of *The Star-Spangled Banner* seem to mean is that the flag was hailed last night just when the sun was going down and then hailed again this morning when we saw it right there where it had been last night. I'm not clear whether they took the flag down last night after it was hailed or not. It's supposed to come down at sunset but "the rockets' red glare and bombs bursting in air gave proof" that it was apparently left up.

In school chapel I used to love to sing *The Battle Hymn of the Republic*. It has a great ring to it but the words don't stand close inspection either.

"MINE EYES HAVE SEEN THE GLORY OF THE COMING OF THE LORD

HE IS TRAMPLING OUT THE VINTAGE WHERE THE GRAPES OF WRATH ARE STORED."

Why "mine eyes" instead of just "my eyes"? It doesn't make sense and yet somehow "Mine eyes have seen the glory" sounds good when you sing it. On the other hand, I find the metaphor of God stamping out the "vintage" hard to believe. Didn't the writer mean "Stamping out the vineyard?" Whatever she meant, I don't think anyone would store grapes of wrath or any other kind of grapes, in either a vintage or a vineyard. You'd pick them there.

If you rewrote *The Battle Hymn of the Republic* to make sense, it would read "He is trampling out the vineyard where the grapes of wrath are grown."

We first read Robert Frost's *Stopping by Woods on a Snowy Evening* in the eighth grade. I didn't understand it or like it then. Now I like it but still don't understand it.

*Whose woods these are I think I know*
*His house is in the village though;*
*He will not see me stopping here*
*To watch his woods fill up with snow.*

There are only a couple of reasons why anyone would stop in the middle of nowhere. I can't believe anyone would stop just to watch it snow. He must have been doing something sneaky because he didn't want the owner to see him. Certainly the owner wouldn't have objected if all he was going to do was watch it snow.

I have several theories about what the man who stopped did but if he's anything like the people who pass our house, he probably threw out an empty Coke can and the cardboard box his Big Mac came in on someone's front lawn.

Frost says he has miles to go before he sleeps so maybe he did what I often do. He pulled over and took a little nap.

Obviously, when it comes to music and poetry, it's best to enjoy it without analyzing it.

## HE WASN'T EVEN
## A HOUND DOG

The mystique of Elvis Presley eludes me. Music is the great divider of generations but age has nothing to do with my thinking that Elvis Presley is the most over-rated singer of all time. His talent was comparable to the forgettable sensation of my high school years, Rudy Vallee.

The Beatles said that they picked up some of their style from Presley but the Beatles were, by comparison with Presley, refreshingly original. Even Bing Crosby had an ingenuous charm about him that rang true. Elvis was phoney clear through. He never learned how to fake being sincere.

In my lifetime I have listened to a lot of bad good music. I include in that category some operas and symphony concerts I've sat through. On the other hand, there has been a lot of bad music that I've enjoyed. The same year that Presley recorded the abominably bad *Hound Dog*, there were a dozen songs that were light and insignificant but delightful. I think of *Que Sera, Sera, Sixteen Tons, Mack the Knife, On the Street Where You Live, The Rain in Spain, Standing on the Corner (Watching All the*

*Girls Go By), I Could Have Danced All Night, Bells Are Ringing (For Me and My Gal)* and *Canadian Sunset.*

There is an element of make-believe in all art. We allow ourselves to be fooled for fun. Elvis Presley's make-believe struck a false note. Frank Sinatra could sing a song and make it sound as if it all happened to him. With Elvis Presley you couldn't forget that he was up there performing. He looked like someone imitating Elvis Presley, badly.

Presley's performance on stage was crude and calculated to be that way. I can understand a young generation being turned on at first and for a short while by his sexual gyrations on stage but it was all so fake and badly acted that I do not understand why it didn't eventually turn them off. In spite of all the pelvic activity, he never seemed very masculine.

I have heard people who claim to have known Presley, speak as if he were some kind of misunderstood intellectual. They talked about his depth of character. Was that when he was on drugs or off them? I didn't know he had any character, let alone depth. He seemed weak and ineffectual. If he had any opinions, he kept them hidden. Did he vote? If so, for whom? Was he philosophically liberal or conservative?

Presley made 33 movies that were memorable only because they were so bad they were hard to forget. This was partly because he was often under the control of tasteless, money-grubbing managers, agents and friends. He was manipulated like a boxing champion who made millions of dollars but couldn't count.

The circumstances of Presley's death were as mysterious as his success. No one seems to know for sure what he died of. Pictures of him before his death show him looking like a bloated, overweight marshmallow.

Other than that though, I liked Elvis.

## MOVIES AND OTHER SMUT

Americans will stand for more filth and violence on the screen in the darkness of a movie theater than they'll stand for on television in the privacy of their homes with the lights on. There they sit in a theater, shoulder to shoulder, elbow to elbow and knee to knee with perfect strangers—strangers are always perfect—listening to language so foul they wouldn't think of using it themselves. They are watching the kind of sex and violence known to them only secondhand through other movies they've seen.

Mike Wallace did an interview on *60 Minutes* with Julie Andrews, the actress who made her name in such All-American films like *The Sound of Music* and *Mary Poppins*.

Several years later, the actress got tired of goody-two-shoes roles and took a part in a picture called *S.O.B.* At one point in this movie, the previously prissy Julie Andrews pulled open her shirt and bared her breasts. In the course of the profile about her on television, *60 Minutes* used that shot. Monday morning after the show producer Don Hewitt was deluged with I'm-Never-Going-To-Watch-*60-Minutes*-again letters.

Are these letter-writers the same people who pay money to see the semi-pornographic movies regularly shown in theaters across the Country? It would be interesting to know how many people go to a dirty movie on Saturday night, then get up and go to church Sunday. The difference between those bare breasts on that television broadcast and the nudity in movies was motivation. On *60 Minutes* it was several miles short of pornography and, considering the modest dimensions of Julie Andrews' figure, not even very sexy. It was a legitimate part of an interesting story.

There's a widespread feeling that standards of morality are going to hell in America. In general, people want the trend to stop. Specifically, they go to the movies and pay $9 to entertain themselves with the very smut they object to.

## IT'S A DISNEY WORLD

It's difficult to act anything but your age. We all have to fight the old-fogy syndrome and remember that the good old days were not all great and life in the United States was neither better nor worse when we were younger.

Having said all that though, I want to act my age and tell you how much I object to all the artificially exciting playlands being built around the world. Disneyland and Disney World on our two coasts are the biggest entertainment extravaganzas in the United States. Disney built another monster outside Paris and giant amusement parks are springing up all over Europe. There's one in Spain south of Barcelona. Time Warner has a place called Movie World in Germany; Lego, the Danish toy company, has a theme park near Windsor, England, and another I've heard is very clever outside of Copenhagen; a Japanese computer-game maker has one in London. A Japanese amusement park in London?

It makes you wonder who's going to look at the scenery, the natural beauty, the architecture, the cathedrals, the museums and the ancient ruins in these old countries once all the amusement parks are operating. Why would an American go to France, Spain or England and then pay to get into an amusement park?

Packaged entertainment is a growing business, in part at least, because of the population explosion. People are looking for more diverting experiences than there is diversion to be had. Parents who used to take their kids camping or who owned a summer cottage on a lake, can't find any place to camp anymore. Lake shores are wall-to-wall with summer cottages. Entertainment parks get millions of visitors a year and one of the reasons is that Yellowstone and all our other great natural parks are full. The lip of the Grand Canyon is crowded with visitors trying to get a look down into the canyon.

Disneyland fills a need we have for amusing several million people in a relatively small space. The best thing about it is that while Disney has

them, people aren't ruining our forests, our mountains or Yellowstone
Park.

Kids used to provide their own amusement. They built tree houses,
walked to ponds or lakes or swimming holes and invented their own
games to play and their own fun to have. They gathered together Saturday mornings at one of the vacant lots in town and played football or
baseball. Girls made chalk marks on the sidewalk and played hopscotch
or they jumped rope. They organized games themselves because there
was no Little League, no parental supervision.

Kids aren't out on their own as much anymore because vacant lots
have disappeared. They're housing projects now. In many cases, neighborhood fields have been replaced as playgrounds by asphalt basketball
courts which take up less space.

The big amusement parks are technological marvels. They are kept
antiseptically clean and well-policed. Their featured attractions are
inventive and well-built but, in spite of all the good things you can say
about any amusement park, they provide canned entertainment and
canned means the same thing for entertainment that it does for peas. It
isn't as good as the real thing.

It's been years since I've seen a little girl skipping rope or a small
group of girls standing around while two of them swing a rope that a
third is jumping over, all in perfect rhythm. Do kids still play jacks? Do
boys make slingshots, walk on stilts or play on pogo sticks? Would a
child eight years old know what I meant if I asked him to play hide-
and-seek or is he too busy trying to find a Disney cartoon to watch on
television? If kids get thirsty on a hot summer day do they make lemonade? Or do kids just go to the refrigerator and get a can of Coke?

There's nothing to be done about any of this. Time has marched on
but in spite of my determination not to join the parade bemoaning the
fact that things aren't like they were in the old days, I can't help wishing
kids weren't exposed to so much pre-packaged play and fake excite-
ment.

# MISS AMERICA

You look for sensible people and there aren't many. That's why I was pleased to read that the producers of the Miss America pageant are going to bar hairdressers and makeup artists in Atlantic City. The girls are going to have to comb their own hair and put on their own makeup when they're getting themselves ready to parade down the ramp.

"I thought, what a shame," one of the producers said. "Here are these wonderfully attractive young women in hairstyles they would never wear and in gowns no one thinks they should wear. You don't get to see these women as who they really are."

Ideally, I suppose, if the girls and not their clothes or their hairdressers are to be judged, they should appear without anything on but that would be difficult to do tastefully so this is the next best idea.

I stopped watching the Miss America pageant years ago because it got to be a joke. Worst of all, a lot of the girls were bordering on being homely. There's nothing wrong with a girl who isn't drop-dead beautiful but if she isn't, she shouldn't parade around in a so-called beauty contest as though she was.

They ought to spend some time getting better-looking girls to enter the contest. It's hard because a lot of the smartest, best-looking women wouldn't dream of putting on a bathing suit and parading around as if saying "Hey, look at me!" They certainly wouldn't do it in Atlantic City.

A lot of pretty women have some minor defect, too. A girl can be a beauty but flat-chested or maybe her nose is too big or her legs too thick. Any single defect disqualifies a girl from the Miss America contest and, because of this, there's a perfect sameness to the ones who get to the finals.

If I were going to produce the Miss America contest, I'd prohibit the girls from dyeing their hair blonde. (You never catch a natural blonde dyeing her hair dark brown.)

I'd rename the contest, too. Instead of MISS AMERICA, it would replace all the others and be called MISS, MS. OR MRS. AMERICA. The Miss America rules now state that the girls have to be between 17 and 24. Married women aren't eligible. I'd change that and open it up to older women, married or not. Diane Sawyer won the Junior Miss competition when she was 17. Diane's in her fifties now and married but in open competition, she'd still walk away with the contest. For her talent performance, Diane could sing the evening news.

The most painful part of the Miss America show every year has been the talent contest. Girls who can't sing come out and sing, girls who can't dance and the ones who have no talent at all read poetry. It's a lot to ask a girl to be both beautiful and talented and these girls shouldn't have to make fools of themselves trying to be both.

## AND THE WINNER IS!

The awards business is booming in New York and Los Angeles. Someone has proposed a television channel that would broadcast nothing but awards shows 24 hours a day, seven days a week.

There are good, legitimate awards given by organizations trying to improve or encourage the work of people in a particular field but a lot of awards dinners are fund-raising gimmicks, designed to call more attention to the organization giving the award than to the person getting it.

Awards proliferate in show business, including television. The Waldorf-Astoria Hotel in New York has about 300 banquets a year in its huge ballroom, at which awards are given.

There is a book called *An International Directory of Awards and their Donors Recognizing Achievement in Advertising, Architecture, Arts and the Humanities, Business and Finance, Communications, Computers, Consumer Affairs, Ecology, Education, Engineering, Fashion, Films, Journalism, Law, Librarianship, Literature, Medicine, Music, Performing Arts, Photography, Public Affairs, Publishing, Radio and Television, Religion,*

*Science, Social Science, Sports, Technology and Transportation.* Each organization has an annual awards dinner, usually its only activity.

Selling tickets to a dinner at which an organization gives a plaque, a
cup, a silver platter or a certificate of honor to someone is a sure-fire way
of raising money. People like to have their names listed as supportive of
some well-known person.

There are tricks to the game. First, the organization has to decide on
a name. Call it The International Do-Good Association of America.

A committee, usually one person actually, makes up an award with
another good name. You might call it The International Do-Good
Association's Nice Guy Award. Next, you find a well-known person
who is willing to be associated with the cause and append his or her
name to the name of the award. Say you choose former President
Jimmy Carter. That makes it The International Do-Good Association's
Jimmy Carter Nice-Guy Award. In view of the honor bestowed on him
with the naming of the award, Jimmy would be expected to show up at
the organization's annual banquet.

You need two more names. It takes a lot of famous people to do it
right. You need a famous name on stage as your master-of-ceremonies
and another famous name to actually present the award to the famous
recipient.

Let's say you choose former New York mayor Rudolph Giuliani.

He's a good speaker and still famous enough to attract a crowd. He
does a lot of this because he probably still has political ambitions. Next
you have someone Giuliani is going to call on to actually give the International Do-Good Association's Fifth Annual Jimmy Carter Nice-Guy
Award. You choose Susan Sarandon for that job. You need a woman in
here somewhere. Susan is a public-spirited person who is usually available. That gives you three famous names in your program to attract a
crowd.

Last you decide who to give it to. You choose someone who doesn't
have to be a nice guy at all but he does have to be well-known. Maybe
you decide to give it to Ted Turner because, while he's not always, or

even usually, a nice guy, he is famous, funny and rich. He may decide on a major donation to your cause in honor of your having honored him.

Even if the famous recipient himself doesn't make a big contribution, you write invitations to as many of his friends and people he does business with as you can make a list of and advise them that, as a token of respect for their friend, it would be in order for them to buy a table of ten at the banquet for $10,000. (Let them know if you're actually coming or just want your name listed as having bought the table.) The poor people who come are charged $500 per ticket.

If you can get 600 people who like to think they are friends of any of the famous people whose names are attached to your award, you'll be collecting $300,000. The dinner you're charging $500 for, may cost you about $60 per head. That's a profit of $270,000.

It is more blessed to give than to receive. More profitable, too.

# PART 6

---

# *Learning*

*You meet a lot of dumb people who went to college.*

# PROUD TO BE DUMB

Considering how highly we prize an education, it's strange that we take so much satisfaction from our ignorance. We're always proudly proclaiming that we know nothing about something. When we do it, there is the faint, far-away intimation of our knowledgeability about almost everything else. We plead ignorance about one subject as if we knew a lot about others.

I try unsuccessfully not to do it myself. As someone who is not an ardent baseball fan, I often find myself saying, the day after a World's Series game, "I don't even know who won." It's as if I thought not knowing who won made me superior. I do the same thing with movies. Because I've hardly ever seen the movie everyone's talking about, I never pass up the opportunity to say I haven't seen it. Why is not having seen a popular movie such a point of pride?

The dumb thing about it is, I am annoyed by people who go out of their way to tell me they don't watch television. There's a whole class of people who love not knowing anything about television. It's a cult. When these people learn that I am on a program called *60 Minutes*, they are bursting with pride when they say, "We don't watch television" or "We don't even have a television set." Well, aren't you special.

It is almost as if they think not watching television makes them intellectually superior to the rest of us. I have no objection to people who don't watch television but I do have an objection to people who pride themselves on it. It's easy to say there's a lot of junk on television because it's true but there's also a lot of good stuff and any American who doesn't watch some of it is ignorant of a lot of things going on in the world.

When you drive through a strange town and stop to ask someone on the street for directions, pride in ignorance is often on display. It seems as if you always get someone who doesn't live there.

"Sorry," they say in answer to your request for directions, "I'm a stranger here myself." They appear pleased with themselves. Why is the average person you ask for directions pleased with not knowing?

"I'm terrible with numbers," almost everyone boasts. At income tax time, many of us repeat over and over how bad we are with the figures. It would be smarter if we spent more time getting better with numbers and less time bragging about our stupidity.

"I'm not good with computers. My 10-year-old knows more about them than I do."

"Geography was never my best subject in school."

"I can never remember a name," we are always saying as if being rude by not making a point of remembering made us interesting.

Teenage kids are apt to say, "I've got a lot of good ideas but I'm not good at expressing myself. You know what I mean?" They always want to know if you know what they mean when they haven't said what they mean. They are suggesting they have some profound thought they are unable to put into words. The fact is if a person can't write it down or say it in plain English, the chances are there is no idea.

Maybe I didn't say this very well. I was never good with . . . you know . . . words but . . . you know . . . you know what I mean?

## THE FLAT EARTH IN KANSAS

In 1999 the Kansas Board of Education assured itself a place in the annals of ignorance by decreeing that Darwin's theory of evolution be removed from the state's school curriculum. It seems likely that board members, looking out their windows at their state's broad plains, might also conclude that the Earth is flat.

It helps restore my faith in the intelligence and good sense of the people of Kansas to know that their decision was reversed two years later.

One of the pleasures of our country house is the recurring memory it evokes of Margie's father, a doctor whose home it was. He was a self-educated intellectual who went from high school to medical college and never lost his fascination with knowledge. On either side of the fireplace in the living room, the bookcases are filled with literary masterpieces more admired than read by most Americans, including this one. Among the treasures is a 20-volume set of red leather-bound books comprising the complete works of Charles Darwin. Over the years I have spent many hours reading them and have a ways to go to finish.

There have been no more than a handful of people who have contributed as much to mankind's knowledge of itself as Darwin did. No one who has read any of what he wrote could question his brilliance or his dedication to searching for the truth. His two-volume book *The Origin of Species* would surprise any member of the Kansas Board of Education who undertook reading it. It seems likely none of them ever has.

"Natural selection is continually trying to economize every part of the organization," Darwin wrote. "If, under changed conditions of life, a structure, before useful, becomes less useful, its diminution will be favored, for it will profit the individual not to have its nutrient wasted in building up a useless structure."

This is merely one paragraph on page 183 of Volume I, but it summarizes Darwin's theory of natural selection and his belief that all living things change as they adapt themselves to flourish or decline under the conditions they encounter. He points out that the tallest giraffes survive the droughts because, even if they are only two inches taller than others, they can reach higher branches for food.

Darwin himself was more aware of the possibility he could be wrong than anyone on the Kansas Board of Education. He laid out some ways he might be wrong in Chapter VII of *The Origin of Species*. It runs for 56 pages and is called "MISCELLANEOUS OBJECTIONS TO THE THEORY OF NATURAL SELECTION."

There are scientists who doubt the broad implications of his conclusions about the origin of mankind but no scientist of any stature doubts the authenticity of his work. For "educators" in Kansas to eliminate study of it from their school curriculum is stupidity. Teach kids to doubt it if they wish, but teach it and let them decide.

Darwin always inspected his own motives and the possibility that he was wrong.

"From my early youth," he says, "I have had the strongest desire to understand or explain whatever I observed—that is to group all facts under some general laws. These causes combined have given me the patience to reflect or ponder for any number of years over any unexplained problem.

"I have steadily endeavored to keep my mind free so as to give up any hypothesis, however much beloved by me, as soon as facts are shown to be opposed to it."

The single biggest difference between those who believe that God created everything at one specific time in history and those who believe everything evolved from one simple cell over millions of years, is that scientists like Darwin are willing, even anxious, to find evidence that will prove them to be wrong. Creationists are looking only for the elusive evidence that God did it.

I have mixed feelings about Kansas. The most time I ever spent there was at a political convention and Kansas City was wonderful on that occasion. On one other occasion I was filming a story in Manhattan, Kansas, and was invited to dinner at someone's home. It was the single most inedible meal I have ever faced and I learned, toward the end of it that our host, the woman who prepared it, taught a class in cooking at Kansas State University. I tell you this so you'll know I had negative feeling about education in Kansas even before the Board of Education banned Darwin.

# THE WAR FOR EDUCATION

We can always find the money for new weapons but we aren't finding enough money for education. It seems wrong that we spend about six times more on our military establishment than we spend on schools. The argument in favor of that is that if we were attacked and lost a war, we wouldn't need our schools.

Schools are doing more than they once did because they are expected to do a lot of the things that parents did before both husband and wife were somewhere other than home when the kids got there. Too much of what they're doing doesn't have anything to do with education.

The longer the school day, the better most parents like it because it means someone is taking care of their kids when they aren't. Women's Lib has been better for women than for children.

In many communities, most people don't have much interest in the school because their children are grown. They no longer have anyone in those schools so their interest in them has diminished to close to none at all. Three quarters of our population is too old to have any active interest in education so they pay no attention to it and often won't support any move to spend more tax money for better schools. They've got theirs. If there is a move to spend money for school improvement, enlargement or teacher pay increase, they vote against it.

Money wouldn't solve all our problems with schools but the money we're spending to educate kids now doesn't come close to how much we ought to be spending.

School buildings ought to be the last priority. Good teachers are more important and teachers are as varied in their ability to teach as students are in their ability to learn. There should be a better system for weeding out inept teachers. Teachers' unions ought to take more responsibility for the quality of their membership. Many of us would be appalled if we sat in on an average class and found out how bad some of the teachers are.

A start toward higher teaching standards would be to raise teachers' pay and give them the kind of salaries that will attract bright people who might otherwise sell insurance or go into business. We have enough insurance salesmen and business men and women but we don't have enough good teachers.

There are more problems than anyone can solve but we have to act as if that wasn't so. For example, punishment, as a way of influencing a kid who has done something wrong not to do it again, is going out of style. Even a loving parent can't give a kid a swat on the bottom for misbehaving or the child psychologists will get after them. It is illegal in most States for a teacher to strike a child and it should be but if a kid who doesn't give a damn about anything misbehaves there's nothing a teacher can do. They're at war without a weapon.

The teacher can give bad marks but if the child doesn't care what his or her marks are, bad marks are no deterrent. Responsible parents will take matters into their own hands if the kid comes home with failing grades but the catch is the phrase "responsible parents." Parents of bad kids are probably as irresponsible as the kids. Teachers can't give parents a failing grade.

Another major problem in schools is how bright kids are taught in the same class or the same school with dumb kids. We're all pretty much agreed that every young person should get all the education he or she can take but we know some can take more than others. The argument in favor of separating the two groups is that separated, the bright kids move ahead faster and get a better education.

The argument against separation is, the slow learners are better off mixed in with smart kids. And then, what do you do about teachers? Do you give the smart kids the best teachers or do you make the best teachers teach the slow learners because those kids need more expert help from the people who are best at giving it?

In New York City, huge numbers of parents who can afford $20,000 a year in tuition, choose not to send their kids to public school because private schools are better. In New York 10 percent of children go to private schools. In Pennsylvania, 16 percent of all children go to something other than a public school. When the President of the United States or any other important government official has a school-age child, it's embarrassing for them but the child does not go to a public school. An exception to this was Amy Carter, who was sent to public school. They can plead that it's a matter of security but the truth is, in our Nation's capital, the schools aren't good enough.

We have money. We find the money to defend ourselves when war is imminent; we should find the money to educate ourselves because this is a war and we're losing it.


# EDUCATION FOR EDUCATION'S SAKE

We all look for hopeful signs that the world isn't going to hell, as it so often seems to be. The single best story I've read in years came from Oxford, England. Oxford University's faculty voted against accepting $34 million from a Saudi billionaire named Wafic Said. He was offering to build a business school for Oxford and free or not, they didn't want one.

Wafic was pretty sore about it. I suppose it would be difficult for someone who has spent his whole life piling up money, to understand why anyone would turn down a gift of $34 million. There is a 400-yard open field in the middle of the Oxford campus and the proposal was to put the business school on it. The field is not known for its great beauty or for anything else. It's known for being simply an open, empty field and a lot of people at Oxford think it should remain just that way. I like that. The world has plenty of ugly buildings and very few open fields left anyplace where there are people.

The idea of college as a place to learn how to make a living is a mistake anyway. Four years of college studying the world's culture, its history and philosophy is the best thing that can happen to a person in his late teens or early twenties. A college education shouldn't be seen as preparation for a life of earning. It should be seen as a time and place where young people acquire a foundation of information on which they can build the rest of their lives. A college education isn't a means, it's an end in itself.

The essence of business is competition, trying to beat someone else. It is seldom friendly. Cooperation is unknown. One of the opponents of the idea of a business school at Oxford was a medieval history professor named Alexander Murray who said that what he wanted was cooperation among the people he worked with, not competition.

Wafic should have looked into other things to do with his $34 million. I wonder if he's ever thought of building a college that would be attended exclusively by people sixty years old or more. People are living longer and the idea of going to college *after* retirement would be appealing to a lot of them. I've always thought I'd like to quit what I'm doing and go back to college and finish. I was drafted at the end of my junior year and I've spent a lifetime feeling uneducated.

If Wafic Said decided to build my kind of college, I'd be willing to have it named after him. When people asked me what I was doing, I'd say, "I go to Wafic Said U."

Because I'm such a bad businessman, I tend to distrust good ones. I know it's untrue but I can't help myself from thinking that business people make money the easy way. They make deals, they draw up contracts, borrow money, buy and sell each other and generally do the things that would be best left undone. It seems to me that it's almost like cheating to study how to make money. Making money is an honorable pursuit but everyone should learn how to make something other than money first.

The question is whether the study of business is a legitimate pursuit of the kind of knowledge that colleges have traditionally concerned themselves with. If everyone in the world went to a business school and graduated with an MBA (Master of Business Administration), the production of all good things in the world would come to an end. There would be no one left but sales people with nothing to sell because there wouldn't be anyone to produce that which could be sold. There wouldn't be anyone left who knew how to make anything except money.

I'm aware of the importance of organization in the world of commerce but when the administrators are considered more important and get more money than the inventors, the designers and the manufacturers of a product, something is wrong. Business schools are in the business of teaching people how to make money and that's all they teach. Oxford, on the other hand, is one of the three or four best educational institutions in the world. It doesn't teach its students how to get rich; it teaches them how to live a full and interesting life.

Great Britain has good colleges. What Wafic Said ought to do is take his $34 million dollars, build a good college in Riyadh, Saudi Arabia, and then go to it himself.

## BIGGER IS WORSER

Bigger is not always better. Bigger isn't even *usually* better. Why we have this compulsion to enlarge everything is hard to understand. There is a perfect size for almost anything, including Miss America, but we're never satisfied with the perfect size. Whatever it is, we want it bigger.

Drive up and down any residential street and you see homes that are being renovated and enlarged. It is infrequently because the family had additional children and needs more room. It is more apt to be that the kids have all left home and the parents have enough money now to build their dream house. Their dream house is bigger.

When children grow up and leave home, I don't ever recall hearing of parents who decided to spend some money tearing off two bedrooms and a den to make the house smaller so there'd be more room for grass and trees.

When I entered college it had a student body of about 594. Today the student body is somewhere around 2,800. In 1942, the entering class numbered 302. The class of 2004 enters with 900 members.

At a reunion last year the compact campus that I knew and loved has been turned into a sprawling complex of buildings that cover all the areas that used to be vacant lots, grassy fields and rolling hillsides. Many of the modern buildings look as if their architects were competing for a design prize. They are more interesting than is necessary for a place to be studied in. The word "campus" itself no longer seems like the right word for the collection of miscellaneous buildings because it suggests a unity that no longer exists.

When I went into a store in the village that is dominated by the college, I spoke to the woman who waited on me about the explosion of construction. I asked her why she thought they kept enlarging the college.

"They do it because someone who went here makes a ton of money and wants his name on a building so he gives them ten million dollars and they put up a new building with his name on it. What are they going to do? Tell him they don't want the money?"

Somewhere there must be a college that has used the money it collects from wealthy alumni to improve the school without enlarging it. They could get the best teachers by paying them more instead of spending it on buildings. They could improve things for students living in what are often slum living conditions in present dormitories. There are a thousand ways any college could improve itself by putting the emphasis on getting better, not getting bigger.

Some of the older classroom buildings at my college need to be rebuilt but it occurred to me that instead of rebuilding them, they ought to spend some of the money tearing them down and making a vacant lot out of where the building once stood. That's what I'd like my name on if I had ten million dollars to give them. The brass plaque would read:

VACANT LOT GIFT OF ANDY ROONEY '42

It is difficult to understand why a good little college wants to get big.

It isn't just colleges that are obsessed with growth though. You see it everywhere. The broadcast network I work for, which was dominated by one man and a board of directors—which he dominated—is now part of a gigantic entertainment goliath comprising other corporations and a wide variety of entities I never even heard of.

It bears no relationship to colleges but when I think of anything that has gotten too big, I always think of the original little hourglass-shaped five-cent Coke bottle. It was a classic design that held six and a half ounces, a perfect amount to drink. The great little Coke bottles are almost a thing of the past and the supermarket shelves are crowded with Coke bottles that hold 64 ounces. If they fit in your refrigerator at all and you open one, it goes flat before three people can finish it.

That's the size I want my college—perfect. Like Miss America or the original Coke bottle.

## COLLEGES

Parents are usually so pleased to have their son or daughter accepted by a good college that they don't ask any questions of it for four years.

As a pleased grandparent of two college students it occurs to me, after several long dinner table conversations with them during various "breaks" and vacations, to ask how many colleges are giving parents their money's worth? It would also be interesting to look into how many college professors are giving colleges *their* money's worth?

College schedules are shocking to inspect.

Stanford University is one of the best and looking at its schedule for the year makes you wonder about how arduous the schedules would be at some of the *worst* colleges.

Classes typically begin at Stanford in the last week in September. Even if it's a Thursday and not much goes on Friday and the following Monday is October, the handbook says classes start in September. October wouldn't sound good even to a regularly abused parent paying the tuition. For one thing, it's too close to the Thanksgiving break. Beginning in early December, Stanford students are off every year for about 32 days. A month after that winter vacation, they get a much-deserved Spring break of 18 days. No statistics are available on the number of nervous breakdowns there are among students who can't take it. Classes end for the year at Stanford in May.

Our granddaughter was taking four courses at a good college her freshman year. She reported that she was in class for three hours on Mondays, an hour and ten minutes Tuesdays, three hours Wednesday and an hour and ten minutes Thursday. She had no classes Friday—or Saturday and Sunday, of course. This is a total of nine classroom hours a week . . . for about 26 weeks . . . for about $40,000.

Should we worry that they're pushing this child too hard?

Many colleges have such huge endowments that they are able to offer some form of aid to a large number of students. As a grandparent of a student who doesn't get any aid, I'd rather see the college reduce the tuition for everyone, rather than give it free to 25 percent.

Our grandson goes to my college and I'm pleased about that. You remain loyal to your college no matter what because you're part of it and it is part of you.

We see quite a bit of our grandson because right after he gets there in October he has a four-day Fall recess. His Thanksgiving vacation his first year was November 20th to the 26th. Classes ended again on December 7th and he was off until January 21st. This gives him time to think—and sleep quite a bit, too.

Then he was back to the old grind until March 16th when he got another eight days off.

Classes ended for the Summer on May 3rd—which isn't summer at all, of course. The faculty has this same grueling schedule.

Our grandson is going to know a lot about things that neither his parents nor we know anything about at all. He didn't waste much time his freshman year on traditional courses like literature, history, science or philosophy. He took really big subjects like the Foundation of Political Thought, Revolutions of the Atlantic World and a required course called the Challenge of Modernity.

I have an idea for colleges. Hold classes on all the days of the year that businesses are open. If they did that, students could finish college in three years and their parents could take the fourth year off—from paying tuition.

# PART 7

---

# *Work Life and Success*

*It's amusing to see who doesn't show up for work when the weather is bad. It's usually the people we could do without any day.*

# ON BECOMING
# A BETTER PERSON
# ON PURPOSE

One of the questions that arises from time to time in our lives is whether or not it is possible to improve ourselves by trying. Experience has indicated to me that resolve has no influence on character. My answer to the question, therefore is "No, you cannot improve yourself by trying but you should live your life as though you could."

Making yourself a better person, a more successful person, a happier person by deciding to be or by studying how to be, doesn't work for the same reason trying to lose weight by reading a book about it doesn't work. We're all trapped by who we are and how we act. No matter how hard we try, we can't step out of character and be someone else.

If you look in a bookstore, especially an airport bookstore, the displays are filled with little volumes on how to organize your life, how to get ahead in business, a hundred ways to become a better insurance salesman, ten ways to attract a rich man, ten ways to attract beautiful women. There are dozens of con artists being pushed by lecture agencies who will speak at your banquet on how to be anything you want. There is absolutely no evidence their advice works for anyone but them because they got the $25,000 lecture fee. This is a negative, defeatist attitude and the best thing to do is ignore the negative evidence and proceed as if you can do things better by trying. I try to improve myself. I try to lose weight. Weight is the most certain sign of defeat. I might think, in optimistic moments, that I'm getting to be a nicer guy; I might dream that, after all these years I'm writing better than I used to because there's no standard against which I can judge myself in either of these areas. Then I step on the scale. I can't kid myself there. I haven't lost a pound. I conclude from this that I haven't become a nicer person or a better writer, either. The problem is living with yourself without getting depressed in the face of hopeless inadequacies.

## ON NOT SIGNING AUTOGRAPHS

It amuses me to think that my appraisal of my own strengths and my weaknesses are close to what they really are. I'm neither egotistical nor falsely modest. (Egotistical of me to think so?) I do some things better than a lot of people but a lot of other things not as well. I pretty much know which they are.

If you're going to succeed, you have to have confidence in yourself and it's difficult to be confident without being too confident. It's a narrow path and in judging yourself, it's best if you can count out what other people say they think of you. We all go to considerable lengths to get people to like or admire us. We try in every way to make our friends and almost every stranger we meet, overestimate us. We don't want them to have an accurate opinion of us. We want them to have a better opinion of us than we deserve.

To accomplish all this for ourselves, we smile when we don't feel like smiling. We offer praise when we don't feel praiseful because we're after reciprocity. We tell stories about ourselves that make us look good and skip the ones that make us look bad.

All this is okay as a game we play but, if we win and succeed in making people think more highly of us than we deserve, it's best if we, at least, don't take anyone's high opinion of us seriously.

In addition to that, you have to take into consideration the fact that people are frequently doing the same thing you've done—offering praise in the hope of getting some back.

I've got myself in the position of being recognizable to a lot of people because of my regular appearance on television and Americans have this dumb way of equating celebrity or well-knownness with excellence. The two don't have much to do with each other except that the well-known person usually knows how to do just one thing well. He or she is not necessarily—or even probably—a wonderful, well-rounded person because of it.

A problem that comes with well-knownness is the autograph. I don't do autographs. I have left hundreds of people all across the United States thinking I'm a conceited ass because I won't write my name on the slip of paper they push at me.

I was thinking I ought to be clear in my own mind why I won't give my autograph. To begin with, if it's important to make an accurate appraisal of yourself, it's certainly best if you make that appraisal without any help from outside.

Just as soon as I write my name on a piece of paper, I'm agreeing with the person who asks for it that I'm a wonderful person whose autograph is worth saving. This is nonsense and I refuse to be put in that position. Anyone who wants my autograph is demeaning his esteem for himself and forcing more esteem on me than I'm worth.

I've been fired twice in my lifetime and it's a devastating experience to be told by someone that you aren't good enough for the job. In retrospect, I think that getting fired may have been good for me. Everyone ought to be fired a few times in his or her life. It brings you back down to earth and usually you can learn to live with it by thinking the boss who let you go was stupid, mean or only interested in money.

I autograph my books. That's different than a piece of paper. I'm proud to have written it and pleased to sign it. A writer dreams that some day a hundred years from now, someone will be browsing through a pile of old books and say "Hey, look! Signed by Andy Rooney. He wrote it. Keep this one."

It isn't immortality but it's better than nothing.

## NO, VIRGINIA,
## THERE IS NO SANTA CLAUS!

Every Christmas for the past 50 years, we've all been subjected to a reprint of that sickeningly sweet reply to the eight-year-old girl who is supposed to have written the *New York Sun* in 1897 to ask if there really was a Santa Claus.

"Yes, Virginia," wrote the editor, Frank Church, "there is a Santa Claus." It has become famous.

As a child, before I knew it was a myth, and as the father of four kids long after I learned it was, I enjoyed the idea of Santa Claus. It seemed like harmless fun and a colorful tradition that gave Christmas an added sparkle.

Now I'm not so sure that promoting the fiction that there's a Santa Claus is a good idea for kids at any age. Not only that, I'm mighty suspicious of Virginia, herself, the girl who supposedly wrote the letter asking. I suspect Virginia's father wrote that letter to the *Sun* for her. Would a girl of eight write "Some of my little friends say there is no Santa Claus"?

No, a girl of eight would not. She would write "Some of my *friends* say there is no Santa Claus." A girl of eight is not conscious of the fact that her friends are "little" and wouldn't say so if she was.

Even though adults get away from believing that Santa Claus actually exists, the notion that some Santa-Claus-like beneficiary is going to come along and make their lives wonderful, without their having to move a finger, seems to prevail in the minds of many little Virginias and their brothers to the day they die.

"No, Virginia," I've often wanted to yell at those perennial reprints of the famous editorial, "there is no Santa Claus! Whatever presents you get, you'll get because your parents worked for the money to buy them and sacrificed something they wanted for themselves so they could buy the toy for you. There was nothing magic about it, Virginia. Get used to it."

In his answer to Virginia, Frank Church said it would be a dreary world if there were no Santa Claus, "There would be no child-like faith then, no poetry, no romance to make tolerable this existence."

I beg to differ, almost 100 years later, with Mr. Church even though he's in no position to defend himself. There's too damned much child-like faith that's carried over into the adult world. What's the virtue of accepting something as fact without first checking the merits of its claim? We'd all be better off if there were more realists who used the brains they have and used their ability with reason and logic to inspect all the facts and arrive at carefully considered solutions to life's problems.

What did Frank Church find hard to intolerable about his existence? Did his feet hurt or did he get up on the wrong side of the bed the day he wrote that? I don't know any stable person who needs poetry to make living tolerable, either. I enjoy poetry as much as anyone else but if I never read another line of poetry, the tolerability of my life would not be substantially diminished. If I'd been that editor about 104 years ago, I'd have made it clear to Virginia that there is no Santa Claus and she shouldn't spend any of the time of her life waiting for him to come down the chimney with a bag of good things. There is no Santa Claus, Virginia, and you don't have a fairy godfather, either. The sooner you give up on the idea you can get something for nothing and learn to make it on your own, the better off you're going to be. Forget the fairy tales.

Our early infatuation with ideas like Santa Claus is what leads people to buy lottery tickets at odds of several million to one. It's the reason idiotic columns on astrology are so popular in newspapers. It's what makes us pull the covers over our heads at night when we go to bed and hope our troubles go away by morning.

We ought to be lying there instead, wide awake, trying to figure out what to do about them.

The Santa Claus fable is why we "hope for the best" instead of working to make the best happen. It's why we think there's a pot of gold at the end of the rainbow. We've become a nation of hopers and wishers.

All this inability to give up our belief in Santa Claus and the Easter Bunny doesn't make us bad people. Actually, it's kind of sweet and modest of us. We have this feeling that if everything we are and everything we're going to become, depends on the decisions we make in a world where we all accept the truth about everything . . . then we're afraid we're in big trouble. We don't think we're smart enough to handle it.

If, on the other hand, our success and happiness depends on hoping and praying and maybe winning the lottery and having Santa come down the chimney on Christmas with a bag full of gifts, then we aren't so nervous. We feel our future is in better hands than our own.

Sorry, Virginia. You're a nice little girl but your future depends on you, not on Santa Claus.


## ON BEING ACCEPTED AT YALE

It has amused me over the years to be invited to speak at colleges I wasn't smart enough to get into when I was in high school. Yale was one of those I never applied to and it was therefore gratifying to be invited to speak there.

Over the years, I've had some terrible speaking experiences and I never get over being nervous before I start because I know how bad I can be. I can be good but I've been bad. At its worst, a bad speech is a combination of the audience, the conditions and the speech itself. Speaking in front of a group of business people in a hotel ballroom is the most lucrative but after they've had cocktails, dinner and given out their bowling trophies, they don't want to hear anything anyone has to say. They're sleepy and they have to go to the bathroom.

The best audience is a few hundred college students confined in a small auditorium. At Yale about 150 students and a handful of faculty crowded into a big room and sat in front of me, elbow to elbow, on chairs, tables and the floor. It was ideal.

The good thing about a confined audience is that the reaction to anything the speaker says is communicated quickly and spreads, almost instantly, to everyone there. If there is laughter, it is a great, spontaneous burst.

After I spoke, there were questions. That's the easiest thing to do because you don't have to remember what you wanted to say next. The questioner is your prompter. You don't need notes. The questions were good.

One young man asked if I felt alienated from younger generations. It was an unexpected question and I fumbled for an answer even though I knew what I thought.

My answer was that I do not feel alienated. There are many things about life that do not change with age. Older people have some advantage over the young because, having been young and having been old, they know both ages. Young people, on the other hand, can only guess what it must be like to be old. I know exactly what it is like to be young and what it is like to be old. I am aware of myself now and remember what I was like then.

One of the great dividers of generations is music but it's a superficial barrier. I confess to not understanding musical groups like the Smashing Pumpkins. I do not understand why my granddaughter, Alexis, had Kurt Cobain's picture plastered on the ceiling of her bedroom but my father and mother didn't understand why I liked Benny Goodman in 1940, either.

It is my biased opinion that young people like loud music because it fills the brain and drives out any thought that might have crept in. They are more at ease when they have some excuse for not thinking and music encourages that condition.

I think I said something like that.

Someone marginally older than the others, a faculty member perhaps, asked if I was disappointed by the failure of television to fulfill its great promise.

In the first place, the question is loaded. He was asking an answer—the answer being that television had failed to fulfill its promise. If I answer it directly, I have accepted the statement that television has failed and I don't concede that. Television isn't as good as it should be—nothing is—but it's great.

If knowledge and the universal distribution of information are good for the people of the world, then television has been a good thing. It's certainly more accessible than the Internet. More people know infinitely more about everything than they knew before we had television. This isn't failure.

When I was growing up in Albany, the General Electric Company in nearby Schenectady was always talking about television but it seemed like one of those never-never land inventions that would not come true. Waves sent out into the open air that hit metal antennas and came down into a lighted box in your living room as pictures? That hardly seemed like anything that would ever happen. It did happen.

GE also had a robot in the rough shape of a man named "Pedro the Voder" at the 1939 World's Fair. He responded to commands. Pedro was going to be doing everyone's household chores in a few years, according to GE. You talk about failure to fulfill a promise. That never happened. The robots in use in factories don't look anything like humans.

Anyone can complain that television isn't good enough but no one can say that television hasn't made everyone more aware of everything. There are even things on television that might enlighten a Yale student.

I told them that. I forgot to tell them I couldn't get in.


## THE JOY OF HARASSMENT

A few jerks around every business office have ruined what used to be a perfectly pleasant and harmless workplace activity—by-play between men and women. In any work place where there are men and women, there is inevitably a relationship established between them that is different from the relationship between the workers of the same sex. There is nothing vulgar or sexist about it. Men are men and women are women. It makes work more interesting and it's too bad we're being asked to behave as if we we're all asexual.

The average man doesn't lust after every woman he sees who's attractive to him. If there are thoughts that come to him unbidden, he suppresses those as quickly and surely as any inclination he might have to shoplift an attractive piece of merchandise in a store.

I was standing at the elevator on the seventh floor of my building when a young woman came along, noted that I had already pushed the DOWN button she smiled, nodded and stood near me. She was attractive and wearing what I perceived to be a new and quite short, dress.

"I like your dress," I said and then I paused and added, "What there is of it."

"I don't know whether that's a compliment or an insult," she laughed.

It seemed to me at the time to be an inoffensive man/woman bit of conversation like ten thousand others I've had over the years but I got thinking afterwards that it's the sort of thing I probably shouldn't say anymore.

The necessity for being neuter in the office is difficult and women are doing their share to help make it easier for men. If men are not expected to take notice of the fact that a woman is attractive or even sexually interesting, then women have got to stop dressing in a manner that evokes such thoughts in men. Women's clothes have got to change and become less interesting if men are to be disinterested. The clothes should stop putting so much emphasis on the difference between a woman's shape and a man's.

This suggestion assumes something that may not be true: that all women are as anxious and angry about sexual harassment in the workplace as the activists in the women's movement are.

There. I've said it and I'm glad.

# ANNUAL LABOR DAY ESSAY

It's so very American that we establish a holiday honoring hard work, call it "Labor Day" and then take off for four days during which time we don't do any.

There are all sorts of Biblical advisories about the fruit of one's labor. One proverb says "Labor not to be rich." I don't know about that. It sounds admirable but I think even Bill Graham likes all that money he rakes in by working hard.

Matthew says Jesus told his disciples "The harvest is truly plenteous but the laborers are few." Jesus would probably be amused to hear things haven't changed. I go to a farm in upstate New York that has lots of corn and tomatoes but they're having trouble finding anyone to work picking them.

Theodore Roosevelt said, "It is only through labor and painful effort . . . that we move on to better things."

That sounds good and we like the idea. It ought to be true but the fact is, a lot of people move on to better things without working at all.

It's why Abe Lincoln said, "Some have labored and others have, without labor, enjoyed a large proportion of the fruits." Those guys enjoying the fruit without working are the ones we all hate. Although we want to be one of them.

There's a difference between workers and laborers. Laborers are almost a thing of the past. I was talking to a New York cab driver the other day. He had big forearms and I said "You didn't get those muscles driving a cab."

"No," he said. "I used to be a laborer. I worked on a road crew cracking rocks with a jack hammer but they got a new machine that does it and they don't need me. I don't need them muscles no more either."

Work changed a lot from very early times when a person pretty much took care of himself and his family working alone. All of us who work now are dependent on what someone else is doing near us or did yesterday or an hour ago. In a car factory, the guy who puts the wheels on can't work independently because there's nothing for him to do until the man on the production line in front of him installs the axles that the wheels go on.

The word "labor" itself has gone out of style. It's used most often in relation to a union. Members of labor unions are called "organized labor." No one ever calls them "work" unions.

"Labor" is also the word used in newspapers when there's a strike or contract dispute. They are "labor negotiations" never "work negotiations." Labor is also what a woman goes into when she's having a baby, of course.

If I was head of a labor union, I'd start a campaign to spell the word the way the British spell it, L-A-B-O-U-R. The word has more class with a *u* in it.

Adam Smith said that any two products "will exchange against each other" in direct proportion to the amount of labor that goes into making them." Karl Marx picked it up. I've been thinking that over ever since I first read it as a sophomore in college. It isn't true. It doesn't take automation or brains into consideration. All labor isn't of equal value. You wouldn't pay someone the same money for digging a hole in your backyard as you would pay someone to fix your computer, even though they both worked at it for three hours. That's probably why communism has fallen on hard times. It's based on a lot of false premises like that.

The most famous statement ever made about work is called "Parkinson's Law" because it was written by C. Northcote Parkinson. He said, "Work expands to fill the time available for its completion."

Labor Day weekend does that, too. The fun expands to fill the time available for having it and that's why we have Labor Day on Monday. We can have fun celebrating work and not do any from about noon Friday until whenever we get back to work Tuesday morning.

# TIME IS NOT MONEY

"The secret to success," says a businessman being handed an award in a picture in the newspaper, "is knowing how to handle time." That's bad news for me if it's true because I don't know how. If time was money, I'd be broke.

It doesn't pay to think much about time because it's depressing. Time has no beginning we can imagine and no end we can conceive of. It's endless in both directions—behind us and in front of us.

No one can change his or her habits regarding time. People who are late are always late. People who get there early, always get there early. I hate myself for it but I'm usually late. A thousand times I've promised I'm going to change but I don't. It's like losing weight. Desire doesn't have any influence on my behavior. Being late is as much a part of me as being overweight.

For anyone so careless with time, it's hard to understand why I like having my watch accurate to the second. I want to know exactly how late I am. I never leave soon enough and I consistently underestimate how long it takes to get someplace. You'd think just by mistake I'd get someplace early once in a while.

It's interesting to consider whether or not, here now in the 21st Century, we're cramming more life into the time of our lives and living fuller lives because of it. We have all sorts of machines that save time for us. We save time by traveling everywhere farther and faster than humans could before there were cars, trains and airplanes. But on the other hand, the hour we spend driving someplace is an hour we didn't spend at all before there were cars. We saved time going nowhere. There are time-saving devices that consume huge amounts of time. It is quite possible that we waste more time with computers than we save.

It's paradoxical that we all want time to last. We hate it when time flies or when we don't know where it has gone. We are always setting out to have a good time fully aware that time passes more quickly during good times than bad. If we really wanted time to last longer, we'd set out to have a lousy time every day.

Quite often we're in a dilemma. While it's certainly true that we're usually reluctant to have time pass by too fast, there are times when we're in some unpleasant situation, and it can't go past fast enough to suit us.

Time passes too slow for me when I'm driving. In the summer I make a long, boring drive twice a week. I dream of having a yacht-length truck luxuriously fitted with two drivers up front.

"Let me know when we're there" I'll tell them and then relax.

In real life I sit there behind the wheel thinking "Gad, two more hours of this. I can't stand it." But then very often I'll suddenly wake up to the fact that I'm almost where I'm going. I don't know what happened to the two hours of time. I can't remember thinking anything. I didn't see anything that registered in my brain. I'm pleased the drive is over but bothered by the fact that I wasted two hours not thinking anything.

Most time passes when we aren't watching. We don't notice it going until we look back and see that it's gone. Our daily habits consume most of our time; things we do automatically without thinking because we do them every day or dozens of times a day. You can't sit around thinking about the passing of time but it slows it down a little if you stop to look where it's going once in a while.

Of all the bad deals human beings were dealt when they were created, the need we have for seven hours of sleep once every 24 hours is the worst. Sleeping away 25 percent of our lives is a terrible waste but there's no way to get around it. Some day they'll come up with a pill that will make us sleep faster.

The world is filled with time-wasters.

Morning radio shows take time. I often listen to Imus driving to work and I enjoy it but I get to the office faced with the necessity of thinking of something to write about and I realize I haven't thought of anything because of listening to Imus.

Television may be the worst major time-stealer in all our lives. I can't get over how often I've sat there in the living room for an hour watching something I can't stand. The show ends and I think to myself "Why did I just waste an hour watching that?" I wish there was some way we could make television give us our time back.

The people who line up in the EXPRESS TEN ITEMS ONLY cashier's lane with twenty items are time-wasters. They not only have too much in their shopping cart but half the time they pay with a check or a credit card, adding to the time they steal from everyone behind them. The cashier calls the manager to have the check okayed while the rest of us stand there, wasting our time.

I'm ambivalent about the time I spend reading the newspaper every morning. Am I helping myself or the world by becoming well-informed about some terrible problem in a remote country that I can't do anything about? I'm not a Congressman, I'm not President, I'm not a general in the Pentagon—why should I spend any time learning about Afghanistan or which is Iran and which is Iraq?

The telephone is a time-stealer. It is a good, quick way of saying something to someone at a distance but most phone calls are too long. If what you have to say takes more than two minutes, write a letter.

Semi-friends you meet on the street can be time-takers or wasters. I am frequently annoyed by the ones who stop to ask how I am, or how I'm doin? They want to know how the wife and kids are. These people have stock phrases they use to waste time: "Whaddya up to?" "How's the world treatin' you?" or "How things goin'?"

Meetings are usually a waste of time. I've never been to a meeting that wasn't twice as long as it should have been. Television producer Don Hewitt says that if you have a lot of meetings, the show looks like a meeting.

My single best time-saver is being rude to people. I cut people off on the telephone when it's clear we've both said what we had to say and are beginning to chat.

The little poem I first read when I was 10 comes to mind when I think of time:

*Backward, turn backward, O Time in your flight*
*Make me a child again just for tonight.*


# I'M A TYPE, YOU'RE A TYPE

Every once in a while it's a good idea to divide people into categories by type. If you know what category someone is in, it saves time. You can base your prejudices on their type or category. We all pretend to be free from prejudice but there isn't time not to have some. You base decisions about people and actions on your previous experience with them. I do not like sweet potatoes. I know what one looks like when I see one and I am repelled by their appearance. Call me prejudiced against all sweet potatoes just because of the few I've eaten and didn't like but that's the way it is.

It would probably be a good idea if we included a person's category with their phone numbers in our address books. There are a lot of categories but many of them tend to cluster in people in the same groups. For instance, people who eat slowly tend to be fastidious dressers. They return their tax return in February. Almost everyone in one of those categories is also in the other.

There are people who are just naturally liberal and people who seem to have been born conservative. They are not only conservative about politics and money but about everything else, too. They even dress conservatively.

Then, there are people who are early plane-catchers and people who show up at the gate at the last minute. The early plane-catchers have time for a cup of coffee after they get there. The late plane-catchers are running for the gate. These people are more apt to have voted for a Democrat.

There are people who drive too slowly and people who drive too fast. Whether they are in a hurry or not does not affect their speed of travel.

We are divided about equally between those who go to bed early and those who go to bed late. Each is proud of their habit.

"I always watch the *Late Show*," the late people are pleased to tell anyone who'll listen.

"I get up by six—even weekends," the early riser crows.

There are people who are always stopping to ask directions of strangers about how to get someplace and people who never ask. Those who don't ask directions will drive for hours, lost in a strange city, without ever stopping to open the window and inquire of a pedestrian about where they are. One of the unfortunate facts of life seems to be that these two extremes are usually married to each other. You seldom hear of a married couple in which both members are direction-askers or both are the type that never asks.

I thought about types today because of a category I fall in with a lot of other people. Every day of my life I underestimate how long it will take me to do something and I am almost always late getting it done.

This week, I promised a magazine editor I'd write something for his December issue. I told him I'd have it for him in two weeks. A month later I've worried about it a lot but I haven't written it.

This isn't an isolated incident, this is a personality trait. I am a type . . . in a category with a lot of other people.

You'd think I'd have learned by now that it takes a long time to do something but I haven't. This trait is as part of my character and genetic makeup as bushy eyebrows. I can't change no matter how hard I try. I was born thinking it wouldn't take long to do something.

A lot of you sympathize with me; others of you have no patience with me.

Some of these impatient friends of ours are no better at judging time than we are. They err in the other direction. They always think it will take *longer* to do something than it does. They finish ahead of schedule and have time on their hands they don't know what to do with. Dinner is ready before anyone is ready to eat it. The alarm is set an hour before it's necessary to get up. These people are more apt to save coupons worth nine cents which they cash in at the Super Market while I wait in line behind them. I'm in a hurry to get home because I'm late.

## "DEAR SIR: YOU'RE FIRED!"

On the business pages of any newspaper, there are regular stories about corporation CEOs or other chief executives who are leaving their jobs. Nowhere are euphemisms for what actually happened more evident.

The language of leaving a high-level job involves high-level hedging. No corporate executive is ever fired. He is not simply quitting as he might get up and leave in the middle of a bad movie. He is retiring, moving on, exploring new opportunities, leaving to spend more time with his family.

The executives left behind in the company, usually including the one who did the firing, say what a great job the exiting executive did for the company and how much he'll be missed. But toodleloo, Pal.

The most famous case of an executive "quitting" a job (quotation marks around a word are a way of winking in print) that has taken place in the United States in modern history was when Richard Nixon voluntarily left the job of being President. The word for it then was "resigned" but the word "resign" has a voluntary sense that doesn't explain what happened to Nixon. There was nothing voluntary about it. The same was true of Spiro Agnew, Nixon's Vice President, who was forced to "resign" a few years earlier for what amounted to stealing. No one ever used the words "fired" or "stealing." Dishonest politicians and business executives whose crimes are enormous, reach a lexicographic level above such descriptions as "thief" and "crook."

Newspapers regularly print stories about "resignations" that are not resignations.

"James Hebe is stepping down at Daimler-Chrysler as head of the unit after sizable losses this year." Stepping down? How about "pushed down"?

"Ford Motor Co. is weighing plans to restructure top management."

You can imagine a Ford executive going home that night. His wife says "How did things go today at the office, Dear?"

"Not too good. I got restructured."

"Two top executives at Time accept buyout packages."

You know how that went. "Here. Take this package and get out." It isn't a buyout, it's a thrown-out.

In a journalism magazine, an item notes that at the *New York Post* "Col Allan replaces Editor Xana Antunes who resigned after six years at the paper." Sure he did. Xana probably hated the job.

"Citing his health, President Ezer Weizman said he will resign before his term ends." The story also noted that Weizman had been caught taking hundreds of thousands of dollars worth of gifts before he made that decision to resign "because of ill health." Something he ate in one of those gift packages, probably.

Palm Pilot president says "We know we need to improve our management talent." Translation: "I'm gonna fire some of these duds and get new managers."

The origin of this tradition in which no one ever gets fired from a job but leaves voluntarily, is unknown. There is a stigma attached to being told to pick up your things and get out that has brought about the creation of a whole new vocabulary for cut from the payroll. Getting fired is a perfectly honorable thing to have happen to anyone but Americans can't take it lying down. Everyone ought to be fired once or twice during a lifetime and the same person probably ought to quit a few times, too. There's no sense staying on a job you dislike just to hang on long enough to get a gold watch. There is great satisfaction to be had from walking out on a job over grievances you either imagine or actually suffer.

The word "quit" itself has half a dozen meanings. It can mean more than just that you're leaving a job. It can mean you're ceasing to perform or that you're leaving where you are in a physical sense and then "quit" can mean you're giving up in defeat. This holds the word's most oppro-brious connotation. If you do that, you're what's known as a quitter. It's funny that while being a quitter is bad, calling it quits is not. That simply means you're bugging out.

# PART 8

*The Writing Life*

We need more plumbers and electricians than we need poets—but we need poets, too. There are more bad poets than bad electricians and plumbers. Maybe poets ought to be licensed.

# THE WRITER AS
# NATURAL RESOURCE

There is a widespread opinion that writing isn't real work.

People often ask me why I spend so much time in my office if all I do is two newspaper columns a week and one three-minute piece for *60 Minutes*.

The diminution of the job of writing in the minds of readers may have something to do with the double meaning of the word "write." When a five-year-old learns to put the letters C-A-T on a piece of paper with Crayola, his mother says he is "learning to write."

When people underestimate how difficult it is to write something that is going to be printed or spoken before an audience, they are confusing that kind of writing with the writing done with Crayola.

While the work writers put into their product may be underestimated, the importance of what they have to say is overestimated. Writers enjoy a status in society that is out of proportion to their real worth. Just by the fact that they are writers, they are accorded a kind of celebrity status and their advice and presence is sought.

There is no way I can say this without seeming churlish, mean-spirited and petty but professional writers are expected to give their services free to organizations that wouldn't dream of asking a carpenter, an electrician, a doctor or even an insurance agent to give his time free.

If I get 100 letters a day, five of them are asking me for something because my name is known as a writer.

- A grade school teacher in San Antonio sends me 24 papers written by her fifth-grade students and asks me to mark them and provide criticism for each one. I am to select a winner who will receive a prize. Reading them and doing the job diligently would take me at the very least, 10 minutes for each of the 24 papers. I do not have four hours to give to a grade school teacher I don't know in San Antonio. I don't have the interest, either.

- A magazine editor writes to say they are doing an article on the healing power of laughter and will I please write back giving him some examples of the sort of thing that makes me laugh. (I throw this out, resisting the temptation to say that people who believe that laughter cures an illness make me laugh.)
- A group of senior citizens in a city near my home town is initiating a new program designed to find useful work for men and women over 75 years old. Will I speak at a dinner they are having in October and explain how I think their goal might best be accomplished?
- A group of women in a town on the outskirts of Chicago is raising money for the work they do with people who cannot read, by putting out a book of favorite recipes of well-known people. Will I please contribute my favorite recipe?
- There are five requests a week from college or high school students. "My teacher has asked us to write about a person we admire. I admire you very much. Could you please tell me who influenced you the most as a writer and what the most important day of your life was? I need to have this by Friday because my paper is due then. Thank you very much for taking the time to do this."
- "Enclosed is the manuscript of my book which I have been working on for eight years. I greatly admire you as a writer and it would mean a great deal to me if you would read my book and tell me what you think of it." The enclosure is 347 pages.
- There are dozens of so-called writers who depend on other writers to write their books for them. Fifty times a year I get a letter asking me to write something to be included in an anthology, for example, "I am currently putting together a book to be called 'MOTHER' and would appreciate it if you would tell me what your mother meant to you and how she influenced your career."

I dislike all these requests because it makes me feel terrible to be rude and when I get one, I am usually rude.

## HOLD THE COMMAS

There are very few people who aren't thinking about writing a book someday. There's a big difference between thinking about writing a book and actually writing one. The difference is that writing one is harder.

Editors have always been a good help to me. I make errors both factual and grammatical which they catch and correct. Several years ago I wrote a book called *My War* that needed an editor's help. When the manuscript was returned to me, the editor had scribbled in a lot of useful corrections.

The manuscript then went to the copy editor who is more concerned with technical aspects of the manuscript. As I sat there reading it, I grew steadily more annoyed with his changes. He had added several hundred commas to my manuscript. It's a funny feeling reading a book you've written and looking for nothing but commas you didn't put in it but that's what I did. I took them out. My attitude was, it's my book and I'll put in the damn commas and leave them out where I feel like it.

The rules about commas are loose. I use them where I hear them. The fuddy-duddy copy editor put a comma in front of the word "but" every time I used it. There may have been a time when a comma was called for in front of a conjunction like "but," but those days are gone forever. I put a comma between those two "buts" just then because it might have been confusing without it. That's the best reason to use a comma—to give a sentence pace and keep down the confusion for the reader. Commas help readers hear the words.

The greatest grammarian of them all, H. W. Fowler, wrote "Anyone who finds himself putting down several commas close to one another should reflect that he is making himself disagreeable."

The copy editor saved me from making a fool of myself many times in the book so I couldn't be angry for long. In one paragraph in *My War*, I referred to the place where American troops got across the Rhine

River and said that there was a small mountain behind the Remagen Bridge where Count Hugo von Zeppelin launched the first lighter-than-air airship. It was Count *Ferdinand* von Zeppelin. I made dozens of mistakes like that which the copy editor caught.

I was careless, as I often am, about putting the word "only" in the right place in my sentences. When I wrote, "I only needed a light shirt" he made it "I needed only a light shirt." I went along with him on almost all my misplaced "onlys" but when I wrote "I only wanted to go home" and he changed it to "I wanted to go home only," I objected.

I was often inconsistent in the book. I'd use "9" for a number in one place and "nine" in another. I spelled it "counter espionage" on one page and "counterespionage" on another.

He made them both one word and that's okay with me.

Some of my mistakes were embarrassing and so dumb that they undermined my ability to argue with him. Twice I used the word "principle" when I meant "principal." There was a colonel whose name I spelled "Dixon" in three places and "Dickson" in two places. When I wrote about the United States Secretary of War and then referred to him in the next sentence as "the Secretary," he changed it to "the secretary" without a capital *s*. I think he's wrong but the AP Style Book agrees with him. In my mind, it wasn't just any secretary, it was *the* Secretary of War.

The copy editor decided that military titles would be "Brigadier General Leon W. Johnson" when I used a full name and "Brig. Gen. Johnson" when I used just a last name. Same with sergeant and other ranks. "Sergeant John Fuller" but "Sgt. Fuller." I went along with all that useful formality. He was right a lot of the time but in other matters the copy editor was a pain in the but.

## PARDON MY ENGLISH

The best book on how to use the English language was written by an Englishman named H. W. Fowler in 1926. *Modern English Usage* is one of the great books ever written. It's the English language bible. If the nuances of our language amuse you as a hobby because of their fascinating complexity, Fowler's (as it is commonly known) is fun to keep next to your bed for reading briefly before you drop off.

The book is old and outdated but its greatness is undiminished. I think of Fowler now because a man named R. W. Burchfield has rewritten *Modern English Usage* and come up with a book called *The New Fowler's English Usage* which I find infuriating.

Professor Burchfield has ruined the original by eliminating all Fowler's delightful little idiosyncrasies without adding any flavor of his own. It's an acceptable book but no better than a lot of other books on grammar and I resent Burchfield trading on Fowler's name. Why didn't he call it *Burchfield's Modern English Grammar* and see how many he'd sell?

My tattered copy of Fowler is 742 pages long and he didn't waste any time getting started. The first entry in the book reads "a, an. 1. A is used before all consonants except silent h (a history, an hour); 'an' was formerly usual before an unaccented syllable beginning with h (an historical work) but now that the h in such words is pronounced, the distinction has become pedantic & 'a historical' should be said and written."

That beginning is typical of Fowler's no-nonsense attitude throughout the book. Burchfield on the other hand, rewriting Fowler 70 years later, goes ring-around-the-rosie. He has three entries before that and then says "a, an. 1. In origin, 'a' (and its by-form 'an'), which usually is called the indefinite article . . ." blah blah blah for a page and a half.

The original has delightful tidbits in it that were removed in the new edition. Fowler was wonderfully opinionated and occasionally wrong, I suppose, but it makes good reading.

Here's Fowler on some things that Burchfield omitted:

- Referring to "the chaos prevailing among writers regarding the use of hyphens . . . the hyphen is not an ornament and should not be placed between two words that do not require uniting and can do their work equally well separate."
- "All right—there are no such forms as all-right, all right, alright . . . confusion with already & altogether." Fowler used a lot of ampersands to save space.
- "Ches(t)nut—Spell with and pronounce without the t."
- "If and when." Fowler says "any writer who uses this . . . lays himself open to the entirely reasonable suspicion . . . that he likes verbiage for its own sake."

Pompous Burchfield, on the other hand, says, "There are circumstances, it seems to me, when the conjoined pair (if and when) has an independent value . . . "

Writing about the confusion Americans had about the spelling of Mohammed and Mohammedan, Fowler acknowledges, way back in 1926, that the spelling was changing from Mahomet to Mohammed. Then he says "The trouble with letting the learned gentry bully us out of our traditional Mahomet is, no sooner have we tried to be good and learnt to say "Mohammed" than they are fired up with a zeal to get us a step or two further . . . which at present seems likely to end in Muhammad."

No such interesting, trouble-making comment in Burchfield's new version. "Mohammed . . . the customary spelling in English."

That's the kind of hot air Fowler never used. I'm even suspicious of Burchfield's phrase "conjoined pair." Is that different from "pair"? Fowler would have made fun of anyone using "conjoined."

If Burchfield didn't like what Fowler wrote, he should have started from scratch and written his own book with his own name on it to see whether *Burchfield* ever became synonymous with English usage as *Fowler* has.

# HANDWRITING

There is a big difference in the way each one of us sounds pronouncing the words of the English language and there is an even greater difference in the way people form the letters of the alphabet they use in handwriting.

The sounds and inflections of our voices differ because of the region of the country we grow up in or because of the manner of speaking of the person who taught us to form words. It isn't so clear why each of us has such a different style of handwriting. There's nothing geographical about it. No one writes with a southern accent.

If what I write was put down on paper by me with a pen or pencil, I'd be out of the writing business tomorrow. I have no patience with poor handwriting when I have to read it as a doctor's prescription or in a letter to me from a friend but mine is as bad as the worst I get in the mail.

I am merciless with letters that are difficult to read. If, within the first two or three lines there are four words I can't make out, the letter goes in the wastebasket with no further attempt on my part to make out what it says. There is no excuse for anyone who has bad handwriting not typing their message. Typing a personal letter is no longer bad manners.

There are two major influences on our handwriting. The first influence is how we were originally instructed to form letters by a teacher early in our school days. The second influence, which must be greater, is our dexterity. It is easier for a person who is naturally dexterous to write well than one who is clumsy. The only thing that makes me question whether that's true or not, are the great artists who can place a dab of paint precisely where they want it to create an effect—but can not write their own name legibly at the bottom of the canvas.

I have never seen any survey indicating whether left-handed or right-handed people have better penmanship but left-handed people taught to write by right-handed teachers must get off to a poor start. (My friend Bill Mauldin once told me that most cartoonists were left-handed.)

I am unnecessarily wary of any man who carries a fountain pen in his inside coat pocket. Some even carry the fountain pen and the mechanical pencil they got as a pair for Christmas. These are special people and I want no part of them. I resent their orderly efficiency but I must reluctantly concede that their handwriting is invariably better than mine. Why would that be?

Teaching handwriting is a difficult job that takes experience that even some good lower-grade teachers don't have. It may be a mistake to leave so important a learning process as handwriting to inexperienced teachers. This instruction is going to last a lifetime and if it isn't good, it will have a negative impact for all a person's life.

I was taught—or they tried to teach me—the Palmer Method. I don't know who Palmer was but I'd like to get hold of him. His "Method" has been as much of a drawback for me as stammering would be if I was a public speaker. I could no more write a neat, legible letter than I could paint a masterpiece. I am constantly making priceless notes to myself on scraps of paper that I am unable to decipher when I try to read them the next day.

It isn't clear to me whether it is a lack of motor skill that makes it difficult to control the movements of my hand or whether it is some kind of mental laziness or even impatience with the process that inhibits me from doing it right.

Bad handwriting is an affectation for some people. They are amused by a writing style they have that's hard to read. I am not amused by mine and when President Bush gets our educational system straightened out, I hope he will have made us a Nation with legible penmanship.

# IN THE BEGINNING—
# THERE WAS A WRITER

I don't want to burden you with a writer's problems but one of the difficulties of writing is how to begin. Because I make my living doing it, I am always alert to how other writers start their reports, articles, essays or novels.

The first words of any piece of writing ought to do several things. They should inform, create some curiosity and begin a story. That's the ideal but few writers try to include all those elements.

No one knows who did it, but the writer of the Bible knew what he or she was doing when the first words to be set down were "In the beginning, God created the heavens and the earth." That's an opening line that would be hard to improve on.

There have been other great ones. Charles Dickens began his epic *Tale of Two Cities* by writing "It was the best of times; it was the worst of times."

I haven't seen the movie and I can't imagine how they could have used the great opening line of Jane Austen's *Pride and Prejudice*: "It is a truth universally acknowledged that a single man in possession of a good fortune must be in want of a wife."

You can tell where that story is going.

One of the great all-time first sentences was the one with which Margaret Mitchell began *Gone With the Wind*.

"Scarlett O'Hara was not beautiful but men seldom realized it when caught by her charm as the Tarleton twins were."

Gore Vidal began his novel *Myra Breckinridge* by writing "I am Myra Breckinridge whom no man will ever possess." Pretty catchy. Anyone reading it would be curious to read on in order to find out whether any man does get to possess her. I know what my bet would be.

Some first lines have become classics for reasons that are hard to determine. Herman Melville wrote one of the most famous first lines ever set down when he began the story of the great white whale, *Moby Dick*. His character said simply "Call me Ishmael."

Tolstoy starts *Anna Karenina* with a general statement.

"Happy families are all alike; every unhappy family is unhappy in its own way."

Ernest Hemingway begins *For Whom the Bell Tolls* in what seems like a mannered and deliberately flat style. "He lay flat on the brown, pine-needled floor of the forest, his chin on his folded arms and high overhead the wind blew in the tops of the pine trees."

Hemingway's style is still popular. I always feel a writer who uses that style probably couldn't think of a good way to begin so he pretended to be deliberately low-key.

My friend Kurt Vonnegut starts his classic *Slaughterhouse-Five* in a disarming way: "All this happened, more or less. The war parts anyway, are pretty much true."

What made me think of the beginnings of written pieces today was, of all things, the *Wall Street Journal*. A reporter or feature writer for a newspaper has a different problem than one a novelist faces. There's more urgency to grab the reader's attention.

The *Journal* is, for the most part, well-written but with maddening frequency they begin a feature story with a synthetic particular. Obviously some editor has insisted "Be specific." They take a person's name—who may or may not have anything to do with the story—and, for a first sentence, attach that name to some insignificant incident. Example:

"Peter Anderson, a freshman at Johns Hopkins University in Baltimore, may have made a costly mistake." The story is about financial aid grants, not about Peter Anderson or mistakes.

"When geologist Susan Waters got the most exciting call of her career one morning at 2 o'clock, she didn't even tell her husband, asleep next to her." The story was about drilling for oil. I was curious about what Susan's husband was taking that enabled him to sleep though a 2 a.m. telephone call. Susan might give some thought to leaving this dull clod.

"Congress is about to taste its own medicine, and Dennis Duffy holds the teaspoon." Clever but the story is about occupational safety around the Capitol.

An essay or a report is even more difficult to end than it is to start. You feel you should end with something clever or decisive and often nothing clever or decisive comes to you so you finish, as T. S. Eliot finished his poem *The Hollow Men.*

*This is the way the World ends*
*Not with a bang . . . but a whimper.*

## IT'S NOT FUNNY

Years ago a carpenter doing some work around our house left two boxes of short ends from several dozen two-by-fours he'd cut. They were to be thrown away. While I don't foresee any time in the near future when I'm going to need 27 pieces of two-by-fours 14 inches long, I rescued them from the trash.

Three years ago a woman named Sue Ryon called me. She was editor of some journalism publication and asked if I'd write an article on humor in newspapers. I wrote it and sent it. I never heard a word from Sue and assumed she didn't like it. Unlike the people in most businesses, writers know when customers don't like what they've done. Insurance salesmen are never told their work isn't good enough.

Anyway, like those ends of two-by-fours, I kept my notes from the article and every once in a while I pick through them to see if there's anything I can use. It's in my computer under the heading HUMOR.

That may have been where I went wrong. Writing about humor or labeling anything "humor" is a mistake. Humor should come unannounced. It's better as a surprise than a promise.

There are few subjects that resist analysis the way humor does. Like beauty, there's no standard of measurement. We know it when we see it, but we can't put our finger on what it is or why it's funny.

There isn't much that's funny in a newspaper and that's the way it ought to be. You can't expect a columnist to be funny Monday, Wednesday and Friday and almost every time anyone sets out to write something funny, the effort falls flat. At its best, humor is a by-product. It comes up in the course of something serious and provides relief. There's usually a good reporter with a light touch on a newspaper staff who can provide all the humor needed. No one should set out, deliberately, to be funny.

(There are a couple of exceptions but it would ruin this theme of mine to name them.)

Some opinion pages run features under the heading HUMOR and I feel sorry for the writers. Any reader seeing that assumes the attitude "Okay. Show me something funny. Go ahead. Make me laugh."

Labeling something HUMOR is the equivalent of labeling an editorial deploring the infrequency of garbage pickups SERIOUS.

Even the best humor has a short shelf life. Funny paragraphs start decomposing as soon as they're written. Over the years I've clipped out things that made me laugh and when I look at them months later, they remind me of pretty stones that I've picked out of the wet sand when they were glistening and colorful on trips to the beach with the kids. A week later, the children have gone, the stones sit there in a pail in my garage, bone-dry and lifeless. I wonder whatever attracted us to them.

If you've read anything written by the classic old American humor writers, you know humor doesn't keep. Kin Hubbard, Josh Billings, Artemus Ward, Finley Peter Dunn, George Ade, Stephen Leacock, Alexander Woollcott all may have convulsed readers of another generation but reading them now, it's hard to understand why. I'll make an exception in the case of the genius, Mark Twain.

I'm glad I saved those notes even though Sue didn't want any part of them. I knew I'd find a use for them. Now to think of something to do with those short pieces of two-by-fours.

## FINANCIAL REPORTERS FAIL

Reporters have never been near the top of any list that rates the popularity of the practitioners of various professions. Every time there's any kind of poll or survey, people in the news business and news organizations themselves, score badly. There are at least three reasons:

Reporters deal with news. News is an event that's a change from the usual or the normal. People like things the way they are. It's not a story if the mayor isn't caught stealing, the forest doesn't burn or no one is found murdered. In almost every case change that makes news is negative and reporters and whole news organizations are associated with that. They are asked "Why don't you ever give us the good news?" The answer is that usually if it's good it isn't news.

The second thing that makes it difficult for a reporter's reputation is, his day's work is out in the open for everyone to see or read. There's no hiding place for a reporter. What other profession has to lay its work out every day where people can review it? Would the work of a banker, an insurance salesman, a garage mechanic stand up to the kind of scrutiny a reporter's work gets?

Third, a reporter's story depends on facts that are difficult to get. People involved in a story would rather say what they'd like to have printed than the truth. Witnesses are more interested in what the story will mean to them when it comes out than in what actually happened. The reporter finds himself or herself, checking one lie or distortion against another.

People are not only poor observers, they are bad at describing what they saw. Their memory of the events is influenced by what they wish they were.

With what facts he can get, the reporter has to try to write a story in a style that is interesting enough to attract readers. Style is not always compatible with fact.

So much in defense of reporters. There is no way news organizations in general and financial reporters in particular, can defend themselves for the terrible job they have done over the years reporting on business. For years there have been daily feature stories and magazine covers on the giants who have taken their company to the top of some business venture. They have been success stories long on personal history, anecdotes and maybe even a little gossip. They have been woefully short on information about shady or illegal practices the tycoon participated in to get him where he is.

Week after week television shows devoted to Wall Street had guests called "stock analysts." Does anyone ever recall Rukeyser pressing a guest to analyze the fraud that was going on in one of the businesses in which the guest was an expert? Not once?

Night after night, the network evening news broadcasts dutifully reported that stocks were up or down. Usually up. They never reported that anything in these corporations seemed to be sideways.

*Fortune* magazine published a report on Enron's questionable business practices eight months before the scandal became public knowledge but other financial reporters never followed up on it.

It is not only the major corporations that have escaped media scrutiny. There must be hundreds of small, local businesses in every city in America that are engaging in practices that would command a banner headline if a good reporter did enough digging to get at the story. The local sports reporting is better.

News organizations need to be as aggressive covering big and small business as they are covering government agencies. It's difficult because companies, unlike government agencies, are closed to outsiders. But a good reporter with a background in business and accounting could have found everything needed to blow the Enron scandal wide open a year before it happened by simply studying published documents. The average reader doesn't know a stock option from a stock yard but someone getting paid to report on business ought to have known something fishy was happening on a scale that makes the great bank robber Willie Sutton look like a small-time pickpocket.

If reporters had gone after Big Business the way they covered the forest fire in Arizona or a kidnapping, they would have been hounding every high-level employee who got fired, looking for whistle blowers who knew the story. Reporters would have gotten to insiders on corporate boards. They would have used all the traditional methods of seeking out information and quite possibly have saved the Country the financial disaster it suffered in 2002 before it happened.

## REWRITING SHAKESPEARE

One of the editors of a slick magazine with a big circulation wrote me to say they were putting together their special Christmas edition and asked if I would write an article about Christmas cards. Funny he wanted it. They would pay me $3,500.

I am already gainfully employed but still not immune to the lure of $3,500 so, while it is almost always a mistake to set out to be funny, I said I would write a funny article about Christmas cards. I wrote it and sent it off. Several weeks later the editor wrote back saying how great it was . . . however there were some minor changes he and other editors wished to make.

My opinion of myself as a writer is neither inflated or deflated. I know how to do it and, while I am not great, I seldom write badly either. The changes the editors made were badly written clichés that were especially offensive because they thought they were writing them in my style. For example, they suggested I begin "Having sent and received my share of cards over the years . . . "

The editing reminded me of an article I wrote for the *Reader's Digest* many years ago. I had referred several times to "children" or "kids" and the editor at the *Digest* changed "kids" to "tykes." The great early television comedian, Fred Allen, made the best remark about editors who changed his script. Fred said "Where were they when the paper was blank?"

This experience made me wonder if the great writers in our literary history had to contend with editors who wanted to change what they had written. What would Shakespeare have done with this:

Dear Will,

Thank you for submitting your little play *Hamlet*. It should stage well but it needs a few minor revisions which we are happy to make for you.

Do you have any strong feelings about the name *Hamlet*? Perhaps you chose it for some reason of your own in which case we'll go along with it but none of us on the editorial know anyone named "Hamlet" and it has a small-town sound that might put people off. Would "George" or perhaps "Roger" be acceptable to you?

Just looking through your script hastily we see several places we feel need help. You write

"To be or not to be: that is the question."

One of our editors who is a stickler for detail feels those are not one but two questions and the line should read "To be or not to be: those are the questions."

Further along you write

"Whether 'tis nobler in the mind to suffer

the slings and arrows of outrageous fortune . . . "

This is a nice turn of phrase but the meaning of the word "slings" in this context is not clear and we're going to take the liberty of making it "the bows and arrows of bad luck."

And then Abe Lincoln might have had an editor:

Dear Mr. President,

Thank you for showing us the advance copy of the speech you plan to give at Gettysburg. While there's a lot in it that's well written, don't forget that you're going to have a big audience and many people will have traveled a long distance to hear what you have to say. Don't you think they may feel cheated because your remarks are so brief? Certainly it wouldn't be difficult for you to extend them so they would last for half an hour. Perhaps you could include some personal anecdotes or stories of your childhood in the log cabin. Was it drafty for instance?

People will expect this of you. It might even make a book called *ABE'S CHAT AT GETTYSBURG.*

Our other comments are very small, Mr. President. For example, you begin by saying "Fourscore and seven years ago . . . "

As editors, we know, of course, that a score is "twenty" but a lot of people in your audience may not. Why don't you just say "twenty"?

Your talk would then begin "Eighty-seven years ago our ancestors started up a new country with high ideals." This is just a suggestion. If you think of a better way of saying it, by all means do so.

A great writer with high principles would refuse to change a word. As a journeyman writer my attitude toward the editors of my Christmas card article was "Do what you want. Just mail me the check."

# PART 9

---

# *Home Life*

*You never see old men sitting in rocking chairs on their front porches whittling anymore. Rocking chairs, front porches and whittling all seem to have gone out of style. Old men, on the other hand, are all over the place.*

# DREAMING OF
# A DREAM HOUSE

Just as soon as I have the time and the money, I'm going to build my dream house. It will be a big, rambling wooden home three stories tall with five bedrooms, a large kitchen with three ovens, a wood-burning grill with its own exhaust system and a small dining area near a window that looks out onto a rocky cove.

Some of the rooms won't be for anything. As the years go by, you always find you need an extra room and we'll have them. They'll be called "Just In Case" rooms.

There would be an attic and a basement. Each bedroom would have its own bathroom with a walk-in, circular shower. Because you'd be surrounded by pipes with pinholes in them, fine streams of water would hit you all over. The temperature of the water would be controlled by a gauge you adjusted on the wall before you got in the shower.

The television set would be in the ceiling so I could watch it lying on my back. Each room would be connected to the floors above and below them with a dumb waiter—a small elevator that would carry food, drink or baggage so no one would have to carry anything up or down stairs.

The living room would be cozier than big and would have a fireplace. Wood for the fireplace would be brought up from the basement on the dumb waiter. A small den off the living room would have just two comfortable green leather chairs, shelves loaded with books, and a television set. There would be a comfortable couch long enough so I could stretch out on it for a nap on Saturdays. (The television set would be equipped with an attachment that automatically switched it off when I fell asleep.)

The ceilings would be high and, because the bookshelves in the den would go to the ceiling, I'd have a lovely, rolling walnut ladder that I could climb to reach the books on the top shelf. I wouldn't go up it very often. I just like library ladders.

There would be a small office room for the computer. Adjacent to the computer room would be a small apartment. This would be where the computer expert would live so he'd be right there at all times when I had a problem with my computer that I couldn't solve.

Each bedroom would have a small door in the wall that opened on a chute down which you could throw dirty clothes. Clean clothes would be delivered the same way. The dirty clothes would drop directly into the washing machine, which could be turned on with a switch in the bedroom. Each room would also have its own small vacuum cleaner recessed in the wall so that no one would ever have to lug one up or downstairs. The closets would be equipped with those moving hanger belts dry cleaners have. You'd press a button and your clothes would start passing in review in front of your eyes. The clothes and shoes below would be dated. Anything older than 15 years, unless expressly exempt from destruction, would be automatically thrown out. There would be a limit to the number of exemptions you could make in one year.

There would be a four-car garage although we'd never put more than two cars in it because the part designed for two more cars would be filled with outdoor tools, a wheelbarrow, lawn mower, hoses and junk that is not worth keeping but that I can't bring myself to throw away. The garage would be wide enough so that there would be plenty of room to open all the car doors. A moving belt, activated by the press of a button, would bring the bags and packages you put on it from the garage to the kitchen. At one end of the garage, nearest the kitchen door, there would be an extra freezer chest for overflow from the refrigerator in the kitchen.

The contents of the garage, the basement and the attic would be displayed on screens near the light switches in each location. When you turned the light on in the garage, the basement or the attic the contents of that room would be displayed with code numbers after each item indicating its exact location.

There would be a small bathroom in the garage. This would be a convenience for people who always seem to have to go to the bathroom the minute they get home.

The driveway and all the sidewalks leading down to the boathouse and out to my woodworking shop would have pipes underneath them with warming wires so that when it snowed, I could turn on the heat and the snow would melt as it fell on them. I'd never have to shovel.

There would be locks on the doors in the house but we'd never lock any of them because we wouldn't have to.

I would not have a swimming pool because, for the number of times you use one, it isn't worth the trouble and, anyway, what I haven't told you about my dream house and why we wouldn't have to lock anything is, it would be the only house on a small island. I am not certain yet whether my island home will be in an ocean or a lake.

The island would be about a mile long and just a few hundred yards wide. I don't have all the details worked out yet but I'm working on the design of some kind of bridge that could be extended out from my island until it rested on the shore of the mainland. After I drove over it, I would press my garage door closer and the bridge would retract into its housing on my island so no one else could come across it. Close friends and the mailman would have one of the openers.

There would be one wooded area on my island, up behind the house, and a good-sized open field where kids could play ball games. One end of the island would have a small, rocky hill you could climb and look out over the water. The other end would be a sandy beach with waves lapping at the shore.

In the small community nearest the house, on the mainland, would be a good, small grocery store, a hardware store, a bakery and, lucky for us, there would be a plumber, a carpenter, a painter, an electrician and a computer expert, all of whom would be looking for work when we called them.

If we left home for a few days, the toaster, the iron and the stove would automatically shut off so we wouldn't have to worry about whether we left anything on while we were away.

## TO EACH HIS OWN—BATHROOM

If I had to choose between living with my family in a house with one bathroom and four bedrooms or a house with four bathrooms and one bedroom, I'd choose the one with four bathrooms.

It's not that I use a bathroom more than anyone else and need a lot of them, it's simply that a bathroom of your own is one of life's most civilized luxuries.

Four years in the Army gives anyone a lifelong appreciation of privacy and a bathroom of your own. The plumbing facilities in many foreign countries gives a traveling American reason enough to hurry home.

We had four children and one of the great things about having them grown now is that six of us no longer have to share the one upstairs bathroom in our house.

There were two bathrooms in our house and the one downstairs had a bathtub but no one wants to go downstairs to take a bath so the only person who ever bathed in that tub was Gifford our white English bulldog.

We all like our own things in our bathroom. We don't want it all mixed in with everyone else's in the closet or medicine cabinet. It should be perfectly clear which toothbrush is mine. I even like my own tube of toothpaste. No one else squeezes it the same way.

When the kids were home, I'd often wash my hands or take a shower and reach for my towel. At least half the time it was damp, good evidence that one of them had used it. I like my own towel, my own comb, my own glass and I like to know where the aspirin and the Alka Seltzer are so I can put my hand on either in the middle of the night without turning on the bathroom light.

When I'm feeling rich, I like to go into a good store and buy a couple of cakes of hard, milled soap or a cake of translucent glycerine soap like Pears. I like good soap. I'm generous with my worldly goods but I don't like sharing my expensive soap with someone who doesn't have the same respect for it that I do. Too many people leave soap in a pool of water.

The first thing I do when I go into the bathroom in the morning is turn on the radio. It's set to a station that carries nothing but news, weather and traffic. I want to know what to wear and I want to make my plans for getting to work. I have the dial set where I want it and I don't appreciate it when someone else has come in and put it on another station. Resetting the dial gets me off to a bad start.

A man's bathroom ought to be his castle.


## WASHING AS ENTERTAINMENT

We look for great moments in our lives but there are so few that it would be smart if instead, we learned to cherish the small satisfactions we get in an average day. I can't offhand think of anything more satisfying than washing something.

Last night after dinner I decided to wash a collection of dirty socks I had thrown in a small waste basket I keep in my clothes closet. I wash my socks because some of them are half wool and I don't want anyone using water that's too hot or soap with bleach in it. Clothes manufacturers warn against using bleach but some people who shall remain nameless insist on using it anyway. Bleach kills stuff like the elastic in shorts or the wool in socks.

The directions on a washing machine advise you not to put clothes with colors that might run in with white stuff but they never warn you about something more apt to happen and that's leaving a Kleenex in a pocket when you put pajamas in the washing machine.

Washing ourselves is a pleasant necessity. Not many things are both. There are still people who like a bathtub but most Americans haven't taken a bath in years. They don't like the idea of sitting in water that has the dirt in it that just washed off the body. They like to see that go down the drain with the soap suds in the shower.

The two things that can ruin a shower is a shortage of hot water or a cake of soap that's too small. The edges often become razor-thin on a cake so that it drops to the shower floor when you try to soap your body by holding the soap in the palm of your hand.

I used to give our English bulldog, Gifford, a bath in the tub downstairs. Giffy didn't like taking a bath any better than I do. Three or four times during the process, he would decide to shake himself, sending a wet, soapy spray over me and the bathroom walls.

Experts don't give advice on anything so simple as taking a shower but I realized last year that I was doing something wrong and I'll pass it on just in case you've had the same problem.

Every day I'd get a terrible back itch below my left shoulder blade. I finally realized that when I was in the shower washing other parts, I stood with the hot water hitting me in the back below my left shoulder blade. I was washing the oils out of that one spot and making it itch. Now I keep turning in the shower. It wouldn't be a bad idea if shower floors revolved.

Washing a car with a hose gives a person the satisfying illusion that he's doing a difficult, important job. The fact that washing a car is neither difficult nor important has nothing to do with how satisfying it is. It can be rewarding, too. The last time I removed the seats to vacuum, I found two nickels, a dime and six pennies. There was also a door key I had lost, a dry cleaning receipt, two McDonald's napkins, a ball point pen and two receipts for a long list of groceries I bought more than a year ago.

Washing dishes is satisfying if you don't have to do them every night. One of the most enduring disagreements in our house is whether or not to use the dishwasher. I don't use a dishwasher.

I've seen the commercials but I know you have to wash a dish before you put it in the washer and wash the glasses after. There is a film left on glass that I don't want mixed in with my drink. There's something else I know that dishwashing machine companies don't want you to know, too. It's the soap, not the washing machine that does it. Washing machine soap is dynamite and it's no wonder they suggest you use a milder liquid detergent when you're washing dishes in the sink. They don't want you to know that it's more the soap than the washing machine that does the work.

Our kitchen door has a huge window in it. Normally I don't notice whether it's clean or dirty but sometimes, when the sun is hitting it, I can see that it's filthy. Washing that is a small, satisfactory job. The trick is to use up-and-down strokes on the inside of the window and back and forth across strokes on the outside. There are always dirty streaks left when you finish the first time and this enables you to tell whether the dirt is on the inside, with the streaks going up and down, or on the outside, with the streaks going across.

I'm washing my hands of this essay now.

## SHOPPING AS
## MENTAL THERAPY

Although nothing really bad had happened to me last Saturday, I had an overpowering urge to do something nice for myself. I got in my car—which is always a comfort because we all think that going somewhere other than where we are will better our condition—and I drove to a clothing store I like. Once inside, I chose three colorful new short-sleeve shirts for summer and put them on a credit card so there was absolutely no pain at all.

Buying sports shirts is something I do. When I got the shirts home and started to put them in my chest of drawers, I realized I liked only one of the three. Worse than that, just a few layers down were three previously purchased sports shirts I had never unpinned. I went to my clothes closet and moved the garment bag I had folded and put on the shelf over the bar that holds my suits. There I discovered three colorful new shortsleeve shirts that I had never worn.

We buy what amuses us, not what we need. In this regard, I can sympathize with Imelda Marcos. You remember that when Imelda's thieving husband was arrested and police searched their palace in Manila, they found that Imelda had closets containing more than 3,500 pairs of shoes.

I am not limited in my impulse buying to summer shirts, either. If I do a few chores around the house Saturday morning and feel I deserve something nice and have a little money in my pocket, I often go to a woodworker's store a few miles from home and buy a tool I don't need or some wood. I am obsessed with good boards.

The machinery in my shop is being crowded out by the racks I built to store wood. In the basement of our house, 25 five/quarter planks are leaned up against every foot of the stone walls. Overhead, I have slipped boards in between the beams. My board collection runneth over.

For her part, Margie collects empty clay flowerpots, rings, art books too big to stand upright in our bookshelves and rakes. She doesn't actually rake anything very often but the walls of our garage are decked with a garland of rakes, hoes and special-purpose shovels. Our little garden tool shed is so full that it's a trick to close the doors. There is so little room in the garage when two cars are parked in it, that I often hit a rake with my shoulder and bring it crashing down as I try to squeeze between the car and the wall from which it is hung. It is made more difficult by the fact that I am frequently carrying two bags of groceries.

I've gotten over buying some things just for the fun of buying them. For many years I bought every old Underwood #5 typewriter I saw at a tag sale or in a junk shop. I bought 23 typewriters before I stopped. I excused myself on grounds that it was a hobby. I'm not talking about a hobby or a collection deliberately assembled. I'm talking about the obsession almost all of us seem to have with buying more than we need of one thing.

Compulsive buying is as certainly a sickness as alcoholism and gambling or drug addiction and I have it. Someone should start an organization called "Buyers Anonymous." We'd meet once a week and talk about all the things we used to buy and how good we were about not buying anything this week just for the fun of it. One "Buyers Anonymous" member would get to his feet and tell horror stories about his buying past and reveal secrets about the piles of unused shoes, shirts, gloves, scarves, cars or even houses that he bought in his dark, impulse-buying past.

## TO SAVE OR NOT TO SAVE

The emotionally wrenching effect on us of one of the most frequent actions we take never seems to go away. Throwing stuff out is always hard.

Over the weekend I built storage space in our garage eight feet high, with five shelves, each eight feet long and two feet deep. Building the shelves and securing the whole thing to the back wall was the easy part. Cleaning out the garage to make room was the tough part because it involved dozens of decisions about what to save and what to take to the dump.

Consider some of the items whose life or death sentence was in my hands:

- A small, iron, wood-burning stove that's cute and compact and would heat the garage but it would cost a fortune to make a chimney outlet for it . . . and who wants to feed a wood stove all night to keep two cars warm.
- Seven cans of paint in assorted sizes and colors. Some may still be good, some not . . . but which is which? If I go to the trouble of painting something, I'll probably buy new cans of paint.
  But maybe not.

- Some attractive empty bottles. The bottles once held something like wine or olive oil and I'm not clear what I thought I'd ever do with them but I like them. There were several fancy tin containers. One had held a round fruitcake from Harrod's in London.
- An outdoor grill that is perfectly good except the grate that holds the coals is missing.
- A dozen boards including a piece of pine 43 inches wide that I picked up at the dump. Occasionally I bring home more than I take to the dump.
- A Dictaphone. It was one of the first recording devices but there's a wide gap between an old piece of machinery and an artifact. Electric typewriters, tape recorders and record players are all useless now, replaced by something better but they are not old enough to be valuable antiques. Should I save them until they are?
- A perfectly good pressure cooker—with the exception of its handle, which is broken.
- A small coffee table I made for Emily who returned it asking me to fix a leg that was broken. It might be easier to make a new one than to repair the leg.
- A box containing several strings of Christmas lights I'd forgotten. They'd have to be untangled and tested. It would be wasteful but easier to throw them out and buy new ones.
- Two pairs of skis. They were Head Masters. Once upon a time, you were king-of-the-hill if you had Head Masters. They still look good but the president of the company, Howard Head, went from skis to tennis rackets and Head Master skis are now in a category with wooden golf clubs and white tennis balls. Perfectly good though. You never know.
- A five-gallon can of kerosene, almost full. The kerosene heater stopped working two winters ago and I threw it out. I don't know how to throw out kerosene.
- A big box with an assortment of snow boots and rubbers belonging to various members of the family, some of whom have left home. No one wears rubbers on rainy days anymore anyway.

My life, like my garage, is filled with things I should decide about whether to keep or discard. My clothes closets runneth over.

Pieces of paper too good to throw away but not worth keeping are crowding me out of my office. Books and magazines I mean to read are piling up in the living room. In the basement I have stacks of scripts I wrote for Garry Moore, Arthur Godfrey and Harry Reasoner.

This dilemma so many of us face is not limited to individuals. Cities and whole countries are constantly faced with the problem of what to save and what to tear down and throw away. Florence and Vienna are awash with evidence of past grandeur, trapped by their glorious past. It creates income in the form of tourist dollars but the upkeep is more than they can pay for. Reverence for their past inhibits progress for the future. Maybe they should build a glass dome over Florence and move to a new place with empty lots.

Every community in America has an argument going on somewhere in town between the conservationists who want to save an old building and the developers who want to tear it down so they can build a bigger, modern one. It isn't so much different from the problem I have in my basement, my garage, my office.


## FIXING THINGS


We are making things faster than we can fix them when they break. The problem comes from the fact that making things is a production-line job and fixing them is different every time.

On a production line, all a worker has to know is one job and it doesn't take much skill. It may be how to bolt a piece of steel to another piece of steel or how to attach one set of wires to the proper terminals. When something breaks, the person doing the repair has to inspect whatever it is, determine what's wrong and then figure out what to do to fix it.

Almost everything needs fixing at one time or another but infrequently enough so you do not establish a relationship with the person who, for example, puts new grout in between the stones on the patio, replaces the gutter that redirects the rain from the roof or replaces complicated hinges on kitchen cupboard doors.

Fixing something takes a lot more ability than making it in the first place. That's why mechanics, plumbers and electricians are so scarce and expensive. They know how to do something. The time is coming when the plumber will command a higher salary than the bank president and rightly so.

It has become difficult to see things on the shelves in our garage because the light that used to go on automatically when the door went up, no longer does. I replaced the bulb but the problem was not with the bulb. It was some other problem. Who fixes garage lights that turn on automatically when the door goes up? Not the same person who puts cement in between the pieces of slate on the patio.

When I got discouraged with the problem with the garage light one Saturday, I came inside and went to the basement where I've been meaning to go through all the old color slides I took of the four kids as they were growing up. We had two slide projectors, one carousel style made by Kodak. I tested that and the little fan that keeps it from overheating came on but the projection light did not. I figured the bulb was dead so I unscrewed the back and removed the strange-looking bulb. Manufacturers do not anticipate anyone keeping a piece of equipment for 10 years and I doubt that they still make that bulb.

The second projector is a Bell and Howell. Slides are stored in a two-inch square cube that drops one slide at a time in front of the lens. That bulb was dead, too. Or at least I *think* it was the bulb. Of course, it may not have been the bulb at all. It's damp in the basement and who knows what happens to projectors in damp basements.

Discouraged, I abandoned the plan to look at the old slides and made myself a tuna fish sandwich which I took to the living room to see if there was a game on television. I turned the set on but the clicker that changes channels didn't change the channel. I thought there was something wrong the other night. It hasn't been working right. Or I think it's the channel-changer that's not working. It could be a problem with the cable that comes into the house. Or maybe there's something wrong with the television set itself. It's eight years old. Maybe I'll call the TV repairman. Or would it be cheaper to just buy a new television set?

After lunch, I decided to set up the card table and go through the boxes of pictures by hand. I noticed the card table was unsteady so I turned it over and found that a hinge on one of the legs was broken. Right after I find someone to cement the patio and fix the light in the garage, I'll go to the store, try to find bulbs for the projectors, look at new television sets and see if I can get a hinge for the card table. Or maybe I should throw the card table away and buy a new one. That's the American way.

## THE DROSS OF DRAWERS

All the little drawers I have in all my desks, chests, bureaus and tables are full. They are filled with things that I hardly ever use but which are too good to throw away.

Last weekend I was determined to make room in a couple of drawers in the top of the chest where I keep clean shirts, pajamas, socks and underwear. The two drawers are relatively small, being only four inches deep, and they fill up because, when I feel obliged to clear off the top of the dresser to neaten things up, I sweep everything into one of them.

I made a list of items in one of the drawers:

- Three nickels, 17 pennies, two 50-cent pieces and a Susan B. Anthony dollar.
- Quite a few elastic bands of different sizes. I hate paper clips and staples but I like elastic bands and try to have one or two in my left-hand pants pocket—especially on weekends.
- More than a dozen pencils and seven ballpoint pens, most of

which have dried up. I took them to the bathroom and put the tips under hot water for a minute or so. I threw the ones that still wouldn't write into the bathroom waste basket with the used Kleenex. It serves them right.

- Two dry cleaning slips for clothes that I have already picked up by signing for them because I didn't have the slips with me.
- Several paper matchbooks with names of famous restaurants on them. The places are Chasen's in Beverly Hills, The 21 Club in New York, Forno's Ovens in San Francisco, Los Olivos in Scottsdale.

    These matchbooks must be quite old because a lot of the restaurants probably don't have them on the tables anymore and Chasen's is closed.

- Two nail clippers I've been looking for.
- Three keys I don't dare throw away because I can't remember what they unlock.
- A small cardboard box from Tiffany that some piece of jewelry came in many years ago. I keep the studs to my dress shirt in it. I wear my tuxedo several times a year—some years. The heavy gold cufflinks with the initials W. S. R on them were my father's—Walter Scott Rooney. I'll eventually give them to my son, Brian Scott Rooney—although I don't know when he'll ever wear a tuxedo.
- A Timex which I wear when I'm woodworking so I don't get sawdust in my good watch and an expensive watch CBS gave me which I don't like because it only has dots where the numbers should be and no sweep second hand.
- Two political buttons. One says ELECT WILBUR MILLS PRESIDENT. The other reads just DOLE.
- A small leather strap with a snap at one end and a loop at the other that I took off a camera I own. The first thing I do with anything I buy that has straps is take them off.
- A cheap pair of dark glasses with only one earpiece.

- Two cases for glasses, given to me by the optometrist the last two times I bought a pair. I don't use glass cases but I don't throw them away, either.
- A tiny sewing kit that I took from the bathroom of a hotel.
- Eight or ten folded pieces of paper with writing on them. They are either lists of things I've meant to do on some Saturday in the past or ideas for a column or a *60 Minutes* piece.
- A whistle, three pairs of chopsticks still in their paper envelope, a roll of film I forget whether I ever shot pictures on and an old razor that takes a single-edge blade. I'm not sure you can buy them anymore.
- Two jackknives. There are more somewhere around the house. I just like the idea of having a jackknife. Some of them are clever and nicely made and the fact that I hardly ever use one isn't the point. My pleasure is in having them, not using them. The jackknife business must be having a hard time because a man has to be careful not to have one in his pocket by mistake when he goes to the airport.
- Two old pictures of myself not looking as good as I prefer to think of myself as looking when I was young.

At the bottom of the left-hand drawer were one black shoelace, two loose aspirin tablets and a bottle of dried-up red nail polish that I used several years ago to put on the keys I carry so I could tell one key from another.

I'm going to throw out the dried-up nail polish along with the ball point pens but everything else I put back in the drawer.

Who knows when I may need this stuff?

# A GREAT PILE OF PILES

It's not clear whether putting things in piles helps or not. I put different things in different piles and what I end up with is a pile of piles.

At the end, I don't know which pile is which or what's in one pile and what's in another. I need a pile file but cannot find one in any stationery store.

There are many accessory tools that go into the making of a paper pile. When I do my taxes, for example, I organize papers by holding certain groups of them together, not with paper clips, but with elastic bands.

Folders are a good addition to a pile of papers but the metal device known as a staple, invented in the late 1920s if memory serves me, are a curse on mankind. Hardly anyone in all history has ever stapled papers together that he or she didn't subsequently regret when, again he or she, discovered they had to be separated.

Fortunately for mankind, shortly after the invention of the staple gun, someone realized their mistake and undertook the task of inventing the staple *remover*. Statistics show that removers have been used on 87 percent of all the staples ever employed. A relatively simple device, the remover will likely go down in the annals of good inventions as one superior to the stapler itself. (This might also be said of the eraser on lead pencils. If forced to choose between having just a pencil or just an eraser, I would choose the eraser.)

Elastic bands, also known as rubber bands, have many uses besides holding pages of income tax information together. They are more helpful than either paper clips or staples in organizing piles of a wide variety of papers. I separate papers in envelopes from loose papers although I do not have a real plan for which things I leave in their envelopes and which things I remove from them. The one clear drawback to rubber bands in holding together a pile of papers is that the pile must be a substantial. A flimsy little pile of papers cannot withstand the ability of the rubber band to contract, pulls together the pages and makes a roll of them. You cannot pile rolled papers.

After I get more piles of paper than will fit on my desk and still leave room for my telephone, I get a box and pile the piles in that. Then I take the box and pile it on top of another box of papers. Four tall is the highest it is practical to pile boxes of papers although I have gone as high as six. A box with its top is about 12 inches high so it is not practical for a person 5 feet 9 inches to pile storage boxes higher than he is. (I say "He is . . ." but you understand I also mean "She is.")

The piles of papers in my basement at home are, generally speaking, higher than those in my office. My basement is not a public place and I am less concerned about what it looks like because it only looks like that to me. No one else sees it.

It is my constant thought that "someday" I will have time to go through all my papers, save the good stuff and discard the junk. I have not set a deadline for accomplishing this and, of course, I worry. It has recently occurred to me that "someday" may never come.

What I've tried to do today is pass on to readers all the information and experience I've accumulated over the years in how to organize your life and all the papers in it.


## VACATION

May and June are the months I enjoy my vacation the most.

My vacation doesn't begin until July but looking forward to it is the best part.

Once a vacation begins, I can't keep myself from counting the days until it ends and that diminishes the pleasure of it. It always goes so fast. I can remember thinking that when I was eight. In July the sun starts coming up later and going down earlier. There's a depressing dwindling sense about the afternoon shadows in late July. It's no longer Spring. The longest day of the year should be in August, not June.

The end of my vacation hangs over my head in July like the income tax deadline in April or a dental appointment in January. As the days dwindle down (to a precious few), it's depressing to realize that what I've been looking forward to for so long, is almost over.

There are some things you can do to lengthen your vacation. Or, at least, give it a sense of length. For instance, it's best if you don't have dates when you have to do something or go somewhere. Dates that interrupt a month make a vacation shorter. If it's interrupted by someone's wedding in another city or by a dental appointment, it divides your days off into little compartments. A good vacation is one during which nothing happens so eventful that you can remember it when you get back to work and people ask "What did you do on your vacation?"

We start going to our summer house on weekends in May and keep on going weekends right through September but for all of July and for three or four days I steal on each end of the month, we're there seven days a week. No commuting. We have an extra bedroom so we can accommodate guests but I don't like having guests during my vacation. If we have friends come to visit us, it's usually on weekends before or after my July vacation. That way, they don't interrupt my vacation. I like having them, mind you, but not during my vacation.

There's a big difference in guests. I like the ones who get up when they feel like it without worrying about "what time do you have breakfast?"

I like guests who don't want to do what I want to do but feel free to wander off on their own. When people are visiting, I don't want to be a tour director. The best guests do what they feel like doing. After breakfast, they may volunteer to drive over and get the newspapers 12 miles away and not show up until several hours later for lunch. I am very fond of guests who enjoy a nap after lunch. If they want to play tennis toward mid-afternoon, that's fine. If it isn't too hot, I'll join them unless they're real good—in which case I'll get someone else to play with them.

Book-readers make good guests. They don't want you to bother them with suggestions like "Would you like to walk down to the lake?" or "There are some good antiques shops in Schuylerville." They're engrossed in their book. The man who won't move from in front of the television set while there's a ball game on makes a satisfactory weekend visitor.

I'm hoping no one we invite to stay with us is going to read this but I don't like guests who stand around asking whether there's anything they can do. If someone asks whether there's anything he or she can do, there almost never is because the people who ask that question aren't the kind of people who know how to do anything.

There shouldn't be many decisions to make on vacation. It's best when the biggest question you have to answer during the day is "What do you want for dinner?" or "Do you need anything at the store?"

Every year I bring several boxes of letters and miscellaneous pieces of paper from my office to go through. I have never yet gone through them. That's what a vacation is for—not doing things.

## THE OLD OAKEN CHAIR

When I left the office a little early Friday, everyone said "Have a nice weekend." They didn't mean it. They were just pointing out that I was leaving early. Having someone say "Have a nice weekend" doesn't usually seem to have any effect one way or another on my weekends but this time it worked. I had a great weekend.

On my last trip to the dump 10 days ago, I brought the garbage, the bundled newspapers and a box of cans and bottles. As I was unloading my Jeep, I saw an old oak desk chair, on top of a mountain of debris. It had been thrown away by someone who didn't want to deal with a chair that needed help. I climbed over several piles of assorted junk, grabbed the chair and pulled it out of the dump so I could get a better look at it.

It was the kind of a chair a lawyer or a sheriff would have sat at in an old cowboy movie. An antique shop would have labeled it "circa 1880" but it's probably more like 1920.

It was well-built. The four slanting legs get their support from each other and from the two rungs that run between the front legs and the front and back legs. An ordinary chair would have had one rung between each leg.

Superficially, this chair was a wreck. The finish was either gone or peeling off. The five-inch wide oak boards from which the formed seat was made, had cracks an eighth of an inch wide between them and, while I told you there were two rungs between each leg, I didn't mention that one rung on the left side, was missing. I loved it.

The gracefully bent oak arms were perfect. There were nine three-quarter-inch oak rounds running from holes drilled in the back edge of the seat up to holes in the underside of the gracefully curved steam-bent piece of round oak. They formed the back. I lowered my old khaki pants into it at the dump and it was good to sit in. I loaded it up and took it home. Margie hates it when I come back from the dump with more than I took.

Saturday morning the first thing I did was slather the chair with paint remover. With a putty knife, steel wool and a coffee can with turpentine, I got most of the old finish off.

Next I set out to replace the missing rung. I cut a piece of oak one inch square and 18 inches long from a nice board I had, mounted it on my lathe and turned it round but slightly barrel-shaped, trying to match the three-quarter-inch thickness of the other rungs. I squeezed glue into the holes for the rungs and into every crack in the seat. With seven long bar clamps I pulled the chair together until glue oozed out everywhere.

The only indication of the maker of this chair so long ago were the initials "E. C." scribbled large on the underside of the seat in thick blue pencil marking. I wish I knew who you were, E. C. You made a great chair.

You can daydream at night. Saturday night in bed I thought about taking my chair to *Antiques Roadshow* for a television appearance.

I'd show the chair I salvaged from the dump to the expert. He'd admire its craftsmanship and my restoration.

"How much did you pay for this chair, do you recall ?" he'd ask.

"Nothing," I'd say proudly. "Picked it off the dump."

"And do you have any idea how much it's worth?" he'd ask.

"I have no idea," I'd say, the way they always say it on the *Antiques Roadshow*.

"Well, Andy," the antiques expert would say, looking at the initials under the seat, "E. C. is the mark of one of the outstanding chairmakers of the 19th Century. This chair is in near-perfect condition. If it were put up for auction, it should bring between $12,000 and $14,000."

"Gosh," I'd say. "I had no idea."

Then I'd pack up and take it home because I wouldn't sell it for a million dollars.

As I write, I am sitting in my beautiful, free, old oak chair, completely restored.

That's as good as a weekend gets.


## A VICTIM OF THEFT

In recent months, I have been the victim of a series of unusual and disturbing thefts. Someone is following me.

Last Friday, I attended the Writers Guild annual dinner at a prestigious New York hotel. ("Prestigious" means expensive.) I brought my cell phone as I often do. After the event, featuring the great Mort Sahl as speaker, I went to my car which I had parked a few blocks from the hotel and drove home. I did not use my cell phone.

The following morning I looked to make sure I had it as I left the house. It was nowhere to be found. I looked in all my pockets, the dresser drawers and hall table. I decided I must have locked it in the glove compartment of the car. I went to the car, unlocked the glove compartment— no telephone.

It was at this point that I realized what must have happened to it. When I checked my coat in the hotel, I deliberately left the phone in the pocket. I was scheduled to speak and did not want the bulk of the cell phone bulging in my tuxedo pocket. I bulge in enough places without it.

When I retrieved my coat, I thought the person in the check room seemed a little suspicious. He spoke little English—which always seems suspicious to me. He never looked me in the eye, either. Aha! It struck me like lightning. Obviously he had gone through my coat pockets and taken my cell phone. He was making extra money by searching through the pockets of the checked coats for valuables. I would call the hotel and ask if they had been having reports of thefts involving their coat room.

Later, before I had a chance to call the hotel, I got back in my car to drive to the office. I felt some object under my brake pedal. Reaching down, I found my cell phone on the floor of the car where I had dropped it.

This was not the only instance of my being victimized by a thief. A week later I parked my car on 85th Street in New York City. Six hours later I went to get it. The car was gone! I walked the whole block and there was no doubt about it. My car was not where I parked it.

I had a car stolen before and now I had the same sinking feeling. The insurance company would probably cancel my coverage or double my premium. So much trouble, so much paperwork. Dealing with the police would be a pain.

As I started to walk back to the office, deep in pained thought about what to do, I walked down 84th Street. Eureka! There was my car. The thief must have taken it from 85th Street, gone for a joy ride and then returned it to 84th Street.

Over the years, I have been the victim of countless thefts like those. I leave valuables like a wristwatch on my desk in the office at night and, in the morning, the watch is gone. Obviously the work of the cleaning people . . . or, wait a minute. There's the watch over on the table across the room.

People take my keys all the time. I don't know why people keep stealing my keys but that's what happens. The keys are no good to them because they don't know which doors they unlock but that's what they do all the time, they take them. They take them and then put them down somewhere else.

Someone has even stolen food from our refrigerator. There have often been things that I know are in there but when I look, they're gone. This kind of petty thievery has had a constant, negative effect on the quality of my life and if anyone has information leading to the arrest and conviction of the people who have been stealing from me, please let me know.

# A NOT VERY
# GRAND LARCENY

Because it took no talent on my part, I was disappointed that nothing I've ever done got me more attention than having my car stolen out of our driveway.

Newspapers everywhere and radio and television stations told of the great heist. People stopped me on the street to commiserate. In the cafeteria at work, the following conversation was typical:

"Hey! Hiya Andy" said someone I've seen but don't know. "Did they steal your car?"

"Yup," I said, hoping he'd drop it there.

"They stole your car, huh?"

"Yup."

"Took it on ya, huh?"

I nodded.

"I read about it in the paper. Sonovagun. Right out of your driveway. It was in the paper."

So far, he hadn't told me anything I didn't know.

"Where did you hear about it?" I asked.

"The paper. I read it in the paper."

"The NEWSpaper?" I said.

"Yeah. They took it out of your driveway."

I am perplexed over why people seem so interested and even pleased to know my car was stolen.

It was the first expensive car I'd ever bought, a BMW. It cost me $35,000 and, while I liked it I wasn't sentimentally attached to it the way you are with some cars.

The car was left in the driveway instead of the garage because Margie had broken her wrist and couldn't drive. When the car is in the garage, it's difficult to put the garbage out. The garbage is normally put out after I leave for work in my old Jeep so I left the BMW in the driveway to make it easier for Margie to get the garbage out. I'm good to her.

When I came home, I left the Jeep in its regular place in the driveway and went upstairs to change my clothes. I had forgotten to pick up the newspaper in the driveway so I went out to get that. It was the first I'd noticed the BMW wasn't there.

Margie likes having a car "serviced" and I thought she had taken it to the "service station." (I'm less enthusiastic about having a car serviced because I've never known what they do.)

The keys had not been left in it although I think people worry too much about car keys. I asked a cop how long it takes a car thief to start a car without a key. He said "About thirty seconds." If you left your keys in the car and had one stolen every five years, it would be less trouble than car keys are when you forget where you put them.

I reported the theft to our insurance company and local police and an efficient policewoman showed up to ask questions I couldn't answer like "What was the license plate number?"

In view of how little help I was to the police, I was surprised the next morning to get a call saying "Your vehicle has been recovered." Cops don't find stolen cars. They recover vehicles.

"The interior has been stripped and the wheels are gone," the officer said. "It's in bad shape."

I called the garage that had picked the car up off the street in a town

20 miles from us. A police officer in the vehicle theft office told me that after they strip a car in a garage thieves take it out of their neighborhood, remove the wheels and abandon it. He also told me cars like old Hondas were more of a target than BMWs because there are a lot of them so parts are needed. He also said the parts for different years are often interchangeable on a Honda. This didn't make me feel any better at all about my all-but-destroyed BMW.

When the insurance company asked what was in the car, swindle crossed my mind. Cheating an insurance company is not considered dishonest in America. What about the expensive wristwatch I had just bought that I left in the glove compartment? And wasn't my brand new Nikon in the car?

My virtuous self emerged triumphant and to the question "What was in the car of value?" I answered "Nothing."

I do have something I'm reluctant to tell you about all this. The insurance company was great. They settled quickly and gave me a very fair amount although I don't suppose it was more than 5 percent of what I've paid them in premiums over the past fifty years.

Not only did the insurance company pay me fairly, several days later an agent showed up at our front door with a cardboard box containing things I'd left in the car that didn't interest the thieves. There were several books, two baseball caps, a screwdriver and a June 1997 *Time* magazine. No wristwatch, no Nikon.


## THE GREAT
## PICKING UP PROBLEM

The important question each of us faces every day is this: Should you clean up when you finish or wait until later?

How we answer this question, divides a nation. Some of us clean up and some of us do not. I don't. I leave things where they are because I may need them in the morning and, anyway, even if I don't I'll feel more like cleaning them up in the morning.

Beginning very early in the day, people start dividing themselves into Group A or Group B. Group A cleans up a mess just as soon as they finish making it. Group B leaves everything where it is until some other time.

Group A people make the bed almost as soon as they get out of it. Group B leaves it at least until after breakfast and possibly until they come home at night and get ready to climb into it again. Or never. That's the other thing Group B people do with beds; they don't make them at all.

When Group A people come downstairs they have a good, wholesome breakfast that's properly balanced and nutritious. They use skim milk on their cereal and then they get right up from the table, wash the dishes and put them back on the shelf where they belong.

Group B people make coffee, get something out of the refrigerator, gulp it down and head for work because they're late. They leave the dishes on the table or, at the very most, pile them in the sink.

Group A people may also put their dishes in the dishwasher. Group B people don't use the dishwasher.

When Group A gets to the office or wherever they work, everything is neat and tidy because that's the way they left it late yesterday afternoon. Group B left everything right where it was and it's a mess but they go right to work without having to get anything out.

There has never been a study done on which group accomplishes the most in life. It is assumed to be the Group A people but this assumption is made by Group A people who do this kind of thing.

This whole subject comes to mind this morning because I was making a table in my shop yesterday. We were going to the house of some friends for dinner and I worked so late that I had to drop all my tools right where I'd been using them and take a shower.

When I got back at making the table the next day, I needed some of the tools I had left out but others cluttered up my work space. I couldn't decide whether I wish I'd cleaned up or not. On the one hand, I'd like to start fresh with every tool hanging where it belongs but, on the other hand, it would have taken me a long while to put everything away and half the stuff I'd have to get out again when I go back at it.

I know people who will read a book at night and, when they finish with it, they'll close it and put it back on the bookshelf. If I'm reading a book, I leave it on the table, open to the page where I stopped reading. I usually put it face down on the pages I was reading with the front and back covers up.

We don't put things back in the box they came in. Usually we don't even keep the box and, if we do, we put something else in it.

We don't file things, we pile things. Quite often, although not always, we can find what we're looking for. Group A can find something quicker but if you add the time it took them to put it away carefully in the first place, I contend we're ahead.

Group A people coil the cord on any appliance they use into a butterfly shape and then they stick the end with the two plugs on it through one loop so it stays coiled up.

Group B puts the appliance in the closet with the cord hanging loose.

There's no question that Group A are more admirable people but as an advocate of my peers in Group B, I think it's possible we get more done. We don't sweat the small stuff.


## THINGS TO DO TODAY


What I think I'll do this weekend is catch up on some things I've been meaning to do. I've got to answer a couple of letters. First though, I better take that stuff in the garage to the dump because the dump is closed tomorrow.

We may be out of big plastic bags. If I'm going to the dump, I'll need those so I'll stop over at the store first.

The car looks terrible with that drop of bird doo on the hood from where I parked it under the tree. I'll hose it down before I go.

Give it a quick wash.

I ought to vacuum the inside after I wash it. There are still needles in back from the Christmas wreath I bought.

I may need gas. I have enough money for gas, I think. I have $30 with me.

Wait a minute though. $30 isn't going to get me far over the weekend. Not if I buy gas first. I'll stop by the bank and cash a check.

While I'm at the store getting plastic bags to put the junk in to take to the dump, it might be a good idea if I got some something for lunch. Tunafish maybe. There isn't much in the refrigerator. Come to think of it, I'm hungry right now. Maybe that's what I'll do. I'll fix myself something to eat before I get the gas to go to the store to get the plastic bags for the junk I'm going to take to the dump after I wash the car and vacuum the inside.

I should read the paper this morning. I wish I were doing a better job reading the newspaper. Yesterday's is still here because I didn't finish it. Hardly started it really. There was something in the Sunday paper I meant to cut out. I'll unwrap the bundle of papers I tied up this morning before I take them to the dump to see if I can find it. I think it was Sunday . . . maybe Saturday's paper though. I forget what it was but I remember I meant to save it.

I did read the story about the Vice President yesterday and I want to talk to Charley about that. I'll call him when I go in the house to get some lunch before I go to the bank with the check to get some money so I'll have enough for the weekend after I buy gas to go to the store to get the bags for the dump.

I should stop off at the post office, too. While I'm there I want to remember to get some four-cent stamps to put on those stamped envelopes I have because of the increase.

Speaking of mailing letters, did I pay the phone bill the other day ? I'll look in my desk before I go anywhere to see if I paid the cable com-

pany, too. That knob came off my desk drawer where I keep my checks
and I want to go to the hardware to see if I can get another one like it. I
think the knob came off because the drawer isn't sliding very smoothly
anymore. I ought to take the drawer out and spray it with WD-40—if I
have any. I may have used it up on the lawnmower. Which reminds me,
I have got to cut the grass before it rains. I think I have gas enough for
the mower. I'll check because if I don't, I can get some when I go to get
gas for the car so I can go to the store to buy the plastic bags before I go
to the dump.

It was late when I went to bed last night. Letterman. Maybe I'll take
a little nap after I have some lunch before I go get gas so I can go to the
hardware to get the stuff for the drawers so I can look to see if I paid the
phone bill before I go to the post office.

That's what I'll do. I'll take a little nap.

## ONE DAMN BIRTHDAY
## AFTER ANOTHER

Someone said "I see you celebrated your birthday yesterday."

"No," I said, gracelessly. "I HAD a birthday yesterday. There was
nothing celebratory about it."

It's true. I do not take birthdays lying down. I hate them.

It's hard to say at what age you reach the top of the hill and start
down the back side. You reach the top physically and start downhill
much sooner than you reach your intellectual peak. Or, at least that's
what people my age like to believe because evidence of our physical
deterioration is evident to everyone while any mental decline that takes
place is not so apparent.

I often try to assess my intellectual powers, now that I've passed 80,
and compare them with what I had when I was 20, 50 and 60. I don't
notice any diminution in them although I realize I'd be the last to notice

if they were gone. There are some small indications that I might be losing it a little but I dismiss those. They are based on minor memory lapses on my part and I don't deny those. Forgetting a few things doesn't bother me. I have filled my life full and have a great deal to remember.

The clearest evidence of age is how eagerly I look for evidence that I haven't slipped. I relish the newspaper story reporting the success of the 94-year-old scientist, novelist or marathon runner. At football games, I used to cheer for Ottis Anderson because he was the oldest running back in the league at 34.

There has always been propaganda in favor of the idea that wisdom comes with age but you can bet no one young started the rumor. The truth is that a person 80 is a totally different person than a person 20 and a comparison of their intellect is as impractical as comparing the home-run hitting ability of Babe Ruth with that of Sammy Sosa. If the young person makes the mathematical calculations quicker, the old one says he understands what they mean better. At my age I take the position he's right. Old people shouldn't let young people take the world away from them.

I look back, with some satisfaction, on what an idiot I was when I was 25. When I do that, I'm assuming I no longer am one. Were I to live another 80 years, I'm sure I'd look back at 2003 and wonder how I could have been so stupid way back then.

If there is one sign of my age that bothers me more than others, it's my tendency to become more conservative in political and social opinions. I admire liberals more than conservatives and am concerned to see myself, more and more often, in agreement with the conservatives with whom I've always disagreed.

There is nothing good about birthdays and true friends would ignore them. My birthday was announced on some radio and morning television news broadcasts and, perhaps I'm too sensitive, but I notice a certain gloating in the voices of the people making the announcement. You seldom hear them give a birth date for someone younger than they are.

It's widely assumed that age is a defect and one from which no one ever recovers. I don't feel physically or mentally infirm and the only thing I reluctantly concede about my age is that I am, statistically speaking, closer to death than someone 70, 60 or 12.

When I was in high school, I got all choked up reading the poet, Edna St. Vincent Millay's verse:

*I only know that summer sang in me*
*A little while, that in me sings no more.*

I no longer choke on that, I gag. Pardon me for saying so, Edna, but these days your verse strikes me as pretentious hot air. Life—summer, winter, fall or spring—sings to me as it always did and I hate birthdays because I don't want the music to stop.

## I DID BUT I DON'T ANYMORE

Our lives run in cycles. There are a lot of things we used to do we don't do anymore. I don't:

- Go up stairs two at a time.
- Go down stairs two at a time.
- Bowl.
- Try to keep a diary. I tried for years and never got past February.
- Worry about wearing socks inside out or that match.
- Lie on the floor in front of the television set. It's harder to get up than it used to be.
- Wind a watch.
- Roll up the car windows by hand.
- Carry a fountain pen or a penknife.
- Read the New York Stock Exchange listings. I stopped looking when they all went down.

- I don't make paper airplanes much anymore.
- Use my CB radio in the car. All I could get was truckers and they never said anything I wanted to hear.
- Buy Tootsie Rolls or chew spearmint gum.
- Play Monopoly, Scrabble, bridge, chess, checkers or Michigan. I never did play pinochle, poker or backgammon.
- Wear white shoes, a vest, galoshes or bow ties. Adolphe Menjou was the only person I ever saw who wore spats and that was only in the movies.
- Smoke a pipe. I did for two years. I liked to think I looked good with a pipe and I enjoyed puttering with it but I got worried about my mouth.
- Own a cigarette lighter. I never smoked cigarettes but I used to like owning a lighter. It was a good toy.
- Use carbon paper.
- See how long I can hold my breath. I used to do it to make the time pass when I was driving. I'd see if I could hold it for a mile . . . or until I counted 10 Chevrolets.
- Pick up my check from the cashier. I have it sent directly to the bank now. I worked for 25 years before I was rich enough not to need the money the day they paid me.
- Wish I could play the piano or touch type. I wished I could do both for years but I've finally come to realize it will never happen so I've put it out of my mind.
- Wear a shirt just one day. Since the laundry started charging $1.50 to wash one, I often wear the same shirt two days in a row.
- Go to a movie that's half over and sit through the intermission to see the half I missed. It didn't bother me when I was a kid.
- Save matchbooks, pennies, tinfoil or empty jelly jars.
- Avoid stepping on a crack for fear of breaking my mother's back. I got over being suspicious of anything.
- Fold over a little corner of the page of a book I'm reading when I decide to go to sleep. I hate it when someone else does it so I stopped.

- Whisper. I guess I don't have as many secrets as I used to. I haven't whispered in years. Who would I whisper to and what would I be saying that I didn't want anyone else to hear?
- Carry a linen handkerchief.
- Stay up past midnight Saturday night.

## LIVING WITH YOUR FACE

"Oh, I look so terrible, Andrew" my mother said, sitting in a rocking chair in our living room when she was 92 years old.

I forget what made her think to say it and she didn't look terrible to me. She looked like my Mother.

When *60 Minutes* starts its new year every September, it reminds me of a lot of things which I'd just as soon not be reminded of. Passage of time being chief among them.

For most of the summer, I sat in our living room Sunday nights and watched myself on reruns looking the way I used to look a year or two ago and thought to myself, "I looked better then."

The funny thing is though, when I look back at pieces I did for television 10 or 20 years ago, I think I look better now than the way I looked when I was younger. I looked funny and old-fashioned way back. What made me think my hair looked good that way? It's like looking at pictures of yourself when you were in high school. You're dopey looking.

You can't tell how you look from what people say. Strangers who see me on the street often say, "You look better in person." Then they go on to ruin the compliment by saying "But I thought you were taller."

Through the years my hair turned gray and the lines in my face got deeper. Inevitably, you get thinking about what you could do to look better, not so old. A few weeks ago a good, old friend of mine—he's older than good—looked himself in the mirror while I was standing near him and, pointing to some wrinkles, said "I think I'll have some of these removed. You know, not much."

All I said was "Don't do it."

There are about 450 plastic surgeons in New York, 750 in California and it says something about how different the cultures are in various parts of the Country to note there are only 69 in Minneapolis.

There isn't a person alive 60 years old who hasn't considered the possibility that he or she could use a little surgical help. I suppose I'd look better and younger. I could dye my hair dark brown, too.

The sad fact is, bad as we all look, if we look our age, we look better than if we try to do anything more about it than combing our hair and dressing neatly. I'll give women a little makeup and a hairdo.

I look at all the people I know or whom I've seen on television who have had cosmetic surgery and I know a surgeon working on wrinkles doesn't make you live any longer and I have yet to see anyone I thought looked better because of it. They look different and sometimes even younger but they seldom look better and they never look like themselves again. There is a strangeness about them that never goes away. They are just a tiny bit someone you don't know.

For some unaccountable reason it is often the best-looking people, the ones who need the least help with their appearance, who set out to get themselves improved, synthetically. Occasionally a television friend will disappear for a month or six weeks, offering some mysterious excuse, and when they reappear they have a different look. Their eyes don't look the same even though the surgeon didn't touch their eyes. When they smile, their face tightens into a shape I never saw before. There is a falseness to their appearance and, if it looks better to them it doesn't look better to me.

One of the most beautiful—okay, THE most beautiful—woman in television news had a job done on herself a few years ago and, while she doesn't look bad, she does not look the same or as good to me as when she had what must have seemed to her to be shortcomings. She looks as if she has been in a minor automobile accident.

When I look at myself on television these days and get thinking I look terrible, I think of my mother and take comfort from the fact that I may look terrible but at least I look like myself.

## OLD

I write using almost everything I know anything about.

One of the things I know a lot about but do not mention in my writing, is being old. It's such an unpleasant subject that I avoid it and hope no one will notice.

I avoid talk about the good old days, too. It not only makes the person doing it sound old . . . but, as we all know, if we're realistic, the good old days were no better than today's days.

One of the worst things about being old is how condescending people are toward you. They offer to help you do things you are capable of doing without help. If I want help, I'll damn well ask for it.

People try to make you feel better about your age by lying.

They tell you how good you look. I know how I look. I look old and old doesn't look good.

People trying to be nice say "What's wrong with being old?"

It's a dumb question to which I have a ready answer. "I'm going to die before you do, that's what's wrong with it."

When I was 10 I had already thought a lot about death. I was scared of it even then. "Nothing ever again" was the chilling thought that went through my mind. It still does.

For years I hoped I'd live to be 83. That was an arbitrary age I picked when it was so far off in my future that it didn't worry me.

Now, being 83, I am no longer anywhere near being ready to settle for dying in my 84th year. I am no more ready to die today than I was when I was 10.

It would be a comfort to me if I believed in a life hereafter but I don't. I notice that people who speak as though they do believe in it, behave as if they do not, too. When they get sick they go to a doctor to save their lives just as I do.

The least selfish thought I have about my eventual demise is immodest. I worry about how sad my family and a few close friends will be when I die. I hate to leave them without me. It's going to make them sad and lonely and that makes me feel worse for them than for me.

My doctor asked if anyone in my family had had cancer of the colon. I said my mother died of it.

"You better have a colonoscopy then," he said.

"Yes," I said, "but my mother was 94 when she died."

"Well," he said "You don't want to die of it when you're 94, either, do you?"

I had the colonoscopy. Now I'm worried that the *New England Journal of Medicine* will publish a report saying that colonoscopies cause cancer of the colon.

A few years ago I spoke in Columbus, Ohio, to an auditorium filled with about 2,000 members of some gerontological group. I told them that there's no doubt you lose some memory as you get older but, if you're lucky, you make up for it with experience. You get to know more.

For instance, I said, I ate in a restaurant in Columbus the night before and wished I could remember the name of it because with the experience I had I want to remember not to eat there again.

You have to think of ways to prevent age from depressing you—like in the middle of the night. Loss of memory is depressing and I have developed a theory that explains it in so satisfactory a manner that it no longer bothers me.

My theory is that the brain has a finite capacity. It can hold just so much information. When you get to be my age, you have put so much into it that your head overflows with facts and every time you add a name or a piece of information, it forces a comparable fact OUT of your brain.

That's where the things go that I can't remember.

It's not my age.

# PART 10

---

# *Animals*

*There aren't as many canaries in cages as there used to be.*

# WHERE HUMANS
# FALL SHORT

I was watching a spider hanging from a copper pipe over my workbench in the basement. We human beings have always considered ourselves to be the superior species on Earth because we can think and reason. However, when I look at what other animals, birds, bugs and insects can do that we can't do, I'm not so sure we are. That spider might have been looking down at me with a feeling of superiority because I can't exude a threadlike substance from my body and hang from a pipe by it.

When you come right down to it, most other living things do what they do better and with more singleness of purpose than we humans. Horses run faster and carry more. Elephants are bigger, stronger and don't eat meat. A bee dips lightly into the flower for nectar and goes back to its hive to make and store honey for months later when it needs food. We have to make a trip to the store.

Every day thousands of humans gather by the side of the lakes and the oceans with poles or they go out in boats to catch fish. They have all sorts of expensive equipment but, more often than not, they fail to catch a fish. The pelicans must laugh.

During a recent storm, a drain pipe leading down from our roof fell in our back yard and I contemplated climbing up to reattach it.

The pipe leading off the roof was above the second floor bedroom. I got out my longest ladder, leaned it against the side of the house and started up. The ladder was nowhere near tall enough so I started back down. On the way, I passed three ants and a slug making their way up the side of the house, bracing their little feet against nothing as they climbed. Ants don't need ladders. This is another case of the superiority of what we consider a lesser species.

On a trip I took a few weeks ago, I carried a suitcase, a briefcase and my laptop computer. The whole mess must have weighed more than 60 pounds. I weigh 200 but it was all I could comfortably carry. Out in the airport parking lot, a colony of ants seemed to have settled in a crack in the concrete near one of my tires. As I locked the truck of the car, I looked down and saw a black ant carrying away a piece of potato chip someone had dropped. It certainly weighed more than the ant. I've heard ants can carry nine times their own body weight. And here I was struggling with baggage less than a third my own weight.

George Bernard Shaw said that no matter how loud a dog barks, he can't tell you that his parents were poor but honest. Shaw's suggestion was that man is superior to dog. That may be true but over the weekend we stopped by to see our daughter Emily and our granddaughter Alexis and their great white English bulldog, Spencer. They all greeted us when we came in and were pleased to see us but none of them were as happy with our arrival as Spencer. Without saying a word, he made it abundantly clear how happy he was. His behavior in almost all situations expresses the condition of his psyche better than the rest of us express ours.

A great many people head for Florida in the winter to avoid the cold weather. Bears have a better and far cheaper way of getting away from the rigors of winter; they hibernate and it doesn't cost them a dime. Bears can slow down their metabolism and live off their fat for months. Why can't we choose to do that with our fat?

Of all the things on Earth that other species can do that humans cannot, flight would certainly be most desirable. There isn't one among us who hasn't dreamed of being able to soar above our problems and above the traffic like the birds do. Birds don't seem to make mistakes flying. You don't see birds crash-land, killing all on board.

It would be interesting to find out where insects, bugs, birds and animals stood on moral questions. We know some of them steal from each other. There are animals that kill other animals. Are there good robins and bad robins? Are there some bad ants?

# MY DOG IS SMARTER
# THAN YOUR DOG

Most people who have a dog think their breed is best and smartest. That's the way it ought to be. Humans should give back a little of the loyalty that dogs give so freely.

A college professor named Stanley Coren wrote a book called *The Intelligence of Dogs*. In it, Professor Coren ranks 132 breeds for what he calls "their obedience IQ." The professor gets off to a bad start here because a dog's willingness to be trained doesn't have anything to do with its intelligence. This is true to some extent with people.

Professor Coren says the border collie is the smartest dog presumably because it's easy to train to round up sheep. From what I've seen of border collies, they're not only dumb, they may be part crazy. We had a friend with a border collie and the damn dog kept circling the swimming pool in their back yard, looking for something in it to round up. No one who doesn't have 100 sheep to corral should want a border collie.

The next four smartest dogs, according to Mr. Coren, are the poodle, the German shepherd, the golden retriever and the Doberman pinschers.

Poodles seem to be nice, smart dogs. My objection to poodles is their owners. They fuss over their dogs more than most owners and the haircuts they give some of them make the dogs look ridiculous. Why do they enjoy making fools of their dog? If they cut their children's hair the way they cut their dog's, the kids would be sent home from school.

When I was a kid going to the movies on Saturday afternoons, one of the great heroes was the dog, Rin-Tin-Tin. We didn't call Rin-Tin-Tin a "German shepherd." He was known to us as a "police dog." All German shepherds were. The favorable impression of police dogs that I gained from watching Rin-Tin-Tin movies was sharply diminished after the Hessbergs across the street from us got a police dog of their own. He was no Rin-Tin-Tin, being half as smart and twice as mean.

After they got him I stopped going over to see if the kids could come out and play because I was afraid of being bitten.

At the Lake, our neighbors in the cottage next door had an Airedale named Bim. I didn't like Bim and he didn't care much for me. If we swam off the dock for an hour, he barked for an hour. They excused him on grounds he was worried about their safety but I never thought worry entered Bim's mind. He was a yapper.

My second favorite dog (I'm saving my favorite) in the world is the golden retriever. I've known two and I've stopped and shaken hands with hundreds of them walking the streets with their owners. They are invariably smart, friendly and personable. They like me and I like anyone who likes me, even dogs. Their temperament isn't much different than the black Labrador, another great dog.

I've never known a Doberman pinscher. They look mean and they have that reputation but I can't say. I'd never pat a strange Doberman on the head though. If there are Doberman pinschers, you'd think there might be some kind of pinschers other than Dobermans. Professor Coren doesn't say who Doberman was.

Now the bad part of this list. The professor says the dumbest dog is the Afghan hound and I don't think it's prejudice on his part because the book was written before we got into the unpleasantness in Afghanistan. Of all the pictures from there, I have yet to see an Afghan dog in Afghanistan.

The second dumbest dog, he says, is the basenji. I have no quarrel with his appraisal here because I've never known one of either breed. My outrage is reserved for Mr. Coren's selection of the third dumbest, the bulldog—also known as the English bulldog.

We're an English bulldog family. I grew up with Spike, a brindle bulldog. Our kids grew up with Gifford and our granddaughter Alexis is growing up with Spencer, a great white bulldog with brown ears and a heart of gold. Spencer summers with us.

One of a bulldog's outstanding characteristics is its disinclination to be trained. If you tell him to do something, he takes it under consideration and then does what he wants to do. I resent the suggestion that because he's not obedient, he's dumb. It's been my observation that, like dogs, the human beings who are easiest to train are usually the dumbest.

## HORSES, HORSES, HORSES

Most people own a dog at some point in their lives. I've known five dogs well but I've never known a horse. Horse-lovers may object but I don't think humans get to know horses the way they get to know dogs. It may have happened but it's not usual.

Everyone says horses are dumb. I hope so because if they're smart, they must often be heartbroken. They are passed from one owner to another all their lives until they're finally sold for a hundred dollars to someone who deals in horses for pet-food companies. That's what happens to old horses.

Years ago I was talking to a man on a farm in Colorado. One of his horses had been out in the severe cold over night and had frozen some of its parts. I shuddered.

I asked what they did with the horse.

"We had to sell him," he said. On a farm "sell him" is a euphemism for sending the animal to the slaughterhouse.

You sometimes read where the trainer of the Kentucky Derby winner says of his horse, "He's really intelligent." Racehorse owners and trainers have an understandable affection for an animal that has won them $10 million but the average race horse is swapped or sold dozens of times and the owner doesn't give it so much as a friendly pat on the nose goodbye. A claiming race is a way of handicapping horses by putting a pre-race purchase price on them. A horse may be sold dozens of times during a mediocre career at the track.

A trainer was arrested for killing or maiming show horses for a price so their owners could collect the insurance. In one case he broke a horse's leg by smashing it with a crowbar so it would look as if the horse hit a jump. That trainer is not typical but there are a lot of hard-hearted people in the horse business.

My mother used to tell about one of the saddest things in her young life. A circus came to her town, Ballston Spa, New York, and a wonderfully talented trick pony broke its leg in an accident. The circus had to move on without the injured animal and my grandfather bought the pony for $25.

He got a veterinarian to set the horse's leg, put it in a cast and fix up a sling in their barn to support the pony's weight while its leg healed. The pony died five days later and my mother never got over it.

The closest I ever came to knowing a horse was one Sunday morning in the country when I looked out the bedroom window and saw a huge, brown horse on our front lawn. (I call it a "lawn" but it's actually a collection of grass and assorted green weeds that we keep mowed.)

I had no idea what to do. I went out and approached the animal and it just stared at me, wide-eyed and innocent. I know mean dogs bite but I didn't know what a horse would do if it was mean.

"Here, boy !" I said, a sexist salutation because I hadn't even checked to see whether it was a boy or a girl. I don't know what I was calling it for anyway because I wouldn't have known what to do if it had come. All I know about horses I learned from Roy Rogers watching in cowboy movies when I was young.

Within a short time, the horse had drawn a crowd. You would have thought it was an elephant on our lawn. Several cars had stopped out front. There was no rope in our garage so I got a 20-foot, flat gray electrical cord with the foolish thought that I could throw it over the horse's neck and capture it.

When I moved toward him, he didn't run but it was apparent I was never going to get him with the cord. Finally two men I knew stopped in a pickup truck down front. They didn't know this horse but it was apparent they knew horses. One of them had a long, hemp tow rope. He walked directly up to the animal and spoke to it. The horse stood indifferently still while the man made a few quick motions with his hands. Before I could see what he'd done, the horse was neatly haltered with the rope over his nose and over his head. If horses are so dumb how come that horse understood that this fellow knew how to handle him and knew that I didn't? I'm unclear about the origin of the phrase "horse sense."

Someone finally located the woman who owned the horse and she came to get him.

"How old is he?" I asked.

"He's about 12, I think," she said. "He belonged to someone with two kids who left home and no one rode him anymore. They sold him to a riding stable but the stable decided to get rid of him so I got him cheap. He's a nice horse."

He was a nice horse without much personality but he doesn't have much to look forward to and I'll bet he wishes he was a dog.

## A BOY, A BIKE AND A COW

It was so long ago that I don't recall how old I was.

I must have been young because I didn't really read the newspaper. I did read Buck Rogers. It was the best action comic strip ever. Buck had a small pack strapped to his back, about the size of a dictionary, that enabled him to make jumps of 25 feet at one leap. While the feats of Superman finally dwarfed what Buck could do with his backpack, I never believed Superman but I did believe Buck Rogers. I have been waiting for inventors to produce the backpack that enabled Buck to make such great leaps. It's what I want most.

The only news story I read that day after I read Buck Rogers was of a boy on a bicycle who was coming down a hill when he hit a cow. There was a picture in the paper of the boy with his badly bent bike. The story did not report what damage, if any, the cow suffered. It may very well have sustained broken ribs. No one would ever know but the cow's ribs must have been sore for weeks. The bike was all but destroyed and the boy's father was demanding that the farmer, who let his cow stray onto the road, pay for a new bicycle.

Even at my age—no more than 10 certainly—I read great significance into this story. It was the first time I ever thought about the law. It seemed to me that it could not possibly have been the cow's fault and if it wasn't the cow's fault, how could it have been the farmer's fault? A bicycle rider, I remember thinking, had as much obligation to watch where he was going as a cow did.

Was there any law, I wondered, about cows using a road? Did a boy riding a bike have more right-of-way to a road than the cow? The cow couldn't have been going very fast. It was probably just crossing the road, having noted that the grass in the field on the other side was greener and longer than the grass in the field on its side, which had been pretty much chewed out by her companions in the herd. That is, if cows in a herd are at all companionable. Because of the inevitability of a cow's fate, we don't like to think about things like companionship among them. These were sophisticated thoughts for me to be having at 10.

This cow, taking off on its own to cross the road, must have been a loner. I admire that in a cow or in anyone else and I remember feeling worse for the cow than for the boy with the bike. The boy, on the other hand, upset with the damage to his bicycle, and his father, intent on retribution from the farmer, had no interest in whether the cow was hurt or not. Cows don't give away their feelings—except in extreme pain. That doesn't mean they don't have them.

If the boy, now a man my age, is still around, I wish he'd write and tell me what he thought—and whether or not his father collected damages from the farmer. The cow certainly didn't get in the boy's way on purpose. There is nothing in any way conniving about a cow crossing the road to get to taller grass. I never heard of a duplicitous cow.

This is the only time I have ever heard of a cow being hit by a bicycle. I don't know why it doesn't happen more often. There's no reason a cow should be leery of cars or bicycles until she is hit by one and I wonder how animals know enough to avoid being hit. Birds, with no experience being hit, get out of the way of oncoming cars. How would a cow or a bird know it would hurt if they'd never had the experience? Who would have told them? Is there word of mouth among cows? It can't be a fear they are born with because cows have been around longer than cars. Darwin notwithstanding, it's hard to believe animals are being born now with an acquired instinct that warns them against crossing roads for fear of being hit by a car—or a bicycle. That would mean the acquisition of a genetic trait in an amazingly brief period of time. It took millions of years for our ancestors to get up off all fours. Why should a cow have any inhibition about crossing a road for fear of being hit by a boy on a bike?

I don't know why our brains don't get filled up and refuse to take in any more information if a brain like mine can get cluttered up with 60-year-old memories of a newspaper story like that.

# PART 11

---

# *Travel*

*No matter how big your suitcase is, it's always a little small for what you're trying to get into it.*

# HOMETOWN U.S.A.

When I was growing up in the capital city of New York State, it never occurred to me that there was any other place named Albany. Over the years I began to hear about Albany, Georgia, and then Albany, California. Now I know there are 18 places called Albany in the United States.

If you think the name of your village, town or city is unique, you're probably wrong, too. There are 19,289 incorporated places in the United States and enough duplicate names to be a pain to the Postal Service. Of those, 9,716 are cities, 4,600 are towns, 3,736 are villages.

There's a wide variation from state to state in what can be called a city. In New York State, the biggest city is, of course, New York. It has 9,000,000 people. The smallest city in New York is called Sherrill with a population of just 2,864.

There are 62 cities in New York State and Montana has almost as many, 51. That's because a wide place in the road with 1,000 people can be a city in Montana. Montana doesn't have any villages, which seems too bad. In Virginia a place has to have a population of 5,000 to be called a city.

The most popular name for a community in America is a surprise. It's "Franklin" and he wasn't even President. There are 33 Franklins.

There are hundreds of places named after one of our Presidents— although they're named after only 15 of them. Those fifteen each have at least five places named after them. The latest President to have at least five places named after him was Wilson. There are a few Woodrows, too.

There are nine Roosevelts but all of them are old enough to have been named after Teddy, not Franklin. There are 31 places named Washington. There are 30 communities in America named Clinton. That's second only to Washington and ahead of Lincoln with 28, Madison with 27, Monroe with 27 and Jackson with 23. All of the places called

Clinton were named before Bill was President. There are no cities
named Bill.

Besides 18 Albanys, there are 21 Clevelands, 18 Buffaloes, 18 Hart-
fords, 15 Rochesters, 15 Nashvilles, 13 Atlantas, 12 Denvers, 12 Houstons,
11 Dallases, 10 Hollywoods and nine places called Miami. I wouldn't
want to live in a place called Miami, Ohio.

Salem is a popular name. There are 30 Salems and 28 Springfields.
There are 20 places named Columbus, another 20 named Columbia.

Cities and towns named "Fair" something are everywhere. There are
26 Fairfields and dozens of places named Fairmont, Fairmount,
Fairview, Fairdale, Fairbanks, Fairplay and Fair Haven.

Names of foreign cities get used a lot in this Country. There are 24
Troys, 15 cities named Paris, 13 Bethlehems, 10 Warsaws, some Viennas,
Cairos, Panamas and Londons.

Five towns are named California although none of them is in California and five are named Virginia and aren't there, either.

So, if you write, don't forget the zip code.


# AIRLINES


It is a mystery to me why anyone wants to go anywhere. Getting
someplace else is such a pain that staying put is an increasingly attractive alternative to travel. Flight, once a grand and exhilarating experience that took you out of your world and into another in hours, has
been turned into an event to be endured with clenched teeth. The terrorists, the airlines and the Government have teamed up to destroy
what was once a magic delight.

It occurred to me in an idle moment the other day that in my lifetime
I'll never see Australia. Too bad. I'd like to but twenty-one hours on an
airplane is more than I can stand to contemplate. I'd as soon be locked
in a tiger cage in the desert for a week with a flight attendant coming by
occasionally to ask if there's anything she can do to make me more com-

fortable. Flight attendants with four times as many passengers as they can accommodate, routinely announce that they are at our beck and call. Experienced travelers know that beckoning or calling a flitting flight attendant is futile.

It is difficult to understand why a service so much in demand as travel is unable to be a profitable and successful business. Both the airlines and the railroads are at bankruptcy's brink.

For years airlines provided infuriatingly bad service and our trains lagged light years behind European and Japanese rail service. Our anger was justified. Now we can only feel sorry for the airlines. They are victims of circumstances largely out of their control.

When I was young and broke, I often traveled by bus. Bus terminals were a synonym for sleazy. Airports have always been upscale in comparison. Tourist gifts and food are more expensive and the rest rooms are cleaner but the basic experience, waiting, is as unpleasant in airports now as it was in bus terminals then.

Ticket clerks are so busy and lines in front of them so long that you have to arrive two hours before the most routine flight to a city a short distance away to be assured a good place in line. Lines at ticket windows are not the work of terrorists. They are the result of a deteriorating airline economy. Airlines don't hire enough clerks. It isn't unusual to stand in line for an hour and a half, shoving your bag along the floor as you wait to be checked in. An airline's answer to any complaint is "We're thinking of your safety."

Making me show a photo ID and answering "no" to the ticket agent's question "Did anyone else put anything in your suitcase?" is not going to prevent a determined terrorist from blowing up the aircraft. Nothing is, and we might as well get used to it or stay home.

Politically, I vacillate between being a right-wing conservative and a left-wing liberal. I can go either way but my socialist tendencies come out when I think of airlines. Telephone service, railroads, power companies and airlines ought to be run by a Government monopoly.

There are too many things that make air travel disagreeable because the airlines are doing them badly. The average flight is late landing because it's late leaving. Airlines routinely fudge their on-time reports. Departure records note the time the aircraft's doors are closed, not actual takeoff time, which is frequently an hour later. Arrival time is listed as the second the wheels touch down, not the moment the doors are opened at the gate.

Flights are frequently canceled for mysterious reasons. The explanation is usually "A maintenance problem. We're thinking of your safety." I suspect it is more often that the flight is unfilled and uneconomical for the carrier to fly. What passenger can insist in the face of "maintenance problem"?

People are allowed to bring too much baggage on board. If an airplane holds 200 people, thirty of them block the aisle for more minutes trying to stow their junk in an overhead compartment that is already full. I believe that passenger planes are built with their overhead compartments full because I have never seen any room in one.

Airlines must either cut down on the baggage a passenger is allowed to carry on or invent a conveyor belt system for the overhead compartments.

"Thank you for flying with us" is the maddening announcement over the public address system at the end of a flight. It is apparently made by a flight attendant ignorant of the fact that hers was the only airline with a flight to the city you wanted to get to.

Airline employees are invariably pleasant and efficient. They maintain their composure dealing with a hostile, almost-always-angry clientele. Ticket agents and flight crews are not what's wrong with flight.

While I don't understand the airline business or its problems, I see them doing small things wrong that I do understand. It makes me suspicious of the intelligence they use with their major problems. One airline I have used frequently proudly serves "warm nuts." I am sitting strapped to my seat, a captive audience seething at being forced to listen to the commercials over the intercom after paying a fortune for my ticket, when a flight attendant offers "warm nuts." What food expert at the airline's home office decided warm nuts were a good idea?

The nuts are not so much warm, as they are soggy, having been put in a microwave oven that destroyed the nuts' appealing crunchiness. Did the airline soften the nuts for our own safety?

## GRACIOUS DINING IN FLIGHT

Nothing is more satisfying and fun than being a reporter. Tracking down facts is difficult but fascinating work. One sliver of information leads to another and the story opens up as you collect bits and pieces of the whole picture from different sources. It doesn't have to be a story of any great importance to be interesting to the reporter writing it; I got into biscuits several years ago.

It's easy to forget that airlines had fallen on hard times even before the threat of terrorism dominated the idea of flight.

You could see them pinching pennies years ago. In pinching pennies, they pinched customers. On a Delta flight from New York to Cincinnati, I was handed coffee and a little mystery package so well-wrapped we probably traveled 175 miles during the time it took me to get into it. I picked at it with my fingernails, poked at it with a sharp pencil and finally bit off a corner that opened it up enough so I could tear the wrapper off.

It was a biscuit two thirds the length of a stick of gum and about twice the thickness of one. Okay, maybe three times the thickness of a stick of gum. The label said it weighed three-sixteenth of an ounce. You know how heavy an ounce is? This was less than a quarter of how heavy an ounce is. It was not a hearty breakfast. Delta was not serving up scrambled eggs, toast and bacon or even pancakes and sausage with maple syrup. They gave me this biscuit and the announcement saying if there was anything they could do to help just ask. The flight attendants could have spent full time helping passengers get into their biscuits.

I ate the little biscuit and it was pretty good but I am puzzled by how many commercial food products that seem to have the same ingredients, taste so different. One ingredient in almost everything is "partially hydrogenated vegetable oil." The wrapper also said the little cookie is "all natural." I guess whether something's "natural" or not depends on your definition of natural. Hydrogenating vegetable oil doesn't seem natural to me.

I kept reading the writing on the biscuit's little plastic envelope. "Caramelised" was a tipoff that it was not made by an American company because we spell words like "surprize" and "caramelize" with a z, not an s.

The biscuit was distributed by a company called The Gourmet Center in San Francisco but aha! "Product of Belgium." That's where the s comes from. Belgium spells it the British way.

There was a lot of writing on the plastic wrapper considering how small it was. In the biggest letters it said "TO PURCHASE OUR COOKIES AND BISCUITS PLEASE PHONE 1 800 422 2924."

There's no doubt about it, a reporter is a naturally suspicious person. Good reporting is often based on suspicion. I am naturally suspicious. What I was suspecting was that Delta didn't even pay for this three-sixteenth of an ounce breakfast they were serving. I suspected that this Gourmet Center representing the Belgian LOTUS corporation gave Delta the cookies to hand out in exchange for the exposure it would give the name LOTUS.

Well, a reporter's suspicious nature doesn't always pay off. I was wrong and I owe Delta an apology. Let me tell you what this reporter found out.

I called the 800 number and Joyce answered. She told me that a box of 200 of the biscuits would cost me $18.95. I asked how much it would be if I bought 1,000 boxes. Joyce was taken aback and said she didn't handle wholesale. I'd have to speak with Gary, their sales manager.

Gary was nice. I asked him about buying 1,000 boxes of the biscuits like the one I had for breakfast on Delta. A box of 200 weighs about three pounds, he said, so 1,000 boxes would be heavy. He told me he could give me a price of $9.90 for each box.

Actually Gary's arithmetic doesn't work out. The way I figure it, 200 times three-sixteenths would be less than two and a half pounds so he must have been including the weight of the wrapping.

I decided to face Gary with my suspicion that the cookie was a promotion gimmick and that Delta hadn't paid anything for my breakfast.

"Do you give them to Delta?" I asked

"No," Gary said "They buy them from us."

So, that's the story. Delta pays $9.90 for a box of 200 biscuits. That comes to a little less than 10 cents each. Please accept my apology, Delta Airlines. This reporter has done you an injustice. I was sure you got my breakfast free and now that I know you paid almost a dime for it, I want to say how sorry—and hungry—I am.

## NOT HOME

One of the pleasant things to do in life is stay in a good hotel. One of the unpleasant things is to stay in a bad hotel. When the big hotel chains took over most of the hotels in this country, it meant the end of the variety of independent hostelries that ran from wonderful to terrible and instead assured us all of a fairly high level of mediocrity. They aren't bad is the best thing you can say about most of them.

I've made a list of good and bad features of hotel rooms I have known:

- Plastic cards instead of keys for opening doors is a step forward. I always felt bad when I left with the key, which was often.
- There is nothing consistent about the way you turn overhead lights and bedside and desk lamps on and off. Sometimes they all go on with the flip of a switch at the door. Sometimes each fixture has to be turned on separately. It's always hard to find the switch on a lamp because you don't know whether it's going to be one you

push, pull or twist. You don't know whether it is located at the base of the lamp, up near the bulb or on the cord leading to it. Light bulbs in hotel lamps are universally too dim. When Charles Kuralt was On the Road for CBS, he always carried two 100-watt bulbs to use in his room.

- There are high-tech developments in hotel rooms but architects who design hotels are not working with engineers who build them. The wiring is still often early 1930s. Hidden under every table or desk or behind each bed or television set, there is a knot of inaccessible electrical cords and wires. There is no convenient way to plug in anything of your own. It is as if they had planned on having only one light or appliance. In the average room there are three lamps, a television set, a coffee maker and a radio. If I want to plug in my computer I have to unplug something else.

- Towels in good hotel rooms are very good and plentiful. I judge a bath towel to be good if it is thick and luxurious and long enough from one end to the other to wrap around my waist while I shave.

- Bellmen who help you to your room with bags ought to be advised not to ask "How was your flight?" I go to the Super Bowl every year and I am invariably asked "Are you here for the game?"

  "No," I always answer, "I came to see my grandmother. She hasn't been well." They are sorry.

- There ought to be a hotel-industry standard for shower controls. It is quite possible to be burned or frost-bitten before you learn how to work the handles that control the heat and flow of the stream of water. The assumption is that you will test the temperature of the water coming from the bathtub faucet before you activate the shower—but it is quite often not easy to understand what turns the shower on and off. And, of course . . . you don't have your glasses on.

- I am always outraged when a hotel adds a 16 percent charge for room service in addition to a $2.50 "gratuity." Even then, you have the feeling that the waiter who brings your food expects a tip. You can hardly afford to eat breakfast in your room anymore. Usually it's so bad you can't eat it even if you can afford it.

- I'd trade that chocolate candy on the pillow at night for a good hard roll in the morning.

- At the newsstand a small roll of Tums is usually $1.25. At that price, Tums give me indigestion.

- Does anyone use all the drawers in a hotel room? I never put anything in one unless I'm staying at least four days, then I use one for dirty shirts, socks and underwear.

- By the time I've been in a hotel room overnight, I have things the way I want them. I put all the advertising junk that the management leaves around, into a desk drawer so there's room for my things.

    When the maid comes in while I'm out the next morning, she puts everything back the way the hotel wants it, not the way I want it. All the advertising literature is out of the drawer and back on top of the desk.

- With the exception of breakfast, it's best not to eat in a hotel dining room. This is unfair but if you want to see something of the city you're in, don't eat where you sleep. Filling out the card for your breakfast order and hanging it on the doorknob before you go to bed is a good idea except you never know what time you're going to want breakfast. At 11 p.m. you don't know what you're going to feel like eating at 8 a.m. either.

- While you're taking a chance ordering breakfast in your hotel room, the advantage is that you can hang around in your pajamas until after you've had it. You can go to the bathroom, shave, shower and dress before facing the world. It's a civilized way of starting a day.

- Of all the things that have gone up in price, nothing has gone up higher than the price of hotel room service. Not much to eat can cost you $27.50 plus a 17 percent tip and a $3.50 service charge. It's more than the room itself cost a few years ago.

- Even the best of our hotels don't seem to have worked out a system for removing the debris when you're finished. That accounts for all the unattractive trays of half-eaten food outside hotel rooms all across America.

I've stayed in five hotel rooms I'll never forget: the penthouse suite of the Fairmont in San Francisco, the Beverly Hills the night after I sold a book to MGM, the Relais Christine in Paris, the Connaught in London and the Metropole in Moscow. The Metropole was not memorable for the same reasons the others were.

## THEY NEVER SURVEY ME

I have never been asked a question by one of those surveys and, furthermore, I do not know anyone else who has been either. It's apparent that the sample number of people they survey is so small that they don't ever get to most of us.

The most striking thing about the surveys I see is how different the answers they get to their questions are from the ones I'd give if they had asked me.

For example, the editors of *Traveler* magazine say they have determined from a survey they took that Sydney, Australia, is what they call "the top destination in the world."

This is one more survey that I've been cut out of and which bears no relationship at all to me. I have no negative feeling about Sydney but it is 9,936 miles from where I live, as the crow flies, although a crow couldn't fly that far and probably wouldn't want to go to Sydney any more than I do anyway. It takes about 20 hours to fly there and 20 hours to fly back. I don't know how long it would take a crow to do it. I checked with American Airlines and they charge $4,526 for an economy roundtrip ticket. When people traveled by steamship, the word for economy was "steerage."

At the risk of being excluded from consideration as a member of the smart set, I hereby announce that I have absolutely no intention whatsoever of spending that many valuable hours of what I have left in my life, paying that much to go to a place I have no interest in getting to. Put that in your survey, *Traveler* magazine!

There are more places to see in the world than anyone has time to fly to and we can't break our hearts about never having been to Sydney just because *Traveler* says it's the place to go. Distance lends enchantment— but pick a closer city. Have the editors of *Traveler* ever been to Milwaukee? What about Bangor, Maine, or Buffalo? Not fashionable enough for a fancy magazine, I suppose, but darn good cities to visit.

I prefer visiting cities I've already been to. There are hundreds of those. I know the name of the main street—quite often "Main Street." I may know a good hotel there, a restaurant and that's about all I need. If I have a friend living there that I haven't seen in years, I'll probably call him as I'm leaving to say I wish we'd had time to get together.

It gives me great pleasure to go back to a city I know. I feel so proud of myself when I can find my way around a place I haven't visited in 17 years. This is the kind of satisfaction I look for when I travel. I don't know Sydney. I'm sure Sydney is a nice city but the name reminds me of a boy in my fourth grade arithmetic class who cheated and I'm adding it to a wide variety of reasons I'm not joining the *Traveler* crowd's rush to Australia.

In more of the same survey, the magazine has determined that Los Angeles has replaced Miami as the world's least-friendly city.

Charleston, S.C., is the most friendly. As a New Yorker, I defy any editor to prove to me that there is any city on earth less friendly than mine.

A city like Charleston gets its friendly reputation because when you go there, everyone asks "How do you like Charleston?" This isn't friendly. It's people looking for assurance from strangers that they live in a good city. Why don't they go about their business and leave strangers alone as we do in New York? What business of theirs is it whether I like Charleston or not? I didn't come to Charleston to hand out a lot of fatuous praise for a city I hardly know anyway. And, by the way, I like Charleston just fine. It's the people who keep asking me how I like it that I can't stand. New Yorkers don't care whether you like their city or not. There are already too many people in it and they don't want to interest more in coming there to live.

I am very suspicious of *Traveler* magazine for picking Sydney, Australia, because its distance is too closely tied to the magazine's own interests. If *Traveler* picked a favorite city that was just a bus ride from where you live, you'd hardly have to travel at all to get there. That's what makes me suspicious of this survey.


## BAD DRIVERS, NOT SPEED, KILLS


Being one, myself, it is natural for me to conclude that it is not usually the fast drivers who cause accidents. It is the slow, super-cautious, deadheads who cause accidents. I have no patience with what are mistakenly called "careful drivers."

It is the so-called careful driver who gets in the left lane moving at 12 miles an hour, starts to make a right turn and, well after he's into the turn, puts on his left-turn indicator.

Too often, careful drivers are not careful, they are inept. Their reactions are slow. They make decisions about which way to turn too late. They get in the way. They are as much of a danger on the road as the irresponsible nut who drives too fast and weaves in and out of traffic.

Twice a week during four months of the year, I drive 145 miles on a six-lane road with a lot of traffic. The speed limit was 60 mph from the time the highway opened about 50 years ago up until 1974. That year Congress passed a law setting 55 mph as the maximum legal speed anyone could drive in the United States. It was ridiculously slow on some roads in wide-open spaces and too slow on my road.

I have been arrested for speeding three times in 35 years. Not bad considering I've made the trip at least a thousand times and I've always driven at 65 to 68 mph.

In 1995 the Federal Government eliminated its blanket 55 mph speed limit and allowed States to set their own. Many states raised their limit—some to as much as 75 mph and several western states have no limit at all. There was great opposition to the move to raise speed limits from individuals and organizations that said there would be mayhem on the highways. They claimed there would be more accidents and more people killed in those accidents.

New York State, where I drive so much, raised its limit on its best and widest roads to 65 mph and it has substantially reduced the time it takes me to make my trip. I am now driving between 70 and 75 mph on the long, straight stretches when there is not a lot of traffic and I'm saving almost 15 minutes. Like most drivers, I am capable of setting my own speed limit. I know what is safe and what is not.

I called the people at the New York State Thruway Authority. They sent me statistics showing that traffic deaths on the Thruway are dramatically down since the new speed limit was put into effect. In 1996 there were 18 percent fewer fatalities than in 1994.

Thruway Authorities aren't sure why—weather has an effect—and it would probably be as wrong to conclude that faster driving leads to fewer highway deaths than it would be to conclude that a 15 mph speed limit would be a good idea. Fewer people would be killed, but not many drivers would vote in favor of it.

In that regard, it was interesting to read a comment about speed from Tom Hicks of the Maryland State Highway Commission. In commenting on the fact that 85 percent of all drivers maintain the same speed on a highway, he said, "Those people are least likely to be involved in motor-vehicle crashes. It's the people who drive much slower or much faster who are at most risk."

The fact is, no one seems to know what causes death and accident rates to fluctuate. Fewer people died after the speed limit was raised in

New York, Florida, Massachusetts, Montana and Utah but more died in Alabama, California, Oklahoma, Pennsylvania, Texas and Nevada. Someone pointed out that the increase in traffic deaths in Nevada after the speed limit was raised was about the same as the increase in the population of the State. More people driving, more deaths.

There is a speed at which a good driver feels safe in a car. No sign by the side of the road can do that. There are places where 80 mph is not too fast and there are other times, other places, where 45 mph is too fast.


## TICKET THE SLOW DRIVERS

When I drive to work, I start the trip down a one-mile stretch of pavement leading from our house to the major highway that takes me into New York City. It's the connecting link between two small towns but there are houses on both sides and it falls somewhere in between being a street and a road. I was driving at a moderate speed, just above the 35-mph posted limit, when I spotted a patrol car in the bushes, on my side of the road, facing me. I know their hiding places.

Instinctively I took my foot off the accelerator and my car dropped down five miles an hour to an even 30 mph. I stared straight ahead, never looking in the direction of the officer. A hundred yards past him, a car came toward me that appeared to be traveling close to 50 mph. I flashed my lights as a warning. He got the message and instantly slowed down before he got to the lurking police car.

Whose side am I on? Law and order or speeders? Why was I in cahoots with the bad guy and against the police trying to make things safe? It is puzzling, too, that radar detectors are openly advertised and sold in most States. These devices are specifically designed to allow drivers to break the law by traveling faster than the speed limit without being caught. Why in the world would those devices be legal in most States? I have one.

Driving is a good time for idle thinking and I got thinking idly about whether the cop I passed was pleased that I was just another law-abiding citizen traveling at a legal speed or was he a little disappointed? If he'd been sitting there for half an hour without getting the chance to stop anyone for exceeding the speed limit, he must have felt frustrated. After all, his job was to catch speeders. If he sat there all morning and didn't catch any, he was a failure. Any normal person in that position would be disappointed every time a car passed at a legal speed.

This is speculation on my part. I have never talked to a cop (I'm using "cop" instead of "policeman" to avoid the awkward gender problem) about how they feel when they arrest someone.

In some cities the police have quotas they are expected to fill. If they don't arrest a certain number of people, it is assumed they aren't doing their jobs. That practice ought to be illegal.

I am ambivalent about police. They have one of the most difficult jobs in any community and while I have sympathy and respect for them, I dislike the aggressive ones. Police forces in cities across the Country differ greatly. Each has its own personality. Some behave with a police-state mentality and others are so casual and laid-back about law enforcement that a crime has to take place under their noses before they do anything about one. You can tell whether a police force is answering to the people of a city or to a political boss who provides them with immunity from criticism for any gross action they take.

It's an unfair temptation that manufacturers provide us with when they make cars that will go 50 mph faster than it's legal to drive anywhere. The average car has a top speed of 125 mph and it's a tribute to our common sense that almost no one ever exceeds 80 mph.

## SEAT BELTS AND SAFETY CAPS

On television, a reporter was interviewing the mother of a Little League player, who had formed an organization to do something about the danger of playing baseball. She quoted statistics on the number of children who were hurt playing the game. One boy had died after being struck in the chest by a ball.

When someone evokes the details of an incident involving the death of an innocent young person, we have no inclination to argue with them. What we need though, are statistics that are less dramatic than the story of one accidental death. They are numbers we don't have and can't get.

How do you draw up a chart that would match the pleasure ten million kids get playing baseball, against the despair felt by one set of parents who lost a son playing the game? Stopping kids from playing baseball or making the equipment prohibitively expensive by forcing manufacturers to protect themselves with insurance policies, is not the answer. If there was no baseball, what would they be doing instead? Would any of them die doing it?

Years ago when radio and television announcers were advising everyone to be cautious driving on the Fourth of July weekend because there were so many deaths on the highway the previous year, I got hold of some surprising statistics. Taking into account the fact that there were five times as many people on the roads on the July 4th weekend, the overall death rate from auto accidents was actually *lower* than on a normal summer weekend.

There are so many people in the world that some of them are going to be hurt doing anything. You can get hurt getting out of bed but there's no organization demanding we stop getting out of bed.

There are no official statistics on how many people burn or drown to death in car accidents because they are unable to unsnap the seat belt that holds them in.

To be completely safe and eliminate all deaths caused by automobile accidents, you could make cars illegal. If we had no automobiles, we'd have no accidents and, best of all, no insurance companies. Should we make crossing the street illegal in order to eliminate pedestrian fatalities?

What the statisticians have to do is quantify the things in our lives that are more difficult to attach numbers to than death or injury. Pleasure, for example, or satisfaction. What number could you possibly attach to the satisfaction a hundred million people derive from getting to work quickly and easily every morning by driving their cars somewhat faster than is absolutely safe?

All of us are constantly being inconvenienced by safety features whose principal value is to idiots. Is the safety feature worth the time-consuming trouble to which it puts the rest of us every day? In some cases, the answer is yes. Traffic lights are worth the trouble. The safety features automobile manufacturers have been forced by government regulations to build into their cars are worth the money they have cost all of us in increased prices.

The idea of mandatory safety caps on pill bottles might be worth reevaluating. The figures in this case might prove the child-proof tops are worth the trouble but they are so irritating that we shouldn't take it for granted that they're good because they're so inconvenient. I'd like to see statistics on the number of people who have died alone in the middle of the night because they couldn't open their life-saving medicine bottle.

You can't make the life of a child or a grownup foolproof and there's a limit to how far we should go in trying. Eliminating baseball as a game kids play in their backyards without expensive protective equipment because a few are hurt every year is ridiculous. Some kids are going to be hurt—a few even killed—in a pillow fight.

No law can make life foolproof.

# TRUE THINGS ABOUT CARS

- Tires are better than they used to be. You don't see many people with flats. Of course, it could be there are fewer nails in the road.
- The average person who does get a flat isn't going to fix it because he has no idea how the jack works—or even how to get it out of where it's stored in the car.
- A study showed that cars that are washed regularly last longer than cars that aren't washed. There's a fallacy in that. It isn't washing the car that preserves it. People who wash their cars are more careful with them.
- My old Ford station wagon with 148,000 miles on it was undercoated when it was new with a lifetime guarantee. After about 125,000 miles it began to rust in spots but I didn't have the nerve to demand my money back on the guarantee.
- A motorcyclist pulled in front of me at a stoplight. At the next light, I pulled in front of him and he started yelling and screaming at me. What's with motorcyclists?
- A car is a snug place in a heavy rain. No matter what complaint you may have with cars, you have to admit, they've made them so they don't leak.
- I'm leery of air bags.
- The height of the front and back bumpers off the road should be standard. Every car and every truck's bumpers should be at the same level with the bumper on every other car.
- Some people have never ridden in the back seat of a car.
- If they had combination locks instead of keys on the ignitions of cars, we wouldn't have to think where we put the car keys.
- One of the important things to know about your car is how much gas you have left after the arrow on the gauge indicates the tank is empty.
- It would be a good idea if they'd put TV sound in car radios.

- I'm surprised by the popularity of front-wheel drive cars. You'd think it would be easier to push something than to pull it.
- Once you pass 60, it's difficult to remember all the cars you've ever owned. We once had a Borgward. My father owned a Hupmobile.
- Cars are better than they used to be. You wonder why they didn't put all the improvements in them fifty years ago.

# PART 12

---

# *Big Issues*

*Investigative television shows like* 60 Minutes *are always finding someone on death row who didn't do it. They never conclude he really did do it. It's puzzling to viewers because someone* out there is murdering people.

# NO SHORTAGE OF HOUSING
## FOR WORSHIP

It's strange that Americans who go to church have divided themselves into so many small groups. There are 350,000 churches in the United States. They belong to 80 religious bodies. If you divided the number of people who go to church every week by the number of churches you'd get a very low number. There are thousands of churches whose Sunday attendance is regularly fewer that 75 people. If some of those churches were businesses, they'd go out of it.

It's difficult to get information on church income or spending because churches are not open about their finances. The Catholic Church is governed from Rome and individual parishes have minimal control over money or theology. When a church is governed by a central body, each member church is assessed a proportion of its income. It gets to keep some for itself.

There are 23,500 Catholic churches and 62 million Catholics. Among Protestants, Baptists are the most numerous. There are 36 million of them but Baptists are more fragmented than Catholics.

The U.S. Statistical Abstract lists 11 national Baptist organizations. The biggest sect is the Southern Baptist Convention. But then there are the National Baptist Convention, USA, Inc., the National Missionary Baptist Convention, National Baptist Convention of America, the American Baptist Association, Inc., the American Baptist Churches in the USA, the National Missionary Baptist Convention of America, National Association of the Free Will Baptists, the Liberty Baptist Fellowship, the General Association of Baptists and the Conservative Baptist Association of America.

That's a lot of Baptists going to a lot of different churches. Are their religious beliefs really so unreconcilable that, as Christians, they couldn't get together and meet under fewer roofs than 91,065? That's the number of Baptist churches in America. There are 36 million Baptists of one kind or another but I doubt that many Baptists would be able to explain what one of those groups believes that another does not.

Every church I see reminds me that there are too many of them for their own good. They have drawn too fine a line between their religious differences—if there are any differences at all. Once they have announced that they believe Jesus Christ is the son of God, Christians should be able to work out the minor points on which they disagree and go to one building to pray.

The proliferation of churches is encouraged by laws that exempt them from real estate tax. Those 91,000 Baptist churches, for example, add a heavy tax burden on other Americans who are not Baptists.

We pay, they pray. Religious Americans should be encouraged to resolve their theological differences and get together in fewer tax-free buildings.

# SEX AND
# THE CATHOLIC CHURCH

The Catholic church has never officially recognized that sexual desire cannot be suppressed by resolve. Sex isn't something anyone can decide not to have and then never feel sexy. The church was unrealistic when it established rules that put both marriage and sex outside the boundaries of acceptable behavior for priests. The church might as well have ordered church bells not to ring when struck.

The question now, with the revelations about illicit sex in the priesthood so prevalent, is to what extent the lives and protestations of belief by priests is sincere. Can a man who claims special goodness because of his professed devotion to the teaching of Jesus Christ be believed when he ignores basic principles of decency with his personal behavior in society?

Religions have always been concerned with sex and it's difficult to understand how so basic a human urge ever got to be considered evil. Religions—Christianity being principal among them—are obsessed with sex. They're against it. Adam and Eve were the original sinners. Mankind has been conceived in sin if you take the Bible or the Koran literally.

One of the results of the revelations of unholy transgressions will be the shadow cast on all Catholic priests. The best, most innocent among them are always going to be suspect. No one is going to look at a priest again without thinking: "Does he do it?"

It won't matter that there is some goodness in the bad priests. We are all better remembered for our exceptional moments, good and bad, than for our everyday accomplishments. The priest taking sexual advantage of young boys might have been a good parish priest but he won't ever be known for that.

I don't know how anyone gets to be a priest. If someone becomes a teacher, a cop, a lawyer, a business person, a plumber, a military leader, an artist or a politician it is probably because he or she showed some ability in that direction and pursued it. It isn't clear why a young man would set out to become a priest now or what steps he would take to get to be one. Fitness for the job is a criterion in most professions but the church is so short of priests, it has almost certainly lowered the standards.

There are 50,000 Catholic priests left in the United States. There were once 100,000. The priesthood has been slowly declining in both number and quality for hundreds of years. There was a time when it attracted intellectuals but as religion was confronted by science, the number of bright young men who wanted to be priests dwindled.

Extinction of the profession was built into the code of behavior demanded of priests. With the prohibition against marriage and sex, it was not a job that was ever handed down from father to son. The fathers of young lawyers are often lawyers. Businessmen bring their sons and daughters into their business. A great many doctors are both the sons and fathers of doctors. Continuity has been one reason for the strength of a variety of professions but the priestly oath of celibacy eliminates, officially anyway, that factor in the Catholic church.

The study of religion is a hobby of mine but I am more interested than knowledgeable about it. Anything can be perceived as religious, no matter how stupid it is, if it is believed by enough people over a long period of time. This accounts for the widespread acceptance of something like genital mutilation by many religions. Circumcision is first among them but in some more primitive religions, the clitoris of women is removed at puberty so they can't enjoy the evil pleasure of sex.

All of us are aware of having done some wrong things—having "sinned"—and a great many sinners who don't want to live with their shortcomings look for forgiveness in religion from a power they perceive to be superior to their own. This is their God. Presumably sinning priests are either rotten clear through or they believe their God has forgiven them.

# PRAYING FOR
# NO SCHOOL PRAYER

The issues of abortion and school prayer are going to be important in the next Presidential election although they don't have to be treated as separate issues because almost everyone who favors school prayer opposes abortion. You know everything about someone's political opinions if you know where they stand on compulsory prayer in schools.

A great many Americans who have not thought through the consequences are even demanding that religion be taught and promoted in our public schools.

The first question that should come up when anyone talks about religion in school is: which religion? Almost everyone, even the leaders of specific religious groups, endorse the idea of religious freedom in America. Not many are so narrow-minded as to insist that religion in schools should mean their religion. Even so, it's difficult for anyone deeply committed to one faith, to be politically neutral and tolerant of other religions.

The willingness of most Americans—including even religious leaders—to be open-minded in public poses a real problem for religious leaders intent on maintaining their own constituencies. A Catholic priest, for example, insists to his parishioners in the privacy of their own sanctuary, that their God is the true God and the only God but when the priest is being an American citizen, supporting religious freedom out in public, he has to act as though there are Gods other than his own. He can't insult the Muslims, the Jews, the Hindus or even the Baptists and Methodists by acting as if Catholics had the only true religion and the inside track to the real God.

The Christian Coalition, the major organization of religious conservatives in America, endorses school prayer but Pat Robertson, its founder, and Ralph Reed, its former director, make it clear that when they refer to school prayer, they mean Christian prayers to their Christian God.

Some States have recognized the problem and have tried to get around it by calling school prayer "a moment of silence." There's a big difference between praying and being silent. A prayer is a request to God by an individual, for God to fulfill a desire of the person praying. It's usually assumed that a prayer has some high-minded content that's more significant than asking for a winning lottery number but is there anyone who thinks that the average kid in school, faced with a minute when there's no one talking or yelling and screaming, will think about God and actually pray in some reverent way? And if the child does form some kind of a prayer, does anyone think the child will ask for anything beyond good marks or that the cafeteria will be serving macaroni and cheese for lunch?

Public schools in most States have been compelled, by law, to be neutral about religion. Teachers have to avoid questions of faith and they have a difficult time explaining some of the questions that come up in science or history classes without using the religious explanation or ignoring the prohibition by using the scientific or logical explanation. Religion was invented to explain the inexplicable. Without it, teachers are in trouble. The truth is either illusive or questioned by the majority of people in the world who choose to believe something else.

## ALLAH IS GREAT,
## ALLAH IS GOOD

Considering that the Koran (or Qu'ran) is believed to be the word of God by one billion, 150 million people in the world, it seems wrong that most Americans know so little about it. One reason is the difficulty anyone who is not Muslim has in writing about it without getting in trouble. It seems likely that Muslims are justified in thinking Westerners do not understand it. They are probably justified.

The Koran was put down on whatever they used for paper about 600 years after the beginnings of Christianity. While it borrows from the Bible, the Koran is not anything like the Bible. The Koran has some history and occasionally mentions historical names but it is not organized chronologically and doesn't pretend to be a history book as the Bible does.

The big thing that set Mohammed's belief apart from Christianity was that, while he accepted Moses, Noah and Jesus as prophets, he did not believe Jesus was the son of God.

The Koran is more a guidebook or a book of short, one-sentence instructions on how Muslims should conduct their lives, their business, their associations with other people, their government, their military and their legal affairs. It isn't organized chronologically and there is more advice than information in it.

The Koran comprises 114 chapters assembled from front to back with the longest chapters generally being first and the shortest ones last.

Muslims believe that the Koran is the word of God given to

Mohammed by the angel, Gabriel. This is the same Biblical angel who told Mary that she was going to give birth to Jesus although Mary said she never had intimate relations with a man.

For anyone brought up in another tradition, the Koran becomes confusing when you try to consider who is speaking. The words are considered to be the words of God (Allah). This is strange for anyone unfamiliar with Muslim thinking because it doesn't seem as though Allah would so frequently praise himself or say things so self-serving as "No one in the heavens and the earth knoweth the unseen save Allah."

If Allah were dictating those words, you'd expect him to be more apt to say something like "None in the heavens and the earth knoweth the unseen but me." Why would he speak of himself in the third person? Perhaps this is a problem that comes with translating the Koran from one language into another.

There is also more effusive praise of Allah in the Koran than you would think even an omnipotent God would bestow on himself:

"Allah controls all things."

"Who is more true in word than Allah?"

"Allah is cognizant of all things."

"Allah is knowing and wise."

"Allah is strong, mighty."

Except that he appears to be stern with anyone who doubts he is God, Allah is thoroughly gentle and good. He prescribes rules that would make this a better world if we all lived by them.

"Allah does not love him who is treacherous, sinful."

"Allah loves those who do good things."

The Koran says he protects us all. Allah keeps the heavens from falling in on the Earth, except with his permission.

One belief that makes Muslims so difficult to get along with is the promise the Koran gives them that they will win Allah's favor and go to heaven if they die fighting "in the way of Allah." On the other hand, the Koran appears to disapprove of suicide, so it is unclear why suicide-bombing terrorists believe Allah approves of what they do.

It is difficult to understand much of the Koran as it has been translated into English and certainly some of the beauty and poetry of it has been lost. Many of the translations of the Koran are poor or inadequate. It should be read in Arabic. Muslims point out that there are not different versions of the Koran, just different translations and the Koran has suffered more from being taken out of its original Arabic than the Bible has in being translated so many times from one language to the next, beginning in Hebrew.

There are passages in any English translation of the Koran that are simply incomprehensible. This one, for example, is a reference to the dead: "We know indeed what the Earth diminishes of them, and with Us is a writing that preserves."

Another translation of the same sentence reads: "We know that which the Earth taketh of them and with Us is a recording book."

Americans who are not Muslim have a long way to go before they understand the great book of Islam.


# THE POPE, BUDDHA AND ATHEISM

If it were anyone else, you'd say he put his foot in his mouth but, because it was Pope John Paul, it seems nicer to say he misspoke or, in this case, misswrote.

In the book *Crossing the Threshold of Hope* which has the Pope's name on it as author along with a professional writer named Vittorio Messori, there is a sentence that reads "Buddhism is . . . an atheistic system."

Buddhists were plenty mad about it and, while the Pope didn't really apologize, he backed off by saying he had "profound respect" for Buddhists. There are over 350 million Buddhists in the world and even the Pope has to be politically correct.

The incident points up the problem with school prayer or religion in government. As America becomes more diverse in its religious beliefs, the question arises "In WHOSE God do we trust?" People who favor school prayer assume everyone prays to the same god. When Baptists say they want school prayer, they mean they want children to pray to the Baptist idea of God and not to any other, such as the one the Hindus or Muslims believe in. It is not clear to me whether Muslims believe that Allah is one and the same with the Christian God. Even the Methodist or the Presbyterian idea of God is not identical in all respects to the Catholic idea of God.

The Pope was probably right the first time. Buddhism is a civilized way of thinking about life but it doesn't have a God the way Christianity does. It's more a philosophy of life than a religion. Buddhists believe that we were born to suffer. This is reason enough for me not to be a Buddhist because I don't believe we were. I believe we were born to enjoy life. Buddhists believe that the best thing that happens to us is dying because death relieves us of our suffering. They think we suffer because we want too many things we can't have. They relieve themselves from the suffering by meditating and convincing themselves they don't want anything. This is a religion that's never going to catch on in the United States because we want it all.

Buddhism is kind of a nice belief really but it would be hard on the malls and the advertising business here. Most Americans would never buy Buddhism because no matter how hard they try, they can't keep from wanting a new car or a television set with a bigger screen. It's suffering they can live with until they get the money to relieve it.

Buddhists make dying easier for themselves by believing that we're all made up of tiny parts of one big whole and that, when we die, our parts reorganize and become part of something else. They believe (I think) that what your parts become part of in the next life, depends on what good or bad things you did with them during this life. It's known as a person's "karma." If a person dies with good karma, he slips into a never-ending state of painless pleasure called nirvana.

Promising all good people nirvana would be an effective way for religion to make people better, so you can't knock it. The threat of going to hell is supposed to do the same thing for hard-line Christians but it doesn't work. The percentage of people on death row who are religious is about the same or slightly higher than the population as a whole.

Buddha's first name, or given name, was Siddhartha. He was born more than 500 years before Christ and taught that there were "four noble truths": 1) Existing is suffering; 2) The origin of suffering is desire; 3) Suffering ends when you stop wanting things; and 4) The way to end desire is to follow "the noble eightfold path."

"The noble path" is described this way: Right belief, the resolve to renounce pleasure, to harm no living creature, (similar to the Hindus who allow the cows to roam the streets in India), right speech, right conduct, right occupation of living, right effort to keep the mind free of evil thoughts (I'm copying this out of a book), right contemplation to achieve, by trancelike meditation, selflessness.

The whole Buddhist belief is based on gentleness, self-denial and compassion. You shouldn't knock that even if you're the Pope.

Buddhism is good to read about but I'm just not sure where it's going to fit into the school prayer program in a small, predominantly Baptist town in the Midwest.

## ONE LIFE TO TAKE

The Federal method of killing someone convicted of murder is by sticking a needle in the person and injecting him with a poisonous fluid. Only one person, Timothy McVeigh, has been put to death by the Federal Government since it reinstituted the death penalty in 1976.

Having a Federal death penalty seems like a step in an uncivilized direction to a lot of people, including me, even though I'm usually all for it in any specific case.

Juries usually convict a murderer for what seems like the least of his crimes. For instance, several hundred people died in the Oklahoma bombing but McVeigh was only found guilty of the murder of eight U.S. Government employees.

The average murderer who ends up being executed spends nine years on death row, waiting. Waiting must be worse than dying. A few years ago Kentucky had a man who had been waiting to be executed for 32 years but he beat the rap. He died of natural causes.

There are 38 States that have the death penalty and they have five ways of killing people. They are 1) electrocution, 2) poison gas, 3) lethal injection, 4) hanging and 5) firing squad. We never had the guillotine although it seems like an efficient method. Last year, one prisoner in a State that gives the prisoner his choice of method, chose to be shot. Another chose to be hanged. I don't anticipate any State having the need to do any of these things to me but if I were faced with a choice, I'd take the firing squad. I always liked the drama of having eight men with rifles, only four of which are loaded with live bullets. None of the eight men knows for certain whether he killed the prisoner.

My last two choices would be hanging or electrocution. I hate getting even a little shock. Hanging doesn't appeal to me at all. They say the victim's neck is broken and he dies instantly but who knows for sure? I remember the cowboy movies I saw as a kid. When they hung someone, they put him on a horse with his hands tied behind his back, put the noose around his neck and then threw the other end over the limb of a tree and the sheriff whacked the horse on the rump. The horse galloped off—without his rider.

There are about 3,000 people on one death row or another in prisons across the United States now. Of those, only 40 are women. This seems like a sexist statistic that must be addressed by women's rights advocates. That would mean men are 75 to one more apt to murder someone than women are.

The Federal Government hardly ever executes anyone but it has recently spent $300,000 on a state-of-the-art execution chamber in Indiana. They may want to start amortizing the cost of it by getting at some of those 3,000 guilty people on death row.

When it comes to actually watching someone put to death, the public is not sanguine. The suggestion so often made when there is about to be a high-profile execution that it be televised is always greeted with an ugh of revulsion. People want it done but prefer not to see it happen. One famous Sing Sing warden regularly invited the judge and prosecutor of a doomed convict to witness his execution but in 20 years, none ever took him up on his offer of free, ringside seats.

Records show that about 19,000 people have been executed in the United States since the 1600s. The number executed has varied during periods of our history. From 1930 to 1964, 3,849 were killed. From 1964 to the present, only 267 have been done in.

Texas puts away the most. They've done about 200 since the death penalty was legalized in 1976. That statistic doesn't do much for the argument that the death penalty deters murder. Texas regularly ranks near the top of the list of States with the most murders.

Louisiana had both the death penalty and the most number of murders per capita in 1995, 17 per 100,000. North Dakota has the fewest murders. It does not have the death penalty.

No one keeps a list of innocent people who have been executed but a lot of mistakes have been made. To name just a few innocent victims of the death penalty, three come to mind—Jesus Christ, Socrates and Sir Thomas More.

## ANGRY SMOKE SIGNALS

So-called "Indian" gambling casinos are hardly ever run by Indians. They produce piles of cash for sleazeball owners using Indians as a front. Indians get enough of the profits to make them happy and keep them quiet.

When I made some comments about casinos on *60 Minutes*, I got a lot of angry letters.

"I was outraged," wrote Marge Anderson, chief executive of the Mille Lacs Band of Ojibwe Indians. "We have used every penny from our Indian-owned casinos to build schools, clinics, homes and so much more. For this, Andy Rooney calls us sleazeballs?"

I don't know Indian chief Marge Anderson but I question whether the Ojibwe Indians have used "every penny" for good works.

Byron Thundercloud of the Ho-Chunk Nation in Wisconsin invited me to come to their "gaming" facilities. In a successful public relations coup ten years ago, casinos got people to drop the word "gambling" for "gaming." It sounds better.

Clifford M. LaChappa, chairman of the Barona Band of Mission Indians in San Diego County, wrote to provide me "with just a few of the facts on Indian gaming." He asked me to call him and I did.

Mr. LaChappa spoke to me with a lawyer at his side, helping him with answers. He said the Barona casino was run by 354 tribal members.

Mr. LaChappa didn't mention it, but the Barona casino is managed by the Inland Casino Corporation, hardly Indian. He said Inland was paid a flat fee, not a percentage, but would not say what the flat fee was. Inland manages other casinos around the Country.

Keller George, of Utica, New York, an Oneida Indian council member, who is highly regarded in his community, was upset with me.

Richard A. Hayward, tribal council chairman of the Mashantucket Pequot Tribe of Connecticut, asked me to read a statement of his on *60 Minutes* about what he called my "incoherent ramblings."

Angriest of all was Roland J. Harris, chairman of the Mohegan Tribal Council, who claimed what I said was "slanderous and libelous." It was not, of course, or I wouldn't have said it.

The Mohegan Tribe's casino is one of the newest and was almost instantly the most successful. In the first few weeks, the casino was making a million dollars a day on slot machines alone.

The Mohegan operation was put together by businessman Solomon Kerzner as a way of taking advantage of the Indian reservation's tax-free status. Mr. Kerzner is president of Sun International Hotels Ltd. whose headquarters is in the Bahamas. Indian leaders agreed to give one of his companies, Trading Cove Inc., 40 percent of the net revenue from the gambling operation.

In response to complaints I wrote the following:

"No one who grew up in the United States could be unaware of the great contribution Indians have made to the American heritage. Nor could they be unaware that Indians were badly treated by invading Europeans. That treatment created a long-term problem for them and for the rest of us.

"It is my belief that gambling casinos are not the solution to the Indians' problem. Gambling produces nothing. Every thousand dollars lost in a casino is a thousand dollars that is not spent on a legitimate product made by a company that employs American workers. A gambling operation, no matter what percentage of the proceeds goes to Indians, does not help one single Indian become independent by learning a trade or a profession. I know of no Indian casino that is actually managed by Indians. If Indians prosper temporarily through the money they are handed from casino profits, it is the worst kind of welfare and beneath the dignity of the glorious Indian tradition."

With the proliferation of gambling in the United States, Indian casinos will gradually lose what has been a monopoly in some States and Indians who have acquired nothing but easy money from their operation, will be right back where they were.

My complaint is not with Indians, it is with gambling casinos.


## A HOUSE OF CARDS

It begins to look as though we'll all be able to get rich gambling very soon now. We won't ever have to work for a living again. The gambling casinos will provide us with all the money we need. "A day's work" will be an old phrase our grandfathers used.

The New York State legislature, one of the last major holdouts, has approved gambling almost everywhere but in New York City. The good thing about the New York move is that it's terrible news for Las Vegas, Atlantic City, the Mob, The Bahamas, Donald Trump and all the foreign gambling combines that have been syphoning off billions of dollars from Americans at their gaming tables. Up to now, those few interests have had a monopoly on gambling in this Country. They alone have profited from the vast amount of money people seem to be willing to bet on the long-shot chance they'll be lucky and get rich in one of the glitzy palaces where sleaze reigns and the operators are the only real winners.

It's bad news for those entrenched casino owners because, if New York has gambling, gambling will soon be legal everywhere. Not many communities in the Country will be able to hold out against it. Community A can't sit still while Community B, a few miles down the road in a neighboring State, allows the opening of a casino that sucks billions of dollars out of Community A's economy. Their answer will be to open their own casino.

The Indian casino scam is a farce. In most cases a handful of semi-Indians are used as frontmen by professional gambling operators as a way of setting up their own empire—tax-free because it is nominally Indian. A few Indians are made magnificently wealthy. Paying the Indians is a small licensing fee those professional gamblers are willing to turn over in exchange for the use of the Indians' exemption from local gambling laws and taxes. Their public relations statements trade on the guilt we feel as a Nation for the terrible things our forefathers did to those early Americans.

It's a sad day for anyone who thought there was really something behind the phrase "the American work ethic." The work ethic has been disappearing for years. The service industry in the United States is now bigger than the manufacturing sector and "work" loses its original meaning when it's applied to people who make their money shuffling papers instead of making a product. (As a writer, I exempt writers from the paper-shuffling category.)

The American dream now is to figure out a way to make a lot of money without doing any work. To get rich gambling on a lottery ticket, at the craps table or simply by playing the slot machines is the American dream. It is the poorest, dumbest Americans who throw away the most money on lottery tickets.

The mystery to me is why people who complain so bitterly over a small tax increase that might provide them with some government service, don't seem to mind dropping big money in a gambling casino whose income does nothing for anyone but the casino owners and some token Indians and a few dime-a-dozen card dealers.

## PSYCHICS ARE PSYCHOS

For a Nation that prides itself on the intelligence of its citizens, we do a lot of stupid things.

For 20 years a secret Defense Intelligence Agency in Washington has kept a dozen, full-time, salaried psychics on its payroll. They were paid $20 million for what they did. What they did was con the bureaucracy.

Dozens of times, Pentagon executives asked the psychics to come up with information about specific military operations in foreign countries; years ago they put their minds to work locating the whereabouts of the Marine colonel, William Higgins, later hanged by Lebanese terrorists.

They were asked to "concentrate on" and "visualize" military targets so they could describe their features and location. How would you like to be a pilot risking your life flying over enemy territory, looking for a "target" that was the product of a psychic's imagination?

Nothing the psychics came up with paid off—except, of course, for the psychics. They are either honest people with a greatly inflated vision of their extra-worldly powers or they are fakes and frauds who cheated us and knew they were doing it.

A psychic is a person who thinks, or claims to think, that he or she is clairvoyant or can successfully get the message of a thought in someone else's brain without the use of spoken or written words, body movements, sign language or any of the other means of communication. This is known as telepathy. Clairvoyance is the supposed extrasensory recognition of an object or an event.

There is no evidence that there is such a thing as a spirit or a soul in any of us and, although it's popular to use the words to express illusive thoughts that come to all of us, the words do not represent anything that has ever been proven to exist. Too bad.

All of us are a little soft on the possibility that there's something going on in our brains that we don't understand. Dreams are unfathomable. We've all had coincidences so difficult to understand that the easiest thing to do is attribute them to telepathy, mind-reading or some other-worldly phenomenon.

We think of someone we haven't seen in 10 years and later that same day, the person will show up. We forget all the dreams we had that came to nothing.

There are a thousand ways we can be fooled into thinking we have participated in some psychic experience. We have not because there is no such thing. It is outrageous for an arm of our Government to spend money on such hogwash. It might as well put the Nation in the hands of astrologers.

If there were such things as clairvoyance and mental telepathy, they could be proven under the strict conditions imposed by scientific experiment. They have not been and, while it's difficult to get one to submit to a test, psychics have failed every time they've been put to one.

For more than 25 years, James Randi, the bright gadfly magician, philosopher and bubble buster, has offered a $10,000 reward to anyone who can produce any psychic, paranormal or supernatural demonstration that he can't explain or expose. In recent years he has raised his offer to $1 million with no takers so far.

The Defense Intelligence Agency is apparently not to blame for keeping psychics on its staff. For years, one staff member of the Senate Appropriations Committee, C. Richard D'Amato, single-handedly defeated all the attempts to kill the psychic boondoggle.

The Central Intelligence Agency conducted a study of the psychics' work and its conclusion was that "no intelligence community funds should be spent on this work." The CIA got it right that time.

# A CASE FOR DIVORCE

An eight-year-old boy in Florida asked for a divorce from his mother, a single parent, who had put him in a foster home. The story gave new meaning to the word "divorce" even though the broader dictionary term has always meant more than the legal dissolution of a marriage. The words "single parent" in referring to an unmarried mother are being used in what seems to be an increasingly forgiving, almost sympathetic, sense. It should not be considered an honor.

If divorce in the future can mean breaking up any relationship between two or more people, it opens up a world of possibilities for us and not all bad either. In my lifetime, I've had two cousins, one aunt and somewhere around eight friends from whom I wouldn't mind being legally separated. Are there lawyers who handle this sort of break-up?

We all have friends we don't like—good friends—and they don't like us either. We assumed nothing could be done about it. We'd run into each other, talk, invite each other over for dinner Saturday nights, play tennis, bowl and have a terrible time together. One summer we went on a ten-day trip with two dear old friends we couldn't stand.

The other day I spent more than an hour with one of my oldest and closest friends. We got talking politics and you're not going to believe who he said he was going to vote for. This is a friend? It certainly makes divorce sound like a desirable option. If we do get a divorce, I'll make a statement saying "We're still friends but I want to spend more time with my family."

Two of my cousins were never anything but a burden and I suspect they feel the same about me. We haven't seen each other in more than 12 years. We don't even do Christmas cards. There is no reason to continue our relationship as cousins simply because my mother and their mother were sisters. A simple cousin divorce would make a clean break of it. All divorces from friends and family would come with the statement "We're still friends."

I don't dislike my cousins the way I dislike some of my friends because I don't know them as well. It's just that we don't have anything in common. Since we stopped exchanging Christmas cards by mutual neglect, we don't have their addresses. One of them lives in Oregon and I was in Oregon a couple of years ago and didn't look him up. Why should either of us bear the burden of continuing to be cousins?

It's always seemed strange to me that the government gets in on a divorce. A marriage or a divorce isn't any of the government's business. Does it ever do anything to help one? You'd think that if two people decided they didn't like each other and didn't want to live together and continue the relationship that involved eating meals together, watching television together and sleeping in the same bed, they could simply make the decision to go their own two ways without filing papers with city hall. We have made the mistake of involving marriage with taxes, bank accounts, credit cards, church membership and those Christmas card lists. The money should be divided in two no matter who made it.

The children are in trouble no matter what happens and the only good thing about a law making it mandatory for two people being married to get a license, is that it makes splitting up harder. There isn't a married couple alive who hasn't entertained the thought of divorce. About half of all marriages end in divorce as it is. If the government didn't make divorce inconvenient, we might have a divorce rate of 100 percent.

The case in Florida of the eight-year-old boy who wanted to get away from his mother was poignant but it never would have made the news if the word "divorce" hadn't been used. There is no court so high that it can dissolve the relationship between a boy and his mother. He's stuck with her.

## THE MALIGNED MALE ANIMAL

When a novelist, a playwright or a screenwriter resorts to using a prostitute with the traditional heart-of-gold, as a character, he must be hard up for a story. The prostitute is usually part of a plot that is too far from fact to be believed. More whores have been created by writers than by women's desperation in real life. It seems certain, too, that even the worst novelist can invent a woman for the purpose of drama who is more interesting than any real one. They are certainly better looking.

Isn't there any other situation screenwriters could regularly fall back on? Are we really expected to believe a rich, handsome young man reunites with his girlfriend who, we are led to believe, has just returned to his arms and bed from a job with another guy? I am simultaneously amused, skeptical and revolted. What kind of guy, knowing this, would take her in? Has she showered?

In my long life through high school, college and the Army, I suppose I've known and liked a thousand guys well enough to call them good friends. Maybe two thousand. It would surprise me greatly if any one among them had ever paid for the services of a whore. I don't know why everyone accepts prostitutes in fiction as though they were a common, everyday part of the lives of most men when, in fact, most men have never had anything to do with one. The average prostitute you see working the streets in a big city in America is someone most men wouldn't shake hands with without first putting on rubber gloves. I can't imagine where these women get their customers.

I've seen the ads in the back of tacky magazines advertising the services of women so I know the business is not limited to a few street-walkers visible in most cities late at night but the number of men who avail themselves of these services is as low as the number of them who buy those magazines. Not many.

In the Army, when we first got to Paris, soldiers talked about the women readily available for a price and it was obvious to me that some American soldiers had paid it but it was not common. Some of the young men with whom I served on *The Stars and Stripes*, in London and Paris, established relationships with English and French women—by which I mean they went to bed with them—but the women were not prostitutes. In three cases the relationships led to war marriages.

American tourists love to return from a visit to Amsterdam, Holland, and tell stories about the glamorous women who sit in plush chairs behind plate glass windows, dramatically lit, displaying their wares to the passers-by. It is amusing but if anyone tells you about the prostitutes of Amsterdam, don't let them get away with saying the women are beautiful. I've seen them on several occasions and they are what we would call "dogs." The word used that way demeans man's best friend.

The glamorization of the prostitute in Hollywood movies is ridiculous and it's a mystery what perverse brain wave makes members of the Academy of Motion Pictures vote for the actress playing the part about every other year. The great-looking Kim Basinger won Best Actress for her highly unlikely part as the prostitute in the over-rated *L. A. Confidential*. She was totally unbelievable in the part. It was to her credit.

Kim Basinger was a bit part of the long Hollywood tradition of giving the award to a prostitute—as if it was a difficult and daring part for an actress to play. In 1960, Liz Taylor was the first actress winning for her part as the prostitute in John O'Hara's *Butterfield 8*. Liz was more believable than some. The part seemed to come naturally to her.

Jane Fonda made prostitutes look good in her Academy award–winning part in the movie *Klute*.

Elizabeth Shue was nominated for her role as one in *Leaving Las Vegas* in 1996.

Jody Foster played the part in *Taxi Driver* but her degree from Yale showed through.

Julia Roberts won a Golden Globe for her portrayal in *Pretty Woman*.

If all prostitutes looked like Kim Basinger, Jane Fonda, Elizabeth Shue, Jody Foster and Julia Roberts, I could change my attitude towards them. They don't. They look like those dogs sitting in the windows in Amsterdam.

# THE SELLING OF US

"You can't sell a bad product with good advertising" my grandfather once told me.

My grandfather was smart but that isn't the only time he was wrong. We have become so good at advertising that a company can sell junk for a long time before people catch on and stop buying it. We are the best salesmen in the world.

My question then, is this: How come Americans have failed so miserably in selling our most basic product, ourselves? Why haven't we been able to sell America to the rest of the world if we're so good at selling things? We have a great Country, accomplishing great things. We are decent, caring and generous people. (We aren't modest but you can't have everything.) So, how come we are so hated? If there were an international poll taken, the United States would be on top of the MOST DISLIKED list.

There is no question we are basically good. With the possible exception of oil, we don't covet anything the rest of the world has. I am not a chauvinist but I like my Country. I believe we have tried to do the right thing in the world. We did the right thing in Kosovo. We probably did the wrong thing in Vietnam but we didn't do it for wrong reasons. We did the right thing in the Middle East even if we didn't go far enough and take out Saddam Hussein. We've tried to help the Irish Catholics and the Irish Protestants solve their problems. We've tried to make peace between the intractable Palestinians and the intractable Israelis. There's nothing in it for us. We're just trying to do the right thing. As a Nation, we approve of justice everywhere.

President Bush did the wrong thing when he refused to sign the Kyoto Protocol. But that's just one.

There are dozens of programs in various government agencies like the State Department's Bureau of Educational and Cultural Affairs and the Commerce Department that try to influence foreigners to like us.

What we need is not another government agency but a big, commercial advertising agency or a public relations company that does it for a living.

President George W. Bush should assemble the heads of the best advertising agencies and the best public relations firms, sit them down around a table in Washington, and tell them what we want. We want the United States to have a better image abroad and we'd ask them to start a major campaign toward that end. They could bid on this billion-dollar job.

These advertising and public relations people would advise every agency of our government that does business with foreign countries. They would have advisers on the boards of companies that do business abroad. They would advise tourists on how to help.

The United States would buy advertising in every foreign magazine and newspaper. It would buy time on radio and television. We would flood foreign countries with honest information about ourselves that would make us trusted and loveable. In order to make ourselves trusted and loveable we'd keep the CIA and the FBI out of this. Our propaganda agencies, Radio Free Europe and Radio Liberty, have had limited success trying to promote democratic values abroad.

Billboards along foreign highways would impress on foreign drivers what nice people we are. The public relations people would try to get stories in foreign newspapers that made us look good. They wouldn't be fake stories. They'd be real but stories with emphasis on good things about the United States. We'd tell them all about how the nine miners trapped 250 feet below the ground were saved. We'd impress foreign countries with the fact that we aren't all rich. We have poor people and problems just like theirs. We'd let them know we aren't after what they've got. All we'd have to do would be to tell the truth about us. We're very nice and good but no one anywhere else knows that.

If an advertising company had the answer to one question, they'd be able to solve our international public relations problem. The question is: Why does almost everyone in the world want to come here if they hate this Country so much?

# TAKING STOCK
# OF THE MARKET

There is plenty of reason to worry. People have lost some of their confidence, not just in the stock market but in the fundamental way we do business. These disillusioned people are not activists trying to overthrow the government. They are average Americans who see that the deck was stacked against them from the beginning. They never had a chance. Business executives knew where the cards were in the deck and they didn't. If an average American does make money in the stock market, it's because he was lucky to have picked what the people who had inside information picked.

The economic disaster of 2002—and it was a disaster—made people think about some basic things in our Country. Two great concepts, democracy and capitalism, got sort of tangled together in our minds. We've been treating them as equals and they are not. Democracy is a great, high-minded idea. As a theory of government, Democracy is unassailable. The prosperity and freedom of the lucky people of the world who have lived, as we have, under a democratic system of government is proof enough of that.

Capitalism doesn't have the same credentials. Its advocates speak of it as though it was a sort of economic religion but it is anything but that. It is irreligious. It depends for its effectiveness on one of the least admirable of our traits: greed. The free-enterprise theory is that if everyone takes as much as he can get for himself, it will work out best for everyone.

If the theory that everything works for the best for individual Americans when selfishness is God, then it ought to work on an international basis. If the United States, as the most productive and powerful nation in the world, takes all of the best of everything for itself like the successful business entrepreneurs, the capitalist theory would have the rest of the world prospering because of it. We know it does not.

Anyone who challenges our free-enterprise system is immediately thought of as some kind of communist or socialist but raw capitalism doesn't work and we've known it since Congress passed the Sherman anti-trust laws in the late 1800s. The question right now in our history is what to do about it. The stock market will recover to some extent but that won't solve the problem of a system that is based on greed.

No one dared say so but there were a lot of good things about communism and socialism that we were never willing to admit. Communism got a bad start in the only start it ever had when it became associated with the dictatorial regime of Joseph Stalin. It's a system that doesn't seem to work anyway and Castro's poverty-ridden Cuba is evidence of that but there are good things about it as a philosophy. We really don't know whether it's working or not in China—or even if what they have IS Communism.

Hitler did the same thing for National Socialism that Stalin did for Communism. The two economic systems never had a chance.

The American people have a serious issue on their hands for the next Presidential election. It will be impossible for Republicans to get around the simple fact that things were never better than when Bill Clinton was President and things have not been worse in more than 60 years since George W. Bush has been President. It isn't fair but it's true.

This is a personal note that might make you think my anger is more personal than professional. I have been writing my newspaper column, first three times a week and now twice a week, since 1978. I am a financial ignoramus but you have to find a place to save some money and I put most of mine in the stock market. In six months, I lost more of what I saved than I have been paid to write my column in all the last 24 years.

# DON'T BLAME THE RICH

It's time we started being nicer to the rich!

People of this Country should be aware of the contribution made by those who make a lot of money. For too long they have been maligned by politicians, trashed by journalists and portrayed in a bad light by such artists as novelists and motion picture producers. If the rich were an ethnic group they could make the case that they are the persecuted victims of financial profiling. The rich are demeaned at every turn, repeatedly reviled in political speeches. To hear politicians tell it, you'd think everything bad that has happened to the economy is the fault of the wealthy.

Politicians are always looking for an easy way to appeal to the greater number of voters and these are the people who make the least. Our leaders should realize they can't routinely lay most of the blame for the country's ills on the relatively small segment of the population which makes a living that is better than comfortable.

Who do politicians think contributes those huge sums to their campaigns? Who provides welfare for the homeless? Which segment of the population gives most generously to the great private colleges of the nation? Who gives the handouts to the charities doing good things for so many? Who is it that supports the cultural institutions of every major city through both patronage and attendance? It's the rich, that's who.

Politicians attack the rich because there aren't many of them and voters who aren't rich, the majority, like it. People hate those who make more than they do. Even rich people hate that.

Politicians praise the homeless and talk as if people with money got that way by stealing.

Most people who have money got it by knowing how to do something and working hard at it.

The rich—the word needs to be rid of its pejorative baggage—pay almost 60 cents of every dollar they earn in taxes . . . Federal taxes, State taxes, school taxes, real estate taxes, excise taxes, sales taxes. Even those who cheat pay a lot.

During his eight years in office, President Clinton set the figure of $100,000 as the income point at which a person became rich. It seems low now.

The minimum wage for a big league baseball player was $109,000 and fewer than 5 percent of the players got that little. Anthony Young, a pitcher who lost 16 games one year and won one game, made $165,000.

At $400,000 a year the President himself would be $300,000 above his predecessor's designation of "rich."

The average doctor in the United States makes $179,000. Should we begrudge them this for the hard, important work they do?

There are multitudes of farmers with incomes that qualify them to be scorned as "rich."

Candidates for office and the majority of the electorate talk and act as if the rich got where they are by luck or dishonesty. Nowhere do we hear anyone say they did it with ability and hard work. No one says it is the financially successful people who make the wheels go 'round.

The well-to-do bear the homeless and jobless no ill will. They are often luckless, occasionally shiftless but always human beings who deserve help but is the pitiable condition of so many Americans in any way the fault of successful people? Why do we speak and act as if that were true when it is not? Why are the homeless so widely praised when those who have worked to buy homes are constantly given the back of every politician's hand? Why are the poor portrayed as though poverty were a virtue and success a sin? The perennially unemployed are to be pitied but does it follow that the gainfully employed, in the upper brackets of that employment, are to be scorned?

Democrats are especially negative toward the rich and conciliatory toward the poor. What is the voting record of the homeless? Is there a shred of evidence suggesting that they cast more votes for the Democrats than the rich? There is not. Many of them don't bother to vote at all. On the other hand, the ranks of the rich are rife with liberal—yes, even left-wing—Democrats.

It is depressing to note how the people of this country have succumbed to the notion that somehow unemployment, poverty, hopelessness, recession and the national debt is the fault of everyone but themselves and particularly the working wealthy. The well-off have become the doormat to entry into the White House. Even so rich a President as George W. Bush with so many rich friends, often appeals to the poor he knows only as a rumor.

It is the rich to whom this Country owes its wealth.

## THE RISE AND FALL
## OF A HERO

I was invited to a dinner honoring Mike Wallace by the secretary of an organization calling itself the Thomas Paine Society. My knowledge of Thomas Paine was vague and I set out to find more about him. In spite of the well knownness of his name, Tom Paine is a relatively unknown historical figure. He became an American hero because of something he wrote called *Common Sense* but then he lost his status as hero when he wrote his book *The Age of Reason*.

If kids in school hear anything about Tom Paine it is simply that he was a man who advocated that colonial America should break away completely from Great Britain and King George III. This was the whole idea of *Common Sense*. Until Paine wrote it, many Americans who objected to British rule of the colonies had merely tried to get the British to change the way they ruled; breaking away completely had not been part of their plan.

Paine didn't leave home in England and come to America until he was 37. He had somehow managed to meet Benjamin Franklin on one of Franklin's trips abroad and Franklin was so impressed with Paine that he wrote several letters of introduction for him. Those helped Paine get his first job here with a magazine in Philadelphia.

Two years later Paine's thin book *Common Sense* was published. In it, he argued that America didn't owe England anything and should break away. The idea brought the separatist movement together and really started the revolution. There were three million people in America at the time of the Revolution, if you can believe it.

Paine was a hero everywhere he went in this Country and he could have lived comfortably for the rest of his life making speeches and accepting awards but he wasn't that kind of a person. He was determined to do more somewhere in the world and in 1787 he went to France where the French Revolution was brewing. He said his motto was "The world is my country and to do good my religion."

Paine's idea of doing good was getting involved in the bloody French Revolution of 1789 and, typically, couldn't stop himself from saying what he thought so he got in trouble there. After their successful revolution, Paine was elected to the new French parliament. When that body started deciding what to do with the deposed King, Louis XVI, Paine fought to save the king's life. This hotheaded British-American said he was opposed to the monarchy, not the monarch. Paine was unable to restrain the French though and in 1793, over his violent objection, they cut off Louis' head. Nine months later they cut off Queen Marie Antoinette's.

Paine had been so loud in his objection to the guillotining that the French threw him in prison as a traitor to the Revolution. He came close to having his own head removed before he was finally released. That wasn't even the worst trouble Paine got into in France. During his months in Paris, Paine wrote what finally did him in, *The Age of Reason*.

*The Age of Reason* is a critique of the Bible. He attacked it with the same logic and enthusiasm with which he had attacked kings and monarchies. He said he wasn't an atheist but he sounded like one and he didn't think Jesus Christ had any divine origin. He didn't think the story about Mary and the ghost was believable. He hated the barbarity of the

Old Testament and questioned the authenticity of the New Testament. He said that "if Christ had meant to establish a new religion, he would have written it down himself."

If he were alive today he'd probably be back in prison for saying things like that.

Paine called himself a "deist" which meant he believed in God but nothing more. He thought that the creation of the universe was evidence enough of the existence of God and the Bible was a flawed invention intended to prove something that didn't need proving.

Paine said, in his introduction to *The Age of Reason*, that he had intended this book to be his last writing because he knew it would make him unpopular. He started it earlier because after he was put in prison, he had nothing else to do.

"I put the following work under your protection," he wrote in the preface. "It contains my opinions upon religion. You will do me the justice to remember that I have always strenuously supported the right of every man to his own opinion, however different that opinion might be to mine."

Tom Paine came back to the United States and found that people had read *The Age of Reason* and he was no longer welcome in many places because of it. People were unwilling to say he had the right to his own opinion if his opinions were those expressed in his book. He was ostracized and died lonely and broke. Six people attended his funeral.

So much being for an American hero.

## DON'T CALL THEM "VETS"

The word "veteran" has been much used and much abused, particularly in its abbreviated form "vet." It is too often associated with the phrase "war hero." The idea that every American who spent time in the Army, Navy or Air Force is a hero is nonsense. The real heroes are least apt to let you know about their war experience. You won't find bumper stickers on their cars announcing their past affiliation.

The yellow pages of any telephone book has dozens of entries made by people trading on their time in the service by calling their business VETERANS' DRY CLEANING, VETERANS' GARAGE, VETERAN'S SHOE REPAIR or "Veterans'" anything else. It lessens the significance of the word and detracts from the sacrifice a lot of men and some women made for their Country.

We have weakened the good meaning of the word "hero," too, by applying it to everyone who ever pulled on a uniform. If an American joins or is drafted into the Army, is assigned to an infantry division and sent into battle, is he a hero? Not necessarily. He had tough duty, you can be sure of that, but the word "hero" should be reserved for those very few who knew what they were doing and risked or sacrificed their own lives for the life of someone else. That's what a hero is.

The Armed Services have diluted the importance of the medals they hand out for bravery by handing them out for everything else. Look at the chest of any general wandering the halls of the Pentagon. He may never have been close to a shot fired in anger but he's got five rows of colored ribbons, some denoting medals he "won" and others indicating things like where he's been stationed. The proliferation of awards lessens the importance of the medals given to the men who did something real and important . . . and maybe even brave . . . to get them.

Most servicemen are neither heroic or cowardly. In battle they keep going. If they're infantrymen, they move up when they're told to. Their responsibility is to the men to their left and to their right. They aren't thinking of winning the war or being heroic. If they're airmen, they fly the next bombing mission when they're assigned to it. In the Navy, they go where their ship goes. Servicemen do these things not because they're brave but because they aren't cowardly and because the men on the line with them are moving up, flying or taking their battle stations. It's not Rambo stuff. They aren't cowards but that doesn't make them heroes. The word should not be used casually.

Veterans who served in our armed forces do not deserve a lifetime of special privileges. We can't do enough for the men who were wounded fighting for our Country but Americans don't owe the rest of us who were in the Armed Services anything. We did a good thing for our Country but let's knock it off with the tendency to deify every soldier, sailor and airman who was in the service. There are thousands of veterans organizations whose members are proud of the organization they served in. They are veterans at their best. They get together and remember and that's the way it should be. They don't convene to ask anyone for anything. They're getting together for old times' sake. They spent three or four of the most intense years of their lives together and it gives them a warm feeling to be in each other's company again. They shared experiences they've only been able to tell to those who weren't there in unsatisfactory fragments. They've repeated the same stories without ever being able to convey the whole idea of what war was really like. When these war veterans get together now, they all know what it was like. No one has to say. They survived the war and they've survived the fifty years since. No need to advertise.

They got what was coming to them—a free country.


## SEPTEMBER 11TH


We all look for something good about the worst things that happen.

The good thing about what happened September 11th is that it didn't happen to just New York and Washington; it happened to our Country. All of us. Americans feel closer together than they did before that terrible day. People who thought of New York as a foreign country, suddenly felt an affinity and an affection for it.

Because the mainland of America had never been attacked before, no one really knew how we would react to an attack. It was possible to imagine millions of Americans panicking and scrambling to flee the danger. If New York was the target, maybe they'd clog the highways headed south and west. Well, they didn't do that. People in New York went about their business.

We have made heroes of those who died in the September 11th attack and it was the right thing to do. Our attitude has turned the event into an emotional triumph instead of a bitter defeat.

I was working as a young reporter in London in 1942 when the Germans were bombing the city every night. Much of London was destroyed. It was terrible.

The editor of a London newspaper talked about how the English reacted to the bombing. I wrote down his remarks. They were so good I've kept them all these years:

"Many of us were anxious about the public reaction," he said. "We didn't know how the people would stand up to it. When the first bombs fell neither the Government nor the newspapers knew what the people who had been hit were thinking and how they would take it. That evening, putting out the newspaper, we decided to assume that they had acted heroically. The next morning we printed all the stories that came in to us of their bravery.

"Right then," the editor said, "the newspapers fixed the pattern of how people ought to behave. Perhaps they would have behaved that way anyway. But there is good and bad in all of us and the right example at the right moment can make all the difference in the way men act."

Our American newspapers and television did the same thing with September 11th. They were filled with stories of heroism. Everyone knew what was expected of them and they behaved as they were expected to.

Reinforcing our resolve to be brave and good in adversity is reason enough for all the attention we have given to September 11th.

# PART 13

*Progress*

*The fastest thing a computer does is become outdated.*

# QUE SERA NO ONE KNOWS

We live for so little time in relation to the history of the world. This makes it difficult for us to see where we are headed even though every move we make, every act, every thought we have is directed toward changing our future for the better. We work to have money for tomorrow. We plan, we save, we dig, we plant—all for the future.

I don't have big thoughts often because dealing with things that are over my head depresses me. However the future is a big thought I have a lot.

Two hundred years isn't much when you hear scientists talking about planets that are a thousand light years away from Earth but when you look at what has happened in just 200 years you have to take the immediate future seriously because it comes fast.

Two hundred years takes us back to the eighteen hundreds, not much longer than two lifetimes. Two lifetimes ago there was no such thing as a light bulb. We didn't have cars, airplanes, television, telephones, or computers and hundreds of thousands of people were owned and lived as slaves. It's not that long ago.

What's next?

Genetic changes in the human race are certainly possible. I read where the French are shorter than they used to be and the Japanese are taller. Somewhere some group of humans is probably smarter than it was a hundred years ago. It's impossible to guess where things like atmospheric conditions on earth are going to take humans in a hundred, a thousand or ten thousand years. Our time on earth as individuals is no more than a spark of light in a vast eternity of darkness on either side of our glorious bit of time here.

I hope a cure for cancer is somewhere in our near future. That seems big to me but it would be no more than a blip in the panorama of history.

I wish they could make long-distance travel safer and faster.

We ought to find some way to reconcile the serious differences between Greeks and Turks, Jews and Arabs, Bosnian Muslims and Bosnian Christians, North and South Koreans, Indians and Pakistanis.

We need a solution to the problem of relationship between the races, especially black and white.

I went to the annual banquet of a black organization in New York with about 500 guests. I was one of perhaps ten white people there. It was dumb of me to be both surprised and impressed with the camaraderie that existed among the people at the dinner. These were successful leaders in business, government and entertainment. When I see black friends every day, mixed with whites, they blend in but together at this dinner event they displayed an air of brotherhood that white people at the dinner were not in on. Nor would a dinner of predominantly white guests have had the same air about it. When my friend Ed Bradley kissed Charlayne Hunter-Gault up on the stage where he was honored, it wasn't just a boy-girl kiss; it was a black-black kiss, too. They'd been through something together that I wouldn't understand.

There was a circle-the-wagons understanding among them that they still shared a problem being black that white people didn't know or care about. They were bound together by something I could not possibly share and it made me feel guilty that they felt they needed it.

Some major trend is going to develop in race relations and it is impossible to anticipate what that will be or how different things will be between races in one hundred or two hundred years. Blacks will lose something good when it happens but I hope they won't be having their own dinners with an air about them.

We could do without any more developments in the computer industry for a few years while we pay some attention to trying to solve the problems that involve human relationships. We are making more progress in the areas of science and technology than we are in human relations. Computers are doing amazing things and information on everything is more instantly available but one out of every two marriages ends in divorce. That's not progress.

Too many of the world's people live under conditions that would have been primitive in the United States 200 years ago. There are African countries without basic medical facilities. Dentists? Forget it. Their teeth ache painfully, rot and finally fall out. They die terrible deaths. Women in some underdeveloped countries would glory in being treated as well as dogs are treated here.

People from the Far East who come to the United States almost invariably do well in America. They are contributing in the classic immigrant way as they become integrated. Chinese, Thai or Korean kids in classes here, are often at the head of it, academically. We're lucky to have them but why did they have to come? How do you explain what's going on in so many countries around the world when the immigrant kids who come here almost always turn out to be good citizens?

Will things certainly change for the better everywhere in the world in the next 200 years? Or is there some dark possibility that in 200 years we will be more like the underdeveloped countries of the world?

We'd all love to come back for a look a hundred years from today—and another look in 500 years.

## MORE OF THE SAME

Some problems are so difficult to understand that you want to close your eyes and go to sleep, hoping someone else will solve them while you're gone.

Cloning is one of the problems facing mankind that is both scientifically and philosophically beyond my ability to understand. ("Facing mankind" may sound like too much but it isn't. It's that big.) I don't have an intelligent opinion about what should and should not be done that couldn't be changed in an argument with someone who knew what he or she was talking about. My one unshakable belief about it is that replicas of living human beings are going to be produced in laboratories whether anyone likes it or not. If we can't stop terrorists from blowing us up or Pakistan, Iran and Iraq from making nuclear weapons, how can we stop scientists anywhere in the world from cloning human beings? Of course they are going to clone them.

If scientists start making people they could change the character of the whole human race. It might be made smarter, stronger and better looking. By selective cloning of the best and the brightest among us, the whole human race could be improved. Or it could go the other way. It might be possible to breed out mankind's worst characteristics. Why couldn't the human race be made better over a period of a hundred years of cloning? They could produce humans who were honest, kind, thoughtful, generous, strong and loving.

The idea of humans making humans is terrifying and it may be unfortunate that we ever learned how to clone but, like the invention of gunpowder or spilt milk, we can't take it back.

No one, not even the scientists involved, seem to believe that there should be free and open cloning of humans. They don't know exactly why but they're against it. There is serious objection to cloning by every church. They feel that by cloning, scientists are moving into creation, an area that has previously been exclusively God's. There is even a moral objection to cloning from people who are not religious. None of that matters. We know how to do it and it will be done.

Part of the sense of dread that lurks behind the word may have been created by a woman named Mary W. Shelley. She wrote the novel *Frankenstein* in 1818. It was a work of genius. She not only anticipated the idea of scientists making a person by about 150 years but she understood the human fear of it. Her monster, Frankenstein, while not cloned, ended up destroying the scientist who created him—or "it" if you prefer. We see that specter now.

It seems likely that the fear of being dominated by something we create is in part, at least, responsible for the objection to cloning.

Dictionaries edited before 1950 do not include the word "clone." Like so many words though, it has already acquired several nuances of meaning. It can be a noun or a verb. The 1985 *Dictionary of Contemporary Usage* says "Cloning is asexual reproduction," in other words, reproduction that does not involve the traditional union of male and female. It goes on to say, "Whether cloning of the human animal is within even the remotest range of possibility is something only science can answer." Well, since 1985 science has answered and the answer is "yes."

It must be discouraging to the scientists who found out how to do it that the word "clone" has acquired a slightly disparaging meaning in popular jargon. "The networks are busy producing clones of last year's successful shows" or "She's a clone of Sharon Stone."

It's more important than that.


## LIFE'S LIFE EXPECTANCY

We're living faster, packing more into our lives but nothing except our lives lasts as long as it used to.

In front of me is my old Toshiba computer on which I've been writing for 10 years. When people see it they laugh. It's that old in the life expectancy of computers.

There's no money left in my computer for the company that made it. Toshiba got theirs when I bought it. They no longer make or even have parts for it. Their prosperous future depends on my throwing it away and buying one of their new models. No industry ever practiced the art of planned obsolescence so expertly as computer companies have.

To the right of my computer, is my typewriter. It is a Model #5 Underwood made in 1919 and it is as good and as serviceable as the day it was built. It does not plug in, hook up, need batteries or say "Please wait." It will last as long as I do. Maybe that's why Underwood went out of business.

We live in a throw-away economy and it seems certain we'll use up and discard all the world's resources in the next few hundred years. How big are the lakes of oil underground in Iraq? Are they as big as Lake Michigan? Even if they are, at the rate we are sucking oil out of them every day even Lake Michigan would shortly run dry.

If President Bush does not get his wish to turn parts of virgin territory in Alaska into an oil field, some President in the future will. There's just so long conservationists will be able to hold out in the face of the dire need that will inevitably come for oil. It may be as far away as 100, 200 or 500 years but it will come.

Maybe the answer is in nuclear energy. A bit of matter the size of a pea might contain enough energy to run a whole city for a month and it wouldn't matter whether the earth's oil was gone or not.

Nuclear energy is civilization's only long-term hope—and one of the hopes that goes with it is that we don't destroy ourselves with a series of nuclear disasters in the process of producing energy to replace coal and oil. And anyway, what good will nuclear energy be when we cut down the last tree, extract the last bit of iron ore, coal, copper, tin and magnesium from the earth?

Nuclear energy can't do anything to provide living space for the population explosion. The number of humans on earth, as far as we are able to count, is six billion people, most of whom can't count. A lot of them don't have enough to eat or places to live because we're crowding ourselves out of space on earth.

The number of people in the world has doubled in 40 years. It will more than double in the next 40—and the number being doubled is double.

In the United States, the population of the inhospitable desert land of Arizona is increasing faster than any other. It would not have been the Pilgrim Fathers' first choice as a place to settle but now it's a popular last resort because there's open space left there. Sure, it's sand but it's space. It won't last long.

Vacant lots in hometowns everywhere are a thing of the past. Backyards are being sold to developers who build two houses there. American kids are not organizing their own baseball games because the lots where they used to play have houses on them now. Their only choice is the communal Little League field. Many major league baseball players are from countries that still have some space but that will disappear, too.

It seems apparent that we should discourage the conception of hundreds of millions of babies who are born not to parents who want them but to parents who haven't learned how not to have them.

## NO TIME FOR A GOOD TIME

Everything's crowding in on us. It isn't just too many people it's too many things to do, too many possessions, too much equipment designed to make life easier, too many wires leading to too many electric appliances, too many relationships to maintain. There are too many events, too many movies and too much television. There are too many books to read. The newspaper keeps coming. There's no time to sit down and stare out the window without feeling you ought to be doing something.

There isn't time to think or to read because there's too much to do. It's possible to fill a day so full of going places and doing things that we can get from breakfast to bedtime without having had a single serious thought.

What could we do to open up some free time in our lives? An Hour of Golden Silence every night on television would help but they'd never do that unless it became law. We have worse laws. For one designated prime-time hour each evening, every channel would cease all programming—go to black. Children with nothing to watch might do their homework. We'd be forced to talk to each other, to read, to sit and think, wash the dishes, call home or go to bed.

One of the great thieves of time is advertising. Advertisers won't leave us alone. We don't want them tugging at our sleeve all day saying "Buy this, buy this." We sit down in our living room at night to read the paper. We thumb through the ads to get to the news while someone on television is trying to get us to buy a new car and the phone rings. Would we be interested in buying life insurance or a magazine subscription? I'm surprised the publishers of novels haven't sold advertising space on some of those blank pages they have at the beginning and the end of their books.

Aside from unwanted calls with pesky sales pitches, the telephone is a major time-waster. Schools might teach courses in how to make phone calls brief. People ought to make notes on what they want to say before they call. Once on the line, they'd go down their list of things to say and hang up without the small talk that takes so much time and relays so little information. There might be one hour in every day when no one made any phone calls. Telephones could be programmed not to ring during that hour or a recording would say "We are at home having a quiet time and don't want to talk to anyone."

We could get ourselves some free time if sporting events were not drawn out in order to provide more time for commercials. Nine innings of baseball seems endless. Every sporting event takes an hour longer than it did 25 years ago. It's an hour of our time they're taking.

The baseball season itself drags on into the football season. Football, a fall sport, ends in February. They're still playing the Stanley Cup ice hockey championship games long after the ice is out of any lake in North America.

One sport overlaps another. There's no open water between seasons. Baseball should finish by Labor Day and be illegal after the football season starts. October is too late for the Boys of Summer. We don't need two sports taking our time.

Mail, which was once one of life's little pleasures, is a time-consuming chore. You sort through the stack with a wastebasket at hand, dropping the obvious junk into it unopened. Some of the junk is not immediately obvious and you open it before throwing it out. It all takes time.

Everyone has you wait to save them time. Doctors' waiting rooms are equipped with chairs and reading materials to make your time-wasting wait less painful. Airports are understaffed at ticket counters and security points. A long line means nothing to them. You wait and waste time while they save the money that adequate staff would have cost them.

Someone told me of the sad case of a relative who had to be institutionalized because he couldn't face the world. He kept going back to bed and pulling the blankets up over his head. He may be the sane one.


## EASY DOESN'T DO IT

It would please a lot of people if the literature and the directions that come with almost everything didn't say how easy the product was to use or put together.

Whether it's a cake mix, an outdoor chair, a foreign language course or a new VCR, the people selling it insist on telling us it's "easy." Easy to make, easy to assemble, easy to learn, easy to use, easy to store. Even a child can do it.

I use the program called WORDPERFECT on my computer. Here's the first line of a brochure that came in the box with it. "WORD PERFECT is so easy to use that it puts even the novice at ease."

This is not true and don't try to tell me it is. Nothing about a computer is easy. If you ask a person who is expert with his computer about a problem you have with yours, he can't help.

I keep a big box filled with manuals and books of direction that came with appliances I've bought. Somewhere in every one of them is the phrase EASY TO USE. If they told us in advance how difficult it was, we wouldn't have anything to do with it. If I'd known in advance how hard my new laptop computer was going to be, I'd never have bought it.

Look in a cookbook or at a menu in the feature section of the newspaper. If they give you a recipe, they invariably tell you it's simple or, perhaps, "Easy as ABC."

Have you ever seen a recipe that said "This is difficult to make and if you aren't an experienced chef, it won't be any good the first eight or ten times you make it"? They never say that. They say it'll be easy to make. Easy as pie. As if a good pie was easy to make.

"Learn to speak Russian in 10 easy lessons!" Sure. In just a few months, at a cost of $800, you'll be able to say "Hello," "Goodbye," "Have a nice day," "Which way to the Kremlin" and "More butter, please" in Russian with an American accent that makes it incomprehensible to any citizen of Moscow.

The reason for all the talk about how easy it is to do something is part salesmanship but not always totally deceitful.

Once a person knows how to do something, it really does seem easy to him or her. Swimming is a good example. I can still remember being taught how to swim. My Aunt Anna had me in the water. First she demonstrated, by swimming a short distance herself, then she asked me to make the same motions. "It's easy" she said. I made the motions in the water and sank.

Once you know how to swim, it's hard to understand why everyone can't do it. The trouble is, if you don't know how, you sink. If my new computer was the ocean, I'd have drowned by now.

## QUICK, EASY AND POOR

The ultimate goal of just about every invention or technological achievement is the elimination of physical labor. An invention is usually something that does the hard work for us. We don't lift or carry as much as our ancestors did before the wheel.

The automobile was invented to make it easier for us to get from here to there without walking. The typewriter was invented to make putting words on paper easier and faster than doing it by hand with a pen or a pencil. The cotton picker and the cotton gin took the hard work out of getting cotton off the bushes and taking the seeds out of the fiber. Pillsbury sells mixes in little boxes that enable anyone to "make" a cake without doing much more than adding water.

Are we doing the right thing replacing ourselves with gimmicks, gadgets and mechanical aids? If we are, what is this great, dissatisfied sensation that so often comes over us when we plunk down on the couch in the living room some nights after not having lifted a finger to do any real work all day long?

You can't make a case for digging a ditch with a pickaxe and shovel if there's a backhoe available but there's satisfaction and pride to be had from doing a job that doesn't come with having it done for you.

We admire the person who walks to work. We marvel at the gardener who grows vegetables. We prefer the homemade cake to the mix not only because it's better but because of some indefinable something in it that a cake made from a mix doesn't have. Although it is better,too. We prefer the intimacy of the handwritten letter or the special look of a sweater knitted by the wearer.

Making something involves straightening or curving or somehow changing the shape of basic material and then assembling it into some useful or decorative form. The process involves frustrating difficulties for the workman or artist but then a final gratification, on the completion of the work, that is unavailable to us in any other pursuit.

It seems likely that we've gone too far having everything done for us when you consider the satisfaction we miss by not doing it ourselves. Working, sweating, getting physically tired are their own reward. It feels great when you're accomplishing something, no matter how simple a job. It's a feeling you can't get by pressing a button. The best kind of work is a combination of intellectual and manual. We're getting too much of one and not enough of the other.

It's interesting to note how much satisfaction people who do not work with their hands for a living get from working with their hands as a hobby.

Collecting wood and making furniture are my hobbies and, even though I work with my brain and not my hands writing for a living, when I am working with my hands at my hobby, I make more mental mistakes than manual mistakes. Why is that?

The good feeling I get is not only on the occasion of the completion of the chair or the table or the chest of drawers. There is constant satisfaction and frustration during the whole course of making it. Doing the work is the good part. It is a letdown when I finish making a piece of furniture. There is that one flash of pleasure but then I realize the fun and satisfaction of doing it are over.

Like cake mixes, a lot of things that come with the hard work done, aren't satisfying.

## COMMUNICATING NOTHING—BUT FAST

A computer doesn't make the writing any better but it makes it easier to correct things or start over. It's a good tool for a writer. On a computer I can rewrite and correct sentences without tearing a sheet of paper out of the typewriter and throwing it away. On my computer, I don't print it until I have it the way I want it.

Communication by email or the Internet has been a disappointment to me. There isn't much content in what's being communicated. When we were kids, we made "telephones" by stretching a waxed string between two empty, cylindrical cardboard ice cream containers. We'd make a small hole in the bottom of each container, put the string through, knot it at each end and then talk to each other at a distance of perhaps fifty feet. It was good fun but we never had anything to say to each other.

"Hello, Bobby? Is that you? Can you hear me?" I'd say to Bobby standing in plain view 50 feet from where I stood.

What happens on the Internet is a lot like that. The technology of communication is ahead of what is being communicated. People good with computers are getting in touch with strangers worlds away but when the two make contact, they frequently have nothing to tell each other. The computer whiz is a cultural idiot.

In the 1970s, citizens band radios were popular. For a while almost everybody had one. Being able to talk to passing drivers was another technological breakthrough. Everyone was saying "Over and out" but the CB fad blew over in 10 years because, while it was easy to talk to a truck driver, he never had anything to say that you wanted to hear.

Now they have a computer on which a person at one end can see and speak to a person at the other end. On a television news broadcast demonstrating it, a man talked to his elderly mother 1,000 miles away.

"Hello, Mom?" he said. "Is that you?" The conversation wasn't much different from that I had 70 years ago with Bobby.

I wish people with brains enough to use a computer were better at having something to say.

## SO SMART YET SO DUMB

To increase sales, manufacturers of almost everything change the product's color, give it a new name or add an ingredient. They know what suckers we are for the latest thing. If our neighbors have the one with the new franakapan we want one, too.

Automobile manufacturers have always created new sales by designing a new hood ornament for cars that are basically the same as the ones they produced last year. They change the model name or number and add or subtract some chromium strips. Only every four or five years do they engineer a major design overhaul. This is the American Way.

The computer industry has taken planned obsolescence to new heights. Whatever you buy for your computer, including a new computer, it's out of date before you get it home and out of the box it came in. In the 12 years I've been using a computer to write on, I have had to buy five new computers to stay with new developments.

The new sales trick in the world of computers is not a change in the shape of the hood ornament or the curve of the lid to the trunk. What computer manufacturers do is make your machine out-of-date by coming up with new programs that don't work on your old machine. Incompatibility is money in their bank.

The range and variety of computers and computer equipment available is more than a mainframe computer itself could sort out to be just what you want when you try to use it. Each machine should come with a technician who could show you how to use it, how to fix it and how to make it compatible with all other computers.

Young people are better with computers than most people who are middle-aged and up. That's me—"up." They use computers at work every day and, when I come in the morning, they've been busy sending messages because there are always a few in my email. Yesterday I read this message from someone in the company who identified herself as "Dana."

Dana's message read :

"A box of tapes were picked up from archives they were for Denise at 'Face the Nation.' The subject of the tapes were on China and the Long Beach Navel Yard in Calif. If you took these tapes by mistake please return it."

How can someone smart enough to use a computer be almost illiterate when it comes to writing a message?

Next to my antique computer, circa 2000, is my 1919 Underwood typewriter, working as well as the day it was made. Underwood never got with "planned obsolescence." It may account for why they're out of business. Their product was so good, no one ever had to buy a new one.

## THE REPAIR MAN COMETH

There are daily articles in the paper about "the communications revolution." The "information highway" is at our fingertips. It sounds good but when it comes to doing anything real, the information highway is a dirt road. There's just so much information that needs to be exchanged. At some point, someone has to stop communicating and get to work. The technology of communications stresses the speed with which information can be sent but no one is paying any attention to the useless quality of too much of the information going out.

We use a small apartment in New York City several times a month. Last week we were using the dishwasher when we got the most dreaded call an apartment-dweller on the 12th floor can have from someone on the 11th: the neighbors downstairs said water was leaking into their kitchen from above. Our washing machine was just finishing its "spin" cycle so we knew the source of the problem.

We called GE and made a date for a repair man to come "between one and four on Thursday." I stayed home from work so I'd be there at the appointed hour. Has a repair man who says he'll come "between one and four" ever, in the whole history of repairmen, ever come at one?

He arrived this day about 3:30 with one small case in each hand. He put down his cases, pulled the washing machine away from the wall and turned it on. I had visions of an angry call from below but he assured me he'd watch for a flood. It was, as I suspected, a leaky drain hose in back.

The repair man opened one of his suitcase-like bags that had a variety of tools in it. He had a second black case which he put on the kitchen counter. He opened it and to my surprise, revealed a state-of-the-art laptop computer. Ignoring the tools like screwdrivers, wrenches, pliers and hammers in his other bag, he turned on the computer and started tapping away. He might just as well have been an airline ticket clerk booking me on a flight to Toledo.

"I'm looking to see if I have the hose for this model," he said.

If there'd been anyone around interested in betting, I'd have bet them $100 that he didn't have that hose.

"I don't see one," he said finally, gazing at the screen. "I'll have to go to the truck and look."

Well, I knew that. Of course he had to go to the truck. Repair men always have to go to the truck. They go back to the truck at best and back to their shop at worst to get the part.

The computer had said he didn't have the part in the truck but he didn't trust the computer any more than I did. He went to the truck. Ten minutes later he reappeared without the replacement hose. The computer was right.

"I'll have to come back Thursday" he told me, turning again to his computer and hitting more keys.

"$46 for today" he said, looking up. "How do you want to pay? The hose will be $45. Unless you want to attach it yourself, there's a $96 installation charge."

I don't do plumbing or electrical work.

So much for modern technology. It was exactly the same as a visit from a repair man would have been before computers but nine times as expensive and nothing was fixed.

Computers simply are not *helping* enough. They don't solve problems. They become part of the problem, adding instead of subtracting from it. You can't apply computer technology to a leaky hose in the back of a washing machine.

The time seems to be rapidly coming when no one will know how to DO anything. We'll all be able to get in touch with one another electronically and exchange information on the highway about our problems but the information we exchange won't have anything to do with solving our problems.

## PENNIES FROM HELL

The time has come to give up on pennies.

The one cent coin's day has come and gone. It was a nice little piece of copper coin in its day but then it turned to zinc and its charm, not to mention its value, was reduced to nothing. Pennies are obsolete, useless, a pain-in-the-pocket. There is no longer anything you can buy with one. No one even bothers to stop and stoop to pick one up when it has been inadvertently dropped on the street. The person who dropped it obviously didn't bother. Maybe it wasn't even dropped "inadvertently." Maybe it was dropped "vertently." On purpose. An itinerant beggar wouldn't bother with one.

There are few things more annoying than to get to the cash register and find you are being charged $11.01 for the items you've chosen to buy. If you pay with a $20, your pocket or purse will be further loaded down with a five, four ones and 99 cents in change, including four pennies.

Our U.S. Mint is still churning out more than ten billion pennies a year. Why? They estimate that there are 106 billion pennies "in circulation" but it's ridiculous to say there are that many pennies circulating among us because pennies don't circulate. They get put in a shoe box or old coffee can.

Fortunately, coffee cans have remained the same size even though the coffee that comes in them has been reduced by 35 percent. They empty more quickly now to make way for more pennies. If Maxwell House ever reduces the size of their cans to fit the actual amount of coffee they put in them, penny-savers nationwide will have to look elsewhere for a place to put their change.

In years past I gave a big box of change to a grandchild at Christmas. The first year, when he was seven, he had a good time counting the coins. The next year he got his father to take them to the bank. Last Christmas, I didn't bother giving him my year's accumulation of nickels, dimes and pennies because I realized that even a nine-year-old is not interested in small change. It isn't as though he could stop at a store near his school and buy penny candy. Penny candy costs a quarter now. A nickel candy bar is fifty cents.

The penny has been devalued everywhere. There used to be an expression people used when they saw a friend in quiet contemplation. They'd say "A penny for your thoughts." No one would say that anymore because it would be insulting to suggest that a friend's thoughts were worth so little.

There was a popular song years ago called *Pennies from Heaven*. No songwriter today would write something with such a worthless title and heaven wouldn't stoop to dealing in pennies anyway. If it started raining pennies today, you'd have to figure it was someone up there emptying his pockets before hanging up his pants.

The U.S. Mint says there are 181 pennies in a pound. They are 97.5 percent cheap zinc, with a thin coating of copper to make them look more valuable. If pennies were made of copper, they'd be worth fifteen cents.

The Mint doesn't have the kind of statistic about pennies that we need. For instance how many pennies are there in a coffee can or a shoe box? The other thing they don't tell us is why they keep making ten billion a year when no one wants even one.

## SAVINGS BANKS
## COULDN'T BE SAVED

It's hard for anyone under 50 to believe but people used to take their weekly paycheck to the bank, go up to the window with the friendly teller whom they'd been doing business with for years and give him their money. They'd put most of it in their checking account so they could pay their bills and a little of it in their savings account. The bank paid them 4 percent interest and that's the way they accumulated money for their retirement. Social Security was a thing of the future.

Banks were dependable, friendly hometown institutions. They were solidly built, usually of stone, a reflection of the rock-solid nature of the institution. Everyone knew where the bank was in town. It often had the date it was built carved in its cornerstone in roman numerals. Roman numerals were a sign of class. Today the bank building has probably been taken over and made into a Duane Reade or Rite Aid drugstore that also sells greeting cards and bottled water.

The names of banks sounded honest and dependable. In addition to the name of the town or city, almost all of them had First, American, Home, Trust, Federal or National in their title. The First National Home Federal Savings Bank of Dayton. They didn't sound like companies that would cheat you. Customers didn't think of them as businesses but as institutions, like hospitals and churches. The only thing dishonest that ever happened in a bank was in the movies when a masked gunman came in and told the teller to "put 'em up" and hand over the money.

Alas, those days are dead and gone forever. Even the bank robbers were a better class of people than they are now. In recent years dozens of banks, all of which have changed their names several times over the years, have been caught stealing. The man with the mask who gets what the teller has in a hold-up, is small potatoes compared to the millions a white-collar thief who cooks the bank's books can take for himself. He doesn't even need a getaway car.

You're more apt to approach a machine than a teller if you go to the bank today and if there is a teller behind the counter, he or she has only been there since March. He's never heard of you. The tellers no longer stay long enough to get to know the customers or be given gold watches. Tellers may handle hundreds of thousands of dollars a day but they are at the low end of the wage scale. There are many women tellers now. If one sister waits on tables and the other works at the bank, the waitress makes better money.

Really wealthy people don't have any money but they can borrow millions. Donald Trump is a good example. Being deep in debt is the true sign of a rich person. A poor person can't borrow anything.

Not many people who make good money put any of it in savings accounts anymore. Inflation is apt to be higher than the interest on the account. If you have $10,000 in a savings account on January 1st, you may have $10,400 with the interest a year later. Meanwhile inflation has been at the rate of 6 percent and your $10,400 will only buy $9,800 worth of stuff.

As a result, saving money has gone out of style. Too bad because it was one of life's little satisfactions. The new way is to spend all you have and borrow as much as they'll let you and hope you can pay it off sometime in the future—so your credit will be good enough to let you borrow more. People no longer take any pleasure from being out of debt. The couple who pay off their mortgage don't understand money. Borrowing more on credit cards than they can afford.

Most moderately well paid Americans put money in the stock market. As amateur investors, with the market on its way up, they're lucky to make a few dollars. The real money isn't made by people who are guessing which way a stock will go. It's made by the insiders who know. There are laws that make buying and selling information you know about a company that no one else knows illegal, but insider traders are hard to catch. Insider trading happens ten thousand times a day on Wall Street but a case comes to court only twice a year. Martha Stewart was just unlucky. The whole business of buying and selling stock is based on inside information or at least on information that the buyer hopes is inside. A really successful stockbroker can make more money buying a stock himself if he knows it's going up, than he can make advising clients to buy it. Why would a broker sell good information instead of acting on it himself? Trainers who fix horse races don't reduce the payoff by selling the name of the winner.

It's naive to believe that people in management positions don't know what's going to happen to a company's earnings better than a stranger who may have read a little about it. Of course that insider is going to find a way to put money in or take money out of the company, based on his knowledgeable guess about what's going to happen to it.

The rest of us plug along, doing the best we can and wondering how in the world we can save some of the money we make now that our friendly bank teller has either become an insider trader or a cashier at Walgreen's in his old bank building.

## AN INCOMPLETE INVENTION

The farmer had been trapped for 10 days with 100 cows to milk and feed during the terrible ice storm that hit the Northeastern part of the United States and Canada. His farm was without heat, light or power of any kind. His family and his cows were cold and hungry.

Late one afternoon, as the sun dwindled down and the cold got colder, he heard the sound of a loud engine. Within minutes a helicopter appeared on the horizon and landed in his field.

An anxious pilot squeezed the farmer on board and whisked him to the nearest small town where he was able to borrow a truck with a plow and return to his family and his animals with supplies, gas and a generator.

This is the kind of happy-ending story on which the helicopter's romantic reputation is based. In the story, it is a magical invention that defies gravity, goes up and down vertically on command and accomplishes missions under difficult conditions. Alas, the truth about helicopters is not so romantic.

The 11,000 privately operated helicopters flying in the U.S. are an engineering marvel that consistently amaze people viewing them from the ground but they are an invention waiting to be completed. There are problems with helicopters that have never been solved. The big rotor whose lift keeps them aloft creates a great amount of vibration because it's impossible to precisely even out the effect of the blade as it goes forward in a tilted, or lifting position with the effect of the retreating blade, which changes pitch so it whirls more nearly horizontal to the ground. If I understand it and I don't, of course, the retreating blade actually creates "negative lift."

More than almost any other modern-day invention, helicopters have failed to live up to their advance notices. Maybe the problem has been more with over-optimistic notices than with the aircraft itself. There was a time when magazine stories promised that, in the very near future, businessmen were going to be routinely taking off from their backyards every morning, landing on the roof of their place of business 20 miles away in a few minutes to take the elevator down to their office. This was going to end the hours of stop-and-go driving. You may recall that other stories in the magazine were about the imminent arrival of cheap, non-polluting battery-powered cars and the small screen attached to every telephone that would enable us to see who we were talking to.

The helicopter is still a contraption. The best of them do good police and rescue work but there are more things they can't do than things they can and they are as socially unacceptable in the city as a cigar smoker at a tea party because they are loud. The crash of one at the Pan Am building heliport near Grand Central Terminal in New York in 1977 ended the fairy tale of the businessman's commute. Helicopters were banned from taking off in the City except over water.

The most advanced military helicopter, the Blackhawk, did some amazing things but was so unreliable it was grounded.

Years ago I spent two weeks in the air over Scotland in a French helicopter gracefully named an "Alouette." You get to be good friends quickly in the air and when the filming was done, I promised my friend the pilot, Francis Campion, that I'd make yearly visits to France to see him. Three weeks after our trip, he was piloting a cameraman over the Tour de France road race and was killed in the Alouette we had flown.

Fifteen years ago, I flew across the United States and back in a big, twin-engine Sikorsky helicopter that was state-of-the-art. On board were the cameraman, two of Sikorsky's ace pilots, Bill Kramer and Dave Wright, and myself. Beneath us, struggling to keep up for daily maintenance, were two of Sikorsky's best mechanics. The rotor spent the day shaking the daylights out of the machinery and they spent half the night putting it back together. We all became fast friends on that trip.

At the end of the month we bade each other a sad goodbye and Bill and Dave promised to come to New York several times a year for a reunion dinner. Three months later, Bill was killed flying a mission to pick up the Shah of Iran when he visited the United States.

So much for old friends who were helicopter pilots. The icebound farmer must think of helicopters as the answer to all of man's transportation problems but he shouldn't hope for too much from them. Helicopters are magic one day but they'll break your heart the next.

# PART 14

---

# *People and Places*

*People don't whistle as much as they used to.*

# NAMES

A lot of people have names I'd rather have than my own. I don't dislike Andy Rooney, it's just that I can think of names I'd rather have.

A good name should sound important and not pompous. "Andy" is frivolous. My name is Andrew, of course, and I prefer that to Andy but only three people call me Andrew. You don't get to decide whether you're important or not.

It's not clear why some people get called by a nickname while others keep their whole first name. You wouldn't call Walter Cronkite "Walt" but, on the other hand, you wouldn't call the cartoon tycoon "Walter Disney." You wouldn't call Peter Jennings "Pete" but no one ever calls Brokaw "Thomas" or Rather "Daniel."

One of the good nicknames in television news is Cokie Roberts. Cokie needed one, too, because her real name is Mary Martha Corinne Morrison Claiborne Boggs Roberts.

During WW II, I knew both Ernest Hemingway and Ernie Pyle. No one ever called Pyle "Ernest" and no one ever called Hemingway "Ernie."

A lot of people trying to be friendly like politicians or preachers, insist on being called by their nickname as if it made them more likeable and accessible: William Jefferson Clinton is just plain Bill. Billy Graham, Jimmy Carter, Dick Cheney.

A really important-sounding name is one that starts with just an initial. "H. Ross" Perot. I doubt if the other kids called him "H. Ross" when he was young. If you have as much money as he has, you can be called anything you want. There was J. Edgar Hoover, F. Lee Bailey, J. Paul Getty and F. Scott Fitzgerald.

Some people prefer to be called by just one name. Cher, Liberace, Madonna and Imus for example. There are more people who have insisted on being called by three names: Frank Lloyd Wright, Sarah Jessica Parker, Andrew Lloyd Webber, William Randolph Hearst, Margaret Bourke-White, Clare Booth Luce, John Cameron Swayze, Martin Luther King, George Bernard Shaw, Mary Baker Eddy, John Phillip Sousa, Snoop Doggy Dog. If anyone called Ralph Waldo Emerson Ralph Emerson, you wouldn't know who they were talking about. It's the same with the man who shot Lincoln. It wasn't Jack Booth—it's always John Wilkes Booth.

There have been well known people who always included their middle initial in their name. Louis B. Mayer, John D. Rockefeller, Edward R. Murrow, Edward G. Robinson.

There are about the same number who always preferred using just their initials. W. C. Fields, P. J. O'Rourke, H. G. Wells, H. L. Mencken, T. S. Eliot, J. D. Salinger.

People who are called by silly nicknames must like it or they'd put a stop to it. For instance, there's "Tipper" Gore and "Whoopi" Goldberg.

It would be strange to have a name that was a noun: "Doris Day," "Billy Crystal," "Johnny Cash," "Ringo Starr," or even "Bob Hope." I guess you'd get used to it but names of things and names of people shouldn't be intermingled.

There are some great names. Vanessa Redgrave is one. Harry Belafonte has a swing to it. David Letterman couldn't be anything else. Dustin Hoffman, Marlon Brando, Alan Alda, Faye Dunaway, Susan Sarandon, Katharine Hepburn, Yo Yo Ma. Great names. On the other hand, I'd rather be Andy Rooney than Arnold Schwarzenegger, Roman Polanski or Engelbert Humperdinck.


# THE CAB DRIVER
# AND THE GOLD NECKLACE

Let me tell you a story about Patrick Coyne. Patrick was a New York City cab driver who liked me and wouldn't let me pay. It's embarrassing because I know I had more money than he did.

Patrick didn't care about money. He liked to take me where I was going free, better than he liked money. It was never a half-hearted gesture. He absolutely refused to take my money. One time I threw a $10 bill at him and he threw it in the street and sped off. I picked it up because I knew he wouldn't.

There are something like 17,000 taxicab drivers in New York so the chances of getting the same one twice is remote but it does happen because cab drivers have favorite locations. They return to the same spot looking for customers and hanging out with their friends—other drivers with the same ethnic background who congregate there. For example, cab-driving immigrants from Russia wait outside the Roosevelt Hotel. They are always there, more interested in fraternizing than getting a fare.

Patrick Coyne drove for 27 years and one of the places he heads for if things are slow is the front door of the office building where I work on 57th Street. Patrick picked me up six times. We were friends. He was a bright, interesting nut.

It had been almost two years since I'd seen Patrick when I got a letter from him. If you have a stereotyped view of what a New York cab driver is like, Patrick's letter should disabuse you of it.

"Do you remember Arlene Francis?" he asked after a few introductory sentences. "Her son was in my cab Tuesday. Arlene is now 83. She lies in a hospital bed at Mt. Sinai. She has broken bones in her feet. She has Alzheimer's. Her son said 'Now my mother is just a little old lady.'"

"When I began to drive a cab 25 years ago," Patrick wrote, the one person I most wanted to pick up was Arlene Francis.

"You may remember Arlene Francis always wore a gold, heart-shaped locket. It was a fifth anniversary gift from her husband, Martin Gabel. Six years ago, the locket was stolen by a chain-snatcher on Lexington Avenue. Today I went into Tiffany's and commissioned them to make a new locket for Arlene Francis from the design sketches they have of her old one.

"Some might say 'Why bother?' but when I was young . . . I wanted to live in a world where all the women were like Arlene Francis, attractive, vivacious and sparkling.

"For once in my life, I want to do something nice, something really nice. I am using the money I've saved.

"I can see you shake your head in disgust and I can hear you say 'Humbug'! (signed) Patrick Coyne, your cabby."

The letter had an address in the Bronx and I wrote Patrick there. Another year went by and I heard nothing from him. He no longer waited for a fare out front of my office building.

Patrick's next letter to me was from Washington, D.C.

"Dear Andrew," he wrote. "I have left New York and am working in a second-hand bookstore in Washington for $100. a week. After driving for 27 years in New York, I was in Times Square at 2 AM one morning. There was only one other car in all of Times Square that night and I hit it. I knew it was time for me to quit driving a cab."

Again I wrote back, this time suggesting he get a job in a store selling new books where he might make a living wage. Our exchanges were always light and inconsequential but I liked staying in touch. I've ignored thousands of letters because I didn't have time but I never ignored Patrick Coyne's.

In the Spring of 1997 a letter postmarked Magnolia, Mississippi, arrived with Patrick's familiar signature on it. He had moved into a one-room log cabin with his brother and his brother's dog. His sister was a nun in a nearby convent. Patrick said he liked the dog but did not get along with either his brother or his sister. "They are my brother and my sister though," he said. He was doing some volunteer work with a local children's library. He had terminal cancer. He didn't make anything of it. He simply said the doctor told him he would not live six months.

I wrote back to Patrick Coyne and enclosed a check for $500. He would have been insulted had I not told him I insisted that he spend it on something he didn't need. At last I wanted to get back at him, I said, for all the cab fares he didn't let me pay.

Less than a month later a fat letter arrived from there. It contained

20 pictures of happy kids running around a garden playground and they were all eating ice cream cones.

"I did what you told me," Patrick wrote. "I bought $500. worth of ice cream and invited all the young children in town to come and eat it."

Patrick returned to New York but I could never find him again. Three months later I received a note from his sister, the nun. Patrick had died alone. She wanted me to know that giving the heart-shaped gold locket to Arlene Francis and having the ice cream party for the kids with the money I'd sent him were the highlights of Patrick Coyne's life.

I don't get into a taxi without thinking of him.

## JIMMY STEWART, WAR HERO

It is probably true of most of us that, when we die, the most significant things about our lives are lost in platitudes about the obvious. By the time you get to be my age, you've known a lot of people who are dead now. It seems heartless but there isn't time to mourn for all of them.

I have never gotten over how disappointed I was by the reports of Jimmy Stewart's life and death because so little attention was paid to the best thing Jimmy did in his life. He was a bomber pilot in WW II and he did it better than he acted.

On Public Television, Jim Lehrer, one of the best interviewers there is, talked with a guest who knew Jimmy the night he died.

"He actually served during World War II, didn't he?" Lehrer asked.

I'll say Jimmy Stewart served during the war, Jim, and he was no tin soldier. He was lead pilot for the 445th Bomb Group of the Eighth Air Force, flying B24s out of Alconbury, England. He was one of the war's outstanding bomber pilots. You don't fly lead in your bomb group if you aren't the best. No one cares that you were a Hollywood star, you have to be good. Jimmy Stewart led the 445th on several of its most dangerous assignments. One was the first raid on the oil refinery at Ploesti during which 60 U.S. bombers were shot down. Stewart got his first Distinguished Flying Cross for that.

You didn't see much about Stewart's wartime career because no one was taking pictures on board a B24 over Germany with FW190s and ME109s boring in and mushroom clouds of flak explosions intermingled with the bombers. Katharine Hepburn and the photographers were not on board.

Stewart was eventually made a colonel but he got there the hard way, up through the ranks. Although already well known for his parts in *The Philadelphia Story* and *Mr. Smith Goes to Washington*, he enlisted in the Air Force as a private.

It's hard to imagine this tall, elegant gentleman immersed in a system designed to reduce everyone to the same level and it's interesting that he rose to the top there just as he had in private life. It makes you understand Jimmy Stewart was something special.

Jimmy had taken some private flying lessons at the Santa Monica airport as a diversion while he was making movies so he knew how to fly when he enlisted.

Within six months Stewart had separated himself from the crowd and was assigned to pilot training school. It soon became apparent to his superior officers that Stewart had exceptional ability as a pilot and, strangely enough that originally worked against him. He was assigned to train other pilots how to fly. Teaching wasn't what he enlisted to do and if there was ever a time he used his star status in the military to his personal advantage, it was writing to the upper-level Air Force officers to get himself out of training and into combat. The military was nervous about having someone famous in their midst because it could be a disruptive factor in actual combat and there were a lot of negative public relations possibilities to having someone so well known killed or taken prisoner.

It seems strange, I know, to have fond memories of the war but I have some and one of my good memories is of meeting Jimmy Stewart when he was awarded the Distinguished Flying Cross after the Ploesti raid. In 1943, I was a sergeant, serving as a reporter for the Army newspaper *The Stars and Stripes*. I went to Alconbury from London with a photographer to write the story of Jimmy's heroism.

I remember being reluctant to intrude on the event by asking the cameraman to walk out in front of the row of men assembled for the purpose of honoring Stewart but I did. We had to have the picture and Jimmy must have been a little proud of himself, too. And after all, it wasn't a Hollywood publicity shot we were after.

After the ceremony I interviewed Jimmy for my story. I had the same reaction to him that everyone who ever met him had: "What a great guy!"

Jimmy told me the story of his arrival in England on a typically foggy night. His navigator couldn't pinpoint Tibenham, the field they were supposed to land at, and they came into one six miles away.

That evening, less than two hours after their arrival, he and his crew were sitting around a Nissen hut listening to the radio when the notorious German propagandist with the heavy-handed British accent, Lord Haw Haw, came on the air from Berlin. It was Stewart's frightening initiation to the efficiency of German intelligence in Great Britain.

"Good evening," Lord Haw Haw began. "Allow me to be the first to welcome the Four Hundred and Forty-fifth Bomb Group to England."

Jimmy said his jaw dropped. "And welcome," the Nazi propagandist continued, "to film actor Jimmy Stewart!"

I treasure having shaken hands with Jimmy Stewart.


## THE MYTH OF GREATNESS


When I first read *The Sun Also Rises*, I was young. I thought Ernest Hemingway was the best novelist I had ever read.

Now, 50 years later, after having shared two brief but intense experiences with him during WW II and having read two bad books of his, *Across the River and Into the Trees* and *A Moveable Feast*, and, most recently having read what they call "a fictionalized memoir" in *The New Yorker* magazine, I feel comfortable saying out loud what I've been thinking silently for years. Hemingway was a jerk and, more often than not, a poor writer. People mistook his mannered style for literature.

"Papa" was his own name for himself, if that gives you any clue to his character. He liked to refer to himself as that and often signed his letters "Papa."

I met Hemingway on August 22, 1944, in the town of Rambouillet. About 40 reporters were following Allied soldiers fighting their way toward Paris. We had descended on the small but charming Grand Veneur Hotel with a band of Maquis, the French freedom fighters with whom he had associated himself. The rest of the reporters were with the First Army press camp but Hemingway had arrived first. He was a constant nuisance to Army public relations both because of his fame and because of his persistently macho style. He insisted on carrying a weapon. No other newsman or woman ever went out armed. If captured unarmed, the protocol of war called for them to be treated as officers. Armed and out of uniform, reporters could be shot as spies.

Hemingway had taken over eight of the 35 rooms in the hotel and the reporters sleeping on the floor in the dining room resented it. Bruce Grant of the *Chicago Sun-Times* went up to Hemingway and demanded he give up some of his rooms for other reporters.

Within minutes the confrontation erupted into a fist fight between the tall, thin, slightly built Grant and the muscular Hemingway. As they squared off and started swinging, Harry Harris, the five foot five inch AP photographer put his 145-pound body between them, extended one raised arm toward their chests and demanded that they stop.

Hemingway turned and strode out the French doors to the garden. Bruce Grant turned away, laughed and started talking again with friends who had seen the preliminaries to the fight.

After a brief period of quiet, Hemingway made a dramatic reappearance and bellowed at Grant, "Well, are you coming out and fight?"

I hadn't seen so juvenile a performance since Alfie Gordon punched Bobby Reedy in the stomach for taking his tricycle when they were five.

*The New Yorker* story is something any editor would run because of Hemingway's name on it but it is terrible. It tells of a hunting trip in Africa where Hemingway and his fourth wife, Mary Welsh, kill a great lion for the fun of it. The only drama involved comes when his wife, whom Hemingway calls "Miss Mary," claims that he spoiled her fun by shooting and killing the lion before she could.

The story is filled with evidence of Hemingway's search for his own virility. He keeps trying to sound like The Great White Hunter. "I could see the lion now and I kept *working* to the left."

He wasn't *working*, he was walking.

"Mary must take him soon, I thought" Hemingway writes.

Well, she wasn't going to *take* the lion. She was going to kill it. They both shot.

"Now we were there with the lion and he was Mary's and she knew it now and she saw how wonderful and long and dark and beautiful he was."

The lion wasn't beautiful anymore. It was dead. Big brave "Papa" and sweet little "Miss Mary" had shot it dead.

Pretty soon Hemingway says everyone else left and "Mary was alone with her sorrow." Sorrowful about not having killed the lion all by herself, I guess.

"Let's go" Hemingway quotes Miss Mary as saying then. "And when we're in bed, we can listen to the night."

That's not the night you hear, Miss Mary. That's the sound of a childhood Hemingway admirer throwing up.

# THE BEAUTY OF THE BRIDGE

There is some mystic quality about a bridge that's unmatched by anything else humans build for themselves. The act of constructing something that spans a body of water from shore to shore produces more poetic beauty in steel than any other mark we make on the face of the earth. It may be partly because bridges are simultaneously practical and pretty. They look good and get us where we want to go.

Bridges make the impossible possible. The body of water between us and our destination is no longer prohibitive. We don't have to wade, swim or board a boat. The bridge is just another street to walk or ride across.

For most of their working lives, bridges are taken for granted. Whenever there is a large or small war somewhere in the world, bridges always come into it because they make good pictures for television.

Bridges and animals don't do well in a war. Just a few years ago when we were trying to keep the Serbs from attacking the Albanians in Kosovo, we bombed down one of the grand old bridges that used to span the Danube. It had the effect of inhibiting the Serbian attacks but it was an ugly thing to have to do to so beautiful a structure.

It would have been sad for the architect who, perhaps 150 years ago, designed the bridge to withstand the load of river-crossing walkers and horse-drawn carts. He had even been prescient enough to anticipate the bumper-to-bumper weight of today's traffic and make it strong enough to stand up under the weight of vehicles he could only have imagined. Why would he know, in 1850, how to build a bridge across the Danube River strong enough to be used in 1999 by wheeled vehicles with diesel engines, weighing tons? How could the architect and the engineer have had that kind of foresight years before there was such a thing as a car or a truck?

We exult in such wartime triumphs as the destruction of an enemy bridge but were the architect who designed it alive today to see what we have done to his work, he would certainly weep.

Bridges are hard hit in a war. They're always being turned into a tangled mess of steel and dumped into the waters of the river running beneath them. An advancing army tries to destroy the bridges behind its enemy to interrupt its supply of food, fuel and ammunition and to cut off its retreat. An army can be more easily annihilated, when it is backed up against water it can't easily retreat across.

Then the aggressors reach the water. To get to the other side, they have to reconstruct the bridge they have destroyed or build a makeshift substitute. Quite often the victorious nation in a war has to rebuild the bridges it spent so much on bombs and air power to destroy.

One of the most dramatic river crossings in the history of war occurred on March 7th, 1945. The U.S. First Army was forcing the German Army, battle-after-battle, deeper back into its own country.

U.S. commanders were worried about what would happen when they got to the wide and swift-running Rhine River. Troops are vulnerable in the face of artillery fire and attacks from the air when they have to cross a body of water in small boats or on hastily built pontoon bridges.

The first Americans to reach the Rhine were members of the Ninth Armored Division when they arrived at the little riverside town of Remagen at the Western end of the Ludendorff Bridge. It was built to carry trains and spanned the Rhine 35 miles south of Cologne. German Army engineers had failed in their last-minute attempt to drop the bridge into the Rhine with dynamite placed in girders at its east end.

Within hours enough U.S. soldiers had raced across the span in the face of incessant shelling from German heavy artillery behind the hills, that they were able to establish a foothold on the German side of the Rhine. It was this stroke of great luck with the bridge at Remagen that led, just one month later, to the liberation of the prisoners at the concentration camp at Buchenwald and the subsequent defeat and surrender of the German Army.

That ugly old railroad bridge was one of the most beautiful in all of American history.

# YOUR PICTURES ARE READY, MR. HOFFMAN!

This will be the last sad chapter of a fascinating episode in my life that began on the west bank of the Rhine River in 1945, as German artillery shells plopped into the water around us.

I have received word from Stanley Cohn that his friend and mine, Marcus Hoffman, died in San Francisco.

It was in the little town of Remagen at the western end of the Ludendorff Bridge, a major link for European east-west freight train travel where I met Mark.

The German army had been slowly driven back across France and finally into its own Country at a great cost in lives to both the German and Allied Armies. The Wehrmacht finally stopped to regroup on the east bank of the Rhine, confident that the 200-yard-wide river would provide a barrier our soldiers couldn't cross. U.S. commanders worried over incurring catastrophic casualties as soldiers trying to cross the fast-flowing water became sitting ducks for German gunners looking down through the barrels of their guns from the hills above the eastern side of the river. (One of those high points overlooking the Rhine had been chosen, many years before, as the site for Count Ferdinand Von Zeppelin's launching of his first gas-filled airship.)

In the single luckiest stroke of luck the U.S. Army had in all of WW II, German engineers who had been ordered to blow up the bridge after the last Wehrmacht soldier had fled across it, failed. Dynamite had been lashed to strategic girders under the bridge in a manner designed to drop it into the Rhine but through some error in communication, the explosives were never detonated. The Ninth Armored Division, arriving in Remagen and finding the bridge intact, thought first that it was a great German trap. There was nothing to do but take the chance and hope. Foot soldiers, tanks and other vehicles of the Ninth Armored poured across it quickly and in force. Getting behind German lines up and down the Rhine at just that one point compromised the safety of German forces from one end of it to the other. They never knew when we might be coming at them from behind. They had no alternative to retreat. It was the beginning of the end for the German Army and Adolf Hitler.

As a young reporter for the Army newspaper, *The Stars and Stripes*, I knew the crossing of the Rhine was an event of great military importance and I was nervous about whether I was good enough to write a story that important.

Reporters got used to writing anywhere at war and I wrote that day with my battered portable Underwood typewriter resting on the hood of my jeep as I sat on a stack of four empty Jerry cans. There was just one other reporter there that day, Howard Cowan of the Associated Press, and no photographers.

Still photographers did not distinguish themselves in the land war in Europe. The great one, Bob Capa, had been killed and many of the journeymen photographers were burdened with cumbersome 10-pound Speed Graphic cameras that were better suited to taking pictures of Hollywood beauties than soldiers at war.

I knew my editor would want pictures to go with my story of that bridge over the Rhine any way I could get them. As I paused from typing to think of the right word, I saw a lieutenant I recall now as tall and handsome, taking pictures of GIs crossing the bridge with a Leica he had appropriated from a surrendering German soldier. Americans were just learning how good Leica and Contax cameras were. I stopped writing, walked from my jeep the 50 yards to the bridge and approached the lieutenant. His name was Marcus Hoffman, an officer in an engineer battalion. After explaining who I was, I pleaded with him to loan me his three rolls of undeveloped pictures.

With my sworn promise to return them when I got them back from *The Stars and Stripes* editorial offices in Paris, he reluctantly gave me the film.

I was able to get the pilot of a Piper Cub reconnaissance plane attached to the Ninth Armored, to take them back to his base and dispatch them by courier to Paris. Army communications channels were pretty good for something like this.

In Paris the editors were ecstatic. I was as much of a hero as if I'd taken the pictures myself. Marcus Hoffman's pictures were good and they used three of them on the front page the next day with my story. No other news organization had pictures of any kind that first day. I had made it clear how important it was that I respect my promise to return Hoffman's pictures and the negatives, along with several dozen prints, arrived back two days later by courier.

Did I search out Lt. Marcus Hoffman and return his pictures? I did not. He moved forward with his unit and I was busy with other stories. It was an incredibly important few days of the war and before I could concentrate on finding Marcus Hoffman we overran Buchenwald. A few rolls of film of a bridge crossing no longer seemed important. It nagged me but I put it in the back of my mind. I kept telling myself I would certainly get his pictures back to Marcus Hoffman shortly. I never did and it haunted me for fifty years.

In 1995 I wrote a book called *My War*. I still had the pictures and in the book I told the story about how bad I felt about never having returned them. I had made a few attempts to locate a "Marcus Hoffman" but there were a lot of them and I had no idea where my Marcus Hoffman came from.

"Marcus Hoffman," I wrote on page 247 of *My War*, "where are you?"

It was at about this same time that Mark Hoffman became aware that *The Stars and Stripes* reporter to whom he had entrusted his pictures had the same name as the commentator at the end of the television broadcast *60 Minutes*. He had not read *My War* when he wrote me the following letter:

"Dear Andy,

About fifty years ago you were at the Remagen Bridge. You borrowed my roll of film but never returned it to me. Would you happen to have the pictures? Probably not."

I was flabbergasted but exultant at the thought of finally getting out from under the cloud of guilt I had felt for so long. Without any note, I packed up Marcus Hoffman's carefully preserved pictures and sent them to him. Three days later Mark wrote again, amazed and with effusive thanks. There have been few more satisfying days in my life.

We corresponded after that and I kept promising I'd come to San Francisco to see him but I never did. In his letter, Stanley Cohn told me things I had not know about Mark—that he had been a swimmer in Billy Rose's famous Aquacade show, for example, and that his art gallery, Maxwell's, was one of the best known in San Francisco. Marcus Hoffman is dead now. We'll never meet again and I feel a little of the guilt I felt during all those years I didn't return his pictures.

## AN AFFAIR
## WITH NORTH CAROLINA

Since my time as an Army recruit at Fort Bragg, I've had mixed feelings about North Carolina. It's the best of States, it's the worst of States.

We were under power on Walter Cronkite's 48-foot sailboat, cruising down the Inland Waterway in the northern part of North Carolina. Walter is such a good old friend that it doesn't occur to me that I'm dropping it when I use his name.

By 4 p.m. the sky was gray, the sun was sinking and we were ready to find a place to dock for the night. We had just come through a bridge that opens only on the half hour. That gives you a sense of accomplishment and you need all those you can get to fill in the day on board a small boat. We looked forward to a drink and dinner on board. We saw a public dock a few hundred yards ahead along the side of the waterway near the small town of Chesapeake and Walter eased the side of his boat up against the telephone-pole size dock posts and we tied up.

A small bridge of boards 10 feet long and five feet wide with a flimsy two-by-four railing ran from the dock, over the water that separated it from land.

Across the bridge, sitting on the incline of the bank was a small boy with a fishing pole. It was a scene from Tom Sawyer and I thought to myself how good and All-American North Carolina seemed. I could forget Jesse Helms.

Suddenly the boy jerked his pole upward and in spasmodic starts and stops, reeled in his line. He lifted his pole and there, dangling from his hook was a 12-inch bass trying desperately to shake itself free of the hook in its mouth.

The boy dropped the fish on the grassy bank and pinned it firmly but gently to the ground with all four fingers across its belly and his thumb under it.

With his left hand the boy deftly removed the hook from the fish's mouth.

"He's got his dinner" someone on board said.

The boy stood up with the fish in both hands and walked to the little bridge. Clutching his fish, he got down on his knees, then his elbows and knees and finally his stomach. With his head hanging over the side of the dock, he reached down and gently put the fish back in the water and released it.

"It hurts them if you throw them back" the boy said. It was the first indication that he knew we were watching.

"You don't keep any of them?" one of us asked.

"No," he said." I'd like to keep him because my brother won't believe I caught him but I never keep them." He stood there for a few seconds, watching the fish to make sure it was all right. "There aren't enough of them," he said.

The boy paused, staring at the water where his fish had been. "They don't eat for three days after you catch them," he said. You could tell he felt sorry about making the fish's mouth sore.

"What a great kid" I thought to myself. "North Carolina. What a great State to have such a great kid."

The following day we stopped again near sundown, this time at a small marina that had a small inconvenient convenience store at dock-side. The good old boy who ran the place was loquacious but not the type who'd ever made me think highly of North Carolina.

"Daddy run this place forty years" he said. "Died three years ago."

When he said he was driving the 10 miles to town, we asked if he could pick up a newspaper. I reached into my pocket for money but he stopped me.

"I'll git it off'n you later" he said. "Don't worry." Then, with a sly grin, he leaned toward me and said "Like a Saturday night nigger . . . I'll cut your pockets right out."

"North Carolina," I thought to myself. "The best of States, the worst of States."

## NO ONE'S PERFECT

I received three checks in the mail. One of them, from my publisher, was the second installment on my share of profits of the book *My War*. The others were my regular monthly retirement check from the Writers Guild and the Directors Guild. I get them even though I am not retired. It's the same with Social Security. I get that even though I am not socially insecure.

One of my simple pleasures is taking a check to the bank. Somehow when a check is mailed to the bank and all I get is a notice saying that it has been deposited, it isn't satisfying.

Wednesday morning I decided to take the three checks to the bank. While I was out, I planned to take four watches that needed various kinds of help to a real watchmaker in Grand Central Terminal. One watch was given to me by CBS, the other by *60 Minutes*. I'd just as soon have had a raise but they gave me the watches. I seldom wear either but they needed new batteries. The $29 Timex, which I wear, needed a new strap.

My bank is near Grand Central so I put the three checks and the four watches in a briefcase and got a taxi. At Grand Central I paid for the ride and crossed the street to take the elevator to the watchmaker on the fourth floor . . . without my briefcase.

I had left the three checks on the back seat. I ran into the middle of 42nd Street and looked east as the cab disappeared in traffic.

How, I asked myself, could I be so dumb, careless, irresponsible? Was senility setting in?

I got back to the office 45 minutes later having decided not to tell Susie because I felt so foolish. It is difficult to look normal when you don't feel normal but I walked in trying to look normal. I didn't want her to suspect anything.

"Did you lose something?" she asked cheerily as I came in. "Here's your briefcase. They just brought it up. They said an English tourist saw your address on an envelope and turned it in to security downstairs."

I was dumbfounded and I don't dumbfound easily.

They had taken the man's name and the name of his hotel. I called. Like most Americans anyone with a British accent sounds educated and cultured to me. I thanked him profusely and asked if I could show him around CBS News and buy him lunch the next day. I wanted him to know how grateful I was, not only about getting my possessions back but for providing evidence that there are still decent people in the world. I planned to take him to a good, expensive French restaurant a few blocks from the office.

He arrived with the same accent I'd heard over the phone but his appearance was a surprise. He was about 40 years old, balding and wearing tattered bluejeans and a tacky T-shirt with some indistinguishable, four-color image on it.

As I showed him into my office, I slipped Susie a note to cancel my reservation at the restaurant. It isn't a T-shirt kind of place.

We spent half an hour touring CBS including a long stay on the balcony overlooking the *Evening News* Studio where Dan Rather was sitting at the anchor desk about to do a breaking news story. After the tour

I took my guest to the CBS cafeteria in the basement. The food is seldom of a high enough quality to be called mediocre. He thought it looked great and took a full plate. At lunch we talked about world problems. He was, like so many Englishmen, better informed than most Americans. He cleaned his plate and, after a moment's hesitation, asked if he might go back for a second helping.

When he finished, we went upstairs to my office and I started saying goodbye to this new British friend to whom I was so indebted. There was no question that offering him any kind of reward would have been wrong and offensive to him. He was genuinely pleased to have helped me. I took down his London phone number and made a mental note to call our daughter Ellen, who lives in London. I thought perhaps she might invite him to her house for dinner. Realizing I didn't know what my new British friend did for a living, I asked where he worked.

"Me and me buddy have a company" he said. "We make porno films."

Listen, no one's perfect. We said goodbye and I erased the mental note I'd made to have him call my daughter.

# ACKNOWLEDGMENTS

My thanks for the editing help of Kate Darnton and Susan Bieber.

PublicAffairs is a publishing house founded in 1997. It is a tribute to the standards, values, and flair of three persons who have served as mentors to countless reporters, writers, editors, and book people of all kinds, including me.

I.F. STONE, proprietor of *I. F. Stone's Weekly*, combined a commitment to the First Amendment with entrepreneurial zeal and reporting skill and became one of the great independent journalists in American history. At the age of eighty, Izzy published *The Trial of Socrates*, which was a national bestseller. He wrote the book after he taught himself ancient Greek.

BENJAMIN C. BRADLEE was for nearly thirty years the charismatic editorial leader of *The Washington Post*. It was Ben who gave the *Post* the range and courage to pursue such historic issues as Watergate. He supported his reporters with a tenacity that made them fearless and it is no accident that so many became authors of influential, best-selling books.

ROBERT L. BERNSTEIN, the chief executive of Random House for more than a quarter century, guided one of the nation's premier publishing houses. Bob was personally responsible for many books of political dissent and argument that challenged tyranny around the globe. He is also the founder and longtime chair of Human Rights Watch, one of the most respected human rights organizations in the world.

For fifty years, the banner of Public Affairs Press was carried by its owner Morris B. Schnapper, who published Gandhi, Nasser, Toynbee, Truman, and about 1,500 other authors. In 1983, Schnapper was described by *The Washington Post* as "a redoubtable gadfly." His legacy will endure in the books to come.

Peter Osnos, *Founder and Editor-at-Large*